GOLF
AN ILLUSTRATED HISTORY
OF THE GAME

GOLF
AN ILLUSTRATED HISTORY OF THE GAME

ROBERT GREEN

Willow Books
Collins
8 Grafton Street, London W1
1987

'To Tot, and to my father'

Willow Books
William Collins Sons & Co Ltd
London · Glasgow · Sydney · Auckland
Toronto · Johannesburg

First published 1987
© Robert Green and Jollands Editions 1987

British Library Cataloguing in Publication Data
Green, Robert
  Golf: an illustrated history of the game.
  1. Golf—History
  I. Title
  796.352'09   GV963

ISBN 0-00-218261-0

Editorial planning by Jollands Editions
Designed by Lee Griffiths

Set in Bembo
by CG Graphic Services, Tring
Printed and bound in Great Britain
by Butler & Tanner Ltd, Frome, Somerset

Contents

Acknowledgements

Writing and researching a book is not a one man job. I am especially indebted to the following for their assistance in bringing this book to publication.

For their help in obtaining various photographs – Dave Oswald and Martin Gannon at *Golf World*, Bill Robertson and his staff at *Golf Illustrated*, Janet Seagle at the USGA, Jean Matthewman at Ganton Golf Club and David Wood at Southport & Ainsdale.

For their help at the 'business end' – Alan Smith, Managing Director of Collins's Special Interests Division, and Michael Doggart and Lee Griffiths, respectively Collins's in-house editor and designer.

Thanks are also due to John Robertson, Peter Haslam and others at *Golf World* for the kindness and consideration shown to me over the past five years; to Nick Mason, Sports Editor of the *London Daily News*, for allowing me to devote so much time to the project over the last winter; to Helen Child, the world's best typist, for her immaculate preparation of the manuscript; to Tim Jollands, my collaborator, for his infectious and unflagging enthusiasm and his expertise in assembling the illustrative material; and to my wife Jane, to whom this book is co-dedicated under one of her politer pseudonyms, for tolerating the ruination of so many weekends and because – if I may be permitted to rephrase Wodehouse – without her never-failing sympathy and encouragement half this book would never have been finished.

Introduction

Golf is a game of fascination and frustration: two entirely different feelings that stem from the same fact.

Golf is, essentially, about man against himself. No other sport offers the average participant the chance to play on the same stage as the stars and face the same problems. Even if one could get on to the Centre Court at Wimbledon, it wouldn't be quite the same challenge if Boris Becker wasn't on the other side of the net. But anyone, literally anyone, can stand over the identical 12-foot putt that Severiano Ballesteros had to win the 1984 Open Championship at St Andrews. Even more thrillingly, the relative novice is occasionally capable of executing a shot of which Jack Nicklaus would be proud.

On the other hand, there is no one else to blame when you miss a 12-inch putt or when your drive hurtles into the nearest lake. One may curse the course, the game and even the Lord, but the ball just sat there, inviting you to hit it, and nobody else put it there (if I may momentarily ignore foursomes) or affected its position. In golf, only you get what you hit.

That is not at all the same as saying that you are only affected by what *you* hit. Never can that have been made clearer to any man than it was to Greg Norman when Bob Tway holed a bunker shot to beat him at the 1986 USPGA Championship (see page 95) and then eight months later Larry Mize chipped in from 140 feet for a birdie at the second extra hole of a play-off to deprive him of the 1987 Masters, which publishing deadlines could not permit to be included in the main text.

Ballesteros was also involved in that play-off, but he was eliminated at the first hole of sudden death. Whether the setback both he and Norman suffered on that Sunday evening at Augusta will prove to be a psychological burden or an inspiration to them in the months between now and the book's publication, and in the years ahead, remains to be seen.

What the future holds for Larry Mize is a matter for conjecture too, but one thing is certain. His shot will never be forgotten as long as championship golf is played. It was as decisive a stroke as Tway's at Inverness and Tom Watson's on the 17th at Pebble Beach in the 1982 US Open – just even more outrageous.

Greg Norman's behaviour in his hour of bitter disappointment was exemplary, as it usually is. He grinned rather than grimaced as he recalled his feelings as Mize's ball disappeared into the hole, as if in acknowledgement of the fact that golf is, after all, only a game.

But what a game.

Robert Green
London
1st June 1987

CHAPTER ONE

Seven Centuries of Golf

St Andrews has a worldwide reputation as 'the home of golf'. Nothing can alter that now because it is how the 'auld grey toun' is perceived by millions of golf's devotees all over the globe, even if they have never been there and are never likely to, but it has at best a tenuous claim to the accolade.

St Andrews is not even the home of the first golf club in Scotland. It cannot be said with any certainty that it is the place where the game began in Scotland. Indeed, it is a matter of grave doubt that golf is of Scottish origin at all.

The question is: What is golf? In a sketch in a stained-glass window at Gloucester Cathedral, illustrating scenes from the Battle of Crécy in France, a man is apparently preparing to strike a ball in a golf-like manner. It dates from around 1350, and perhaps it shows not golf but the game of *cambuca*, a popular pastime of the day enjoyed by the English and similar to the earlier Roman game of *paganica*. It involved someone standing side-on to a ball, intent on striking it with the club in his hands. The ball in *paganica* consisted of leather and feathers, in *cambuca* it was of wood. In

This 14th-century detail from the Great East Window of Gloucester Cathedral has led some people to declare that golf must have been known in England around 1350. In fact, that is highly unlikely. It is probable that the medieval English pastime of *cambuca* or the Flemish game of *chole* are depicted in this stained glass roundel.

the ancient Flemish game of *chole*, the ball was made of beechwood and it was struck with clubs forged from rigid shafts and iron heads. Since the colourful windows in Gloucester Cathedral are concerned with battle campaigns in France, it may be instead that *chole* is the game depicted.

Chole could be a genuine forerunner of golf. Still played occasionally in southern Belgium, it is a field game in which the ball is hit by a team towards a distant target – sometimes very distant, literally miles away. The target can be anything from a door to a tree, a pole to a stone. The team has three strokes to make progress before standing aside while its opponents, known as *decholeurs*, have the next blow with which they attempt to dispatch the ball as far backwards as they can, or into a spot which will make matters as awkward as possible for their rivals. And so it goes – three steps forward, one back.

This obviously sounds more like large-scale croquet than golf, and one of the great difficulties confronting anyone who delves into the earliest days of the sport lies in deciding how many, if any, of these potential candidates actually spawned the game of golf we now know. Even back in 1338, German shepherds were granted special dispensation to mark out their territories by striking a pebble with their crooks, the distance which the shot covered being the extent of their grazing rights. Could that be said to have anything to do with golf? Probably not. Quite simply, if a man has a club in his hands he will look for something to hit with it: hockey, shinty, polo and lacrosse are just some of the games which evolved from the same basic instinct.

The late Dutch golf historian Steven J. H. van Hengel, acknowledged as one of the foremost experts on the origins of golf, felt that it probably developed via an amalgam of the implements used in *chole* and the rules of *jeu de mail*. The technique of the latter was similar to golf and it was played on a court prepared specifically for the purpose. It started in Italy and was taken up by the French, becoming especially widespread in the early 17th century. It went out of fashion some 100 years later but until 50 years ago it remained a regular activity in southern France as *jeu de mail à la chicane*, a cross-country version of the same game.

Incidentally, *jeu de mail* arrived in England from France. Translated, it was known as 'pall mall', and the original course in London was laid out in what is now the busy one-way thoroughfare of that name. Charles I was a keen disciple of the game around the same time as it was celebrating its halcyon days in France, but during the reign of Charles II, in the latter part of the 17th century, the court was moved south on to The Mall, which nowadays joins Buckingham Palace to Trafalgar Square.

Golf had already been played in Scotland for centuries by the time Charles I came to the throne. He followed the example of Mary Queen of Scots in enthusiastically enjoying golf and *jeu de mail*. Mary was vilified for playing both shortly after the suspicious death of her husband, Lord Darnley, in 1567, and this apparent lack of grief at his demise did her chances of avoiding an appointment on the executioner's block no good at all.

However, this is getting rather ahead of the story. I have, to be honest, slightly mis-represented the researches of van Hengel in saying that in his opinion golf emerged from a combination of *chole* and *jeu de mail*, both of which date from the Middle Ages. He doesn't say golf but *colf*, also known by other medieval phrases such as *spel metten colve* (game with club), but essentially *colf*.

It doesn't require an international interpreter to make the connection between *colf* and golf, but van Hengel had a fundamental advantage in tackling the wealth of information available to golf historians in the Low Countries. The fact that he was a Dutchman meant he was able to investigate the old archives of pictures, maps and other materials written in medieval language with an ease which can only come to one who has the current version as his mother tongue. The task for Britons is as forbidding as it would be for a Frenchman, however conversant with modern English, to understand Chaucer.

Van Hengel traced *colf* back to Boxing Day 1297, to Loenen aan de Vecht in northern Holland. Then the local townsfolk played four 'holes' measuring a total of 4950 yards to commemorate the relieving of Kronenburg Castle exactly one year previously. The castle had

been the besieged refuge of two noblemen wanted for murder; that they were eventually captured and summarily dealt with by the crowd was deemed cause for celebration. The fact that *colf* was chosen to mark the occasion is, suggested van Hengel, proof that it was already popular by 1297, though not even he could say for how long.

Holing out at what might today be known as the Kronenburg Country Club was not performed by putting into a hole of 4¼ inches diameter. The targets consisted instead of four doors – respectively in a kitchen, a windmill, a castle and a courthouse. This unique ritual continued until 1831, when the castle was pulled down, but golf has remained.

Landscape artists portraying life in contemporary Holland towards the end of the 16th century regularly included golfers, or *colfers*,

Victorian impressions of the Royal & Ancient game.

Left **Mary Queen of Scots was a keen player of both golf and *jeu de mail*. This picture shows her at St Andrews in 1563. Four years later she was seen playing golf at Seton House shortly after her husband's death, a fact used as evidence at her trial of her complicity in his demise.**

Above **Like Mary, Charles I lost his head on the block, though not for playing golf. He is seen here on Leith Links receiving news of the Irish Rebellion in 1641.**

The Flemish artist Paul Bril painted this scene of *chole* players in 1624. The implements are similar to those employed in golf, although both clubs and balls are on a rather larger scale. Note how the players' target is a door. Doorways also formed the ultimate goal in the first recorded game of *colf* unearthed by the Dutch historian Steven van Hengel. He believed that golf was directly descended from *colf*, which flourished in Holland in the Middle Ages.

in their works, unquestionably because they were a common sight. The game was played in both matchplay and strokeplay form, to use the modern terms, and contested by singles, foursomes, fourballs or even, in that pre-slow-play era, eightsomes. It was predominantly practised in spring, autumn and winter (hence the apparently surprising number of paintings which depict the game on frozen canals and lakes) because in summer the grass was too long and in those days there were no prepared courses, except for one at Haarlem. Doorways were gradually substituted by a hole in the ground, often with a pole protruding from it, as the ultimate target.

Colf continued until the early 18th century when it suddenly fell out of fashion. There are no satisfactory explanations for this, but it was quickly replaced by *kolf*, a considerably shorter game, played on a course of some 20 metres in length. *Kolf* was popular in the Netherlands until just before the turn of the last century when the Scottish version of golf was imported.

And so back to Scotland. To suggest to a Scotsman that the game was not the creation of his countrymen is as dangerous as saying to a gurkha that his ancestors were cowards. And maybe he would be right to take offence. As I said before, it all depends on what one understands by 'golf'. Though the Dutch were familiar with golf as a game with a hole in it, it is probable that the Scots have never played it any other way. To that extent they could be said to have invented golf as we know it; and St Andrews, despite the optimistic claim to have fostered the game that is inherent in the label 'home of golf', was indubitably responsible for 18 holes becoming established as the norm for a full round, a step taken in 1764. But van Hengel's theory of *colf* begetting golf is supported by the frequent trading links between Holland and Scotland from medieval times. These presented an abundance of opportunities for the game to travel across the North Sea, and the strongest indications are that the movement was from east to west.

Until well into the 19th century, golf in Scotland was almost confined to the east coast, where the sandy turf among the dunes along the shore made for ideal golfing ground. Had the game begun in Scotland it is likely that it would have enjoyed a greater geographical spread, such as was to be found in the Low Countries, though granted the North Sea coast was favoured there too. Furthermore, it is reckoned that *c*.1650 golf was played in only about 12 locations in Scotland (at Dornoch, Banff and Aberdeen in the north; at Montrose, Carnoustie, Perth, St Andrews and Leven further down; and at a few spots around Edinburgh), whereas there were over 40 places in Holland where there is incontrovertible proof that *colf* was practised by then. The first documentary reference to golf in the Netherlands dates from 1360 (though that is not to deny the truth of that splendid saga at Loenen); in Scotland from 1457. In short, the odds are that Dutch traders introduced *colf* to the Scots, who in turn refined it into golf and eventually spread the gospel to the world. Let's call it an honourable half.

That reference of 1457 to golf in Scotland was contained in a parliamentary decree promulgated by King James II of Scotland, declaring 'that Fute-ball and Golfe be utterly cryit doune, and nocht usit'. His Majesty was worried that these two sports were keeping his subjects away from precious archery practice, which was needed to repel the frequent incursions of the English, and hence the order.

The date is instructive for two reasons. First, no such law would have been necessary had the game

Golf began to be portrayed on ceramics from the 17th century. This Dutch ice scene dates from that era and is taken from an encaustic dish.

been played by only a few. Second, a similar enactment of 1424 prohibited 'fute-ball' but not golf, thus indicating that the latter had enjoyed significantly increased popularity in the intervening years. Interestingly, Edward III of England had issued a similar Act in 1363 banning *cambuca*.

From 1457, references to golf gradually become more common, even in England. Catherine of Aragon, the first of Henry VIII's six wives, wrote to Cardinal Wolsey in 1513 that 'all his [Henry's] subjects be very glad I thank God to be busy with the Golfe for they take it for a pastime'. In 1552, a local licence made it plain that the people of St Andrews had the right to play golf, among other

Adriaen van de Velde's oil painting of 1668 shows a frost scene at Haarlem but it has been used to suggest that the Scots, not the Dutch, invented golf. The man about to strike the ball is wearing a kilt, but it is very possible that he was supposed to be an itinerant trader or soldier. The date itself is not very helpful since it is certain that the Scots had been playing golf for at least two centuries by then.

One of the first paintings of golf in Scotland. This watercolour by Paul Sandby was completed in 1746 and is entitled 'View of Bruntsfield Links looking towards Edinburgh Castle'.

The Honourable Company of Edinburgh Golfers is recognized as the oldest golf club in the world. Edinburgh Town Council marked its foundation in 1744 by presenting a Silver Club to be contested annually by the members. This engraving after a drawing by David Allan illustrates the Procession of the Silver Club in 1787, with the Town Crier and his drummers announcing the date of the next competition.

things, over the now-hallowed ground, though even as late as 1593 a luckless couple called John Henrie and Pat Rogie were apparently jailed in Edinburgh for 'playing of the gowff on the links of Leith every Sabbath the time of the sermonses'. The spelling of 'golf' in those days was, as you can see, anything but uniform.

There is evidence that in 1608, five years after King James VI of Scotland had also become James I of England, a seven-hole course was laid out at Blackheath, London, by Scottish courtiers who were homesick for their beloved game. This gives rise to Royal Blackheath's claim to be nearly 400 years old, although in their comprehensive work, *Royal Blackheath*, Ian Henderson and David Stirk suggest that a club was not formed there until 1766. It is, nevertheless, the oldest golf club in England, notwithstanding that there are references to golf being played at Molesey Hurst near Hampton in 1758.

Dating golf clubs is a hazardous business, partly due to the identity of the founders in those bygone days. Most of the earliest societies were established by freemasons. The inherent secrecy of the masons meant that when the golf clubs were eventually opened to those outside the fraternity, many of the existing minutes of meetings and other documentary materials were destroyed. For example, the Royal Burgess Society of Edinburgh Golfers was apparently formed in 1735 but there are no minutes to support the claim. Similarly, no records can be

traced to substantiate the belief that Musselburgh was instituted in 1774 rather than 1784 as is suggested by the minutes.

Accordingly, the distinction of being recognized as the oldest golf club in the world falls to the Honourable Company of Edinburgh Golfers, now based at Muirfield on the Firth of Forth to the east of Edinburgh but in 1744 located at Leith, just outside Scotland's capital city. The club has maintained continuous records since then, although the scene of its members' activities was moved from Leith in 1831, initially to Musselburgh in 1836 and eventually to Muirfield in 1891.

The Honourable Company also bequeathed to the game its first set of Rules; 13 articles of faith which have multiplied and been embellished in the ensuing years, ostensibly of necessity but, it must be said, to the dismay of many people, such as the late Henry Longhurst, who felt the basic principles of golf could comfortably be accommodated on the back of a matchbox. The code devised by John Rattray (the club's first captain) and his colleagues captured the spirit of the game, with its reliance on trust and on the honesty of its adherents, and that remains the underlying theme of the Rules today – albeit with suitably severe penalties to deter would-be transgressors.

In 1744, to mark the creation of the club, Edinburgh Town Council presented the Honourable Company with a Silver Club to be contested by the members. Thus was born the first club competition. Rattray was the winner and hence became captain. The event (matchplay, of course, since strokeplay was in its infancy) was played over Leith's five-hole layout, a forbidding test with holes measuring 414, 461, 426, 495 and 435 yards respectively. Given the nature of the equipment back in 1744, that represents an equivalent of around 600 yards per hole by modern standards.

It is immediately apparent that the long game was then the thing, putting playing nowhere near so dominant a role as it does now. The notion that these days too much emphasis is placed on putting will never wilt for want of advocates, but they have been fighting a losing battle since the invention of the mechanical mower in the first half of the last century. The scythe gradually became redundant as an instrument of greenkeeping and the general quality of putting surfaces improved rapidly. Putting became an art, rather than a case of hit-and-hope, on these new manicured surfaces and through the 19th century 4¼ inches became the accepted diameter for the hole itself.

It is likely that this seemingly random size was just that: it happened to be the width of the implement used to cut the holes at Musselburgh. It was obviously considered of satisfactory dimensions for general application because in 1893 the Royal and Ancient Golf Club of St Andrews (the R & A, as the club is now universally referred to in shorthand) decreed that a 4¼-inch hole was mandatory. Thus it has remained, despite the efforts of the lobbyists who tried to get the size of the hole increased when the United States adopted the 1.68-inch diameter ball in 1931 (as opposed to 1.62 inches elsewhere). In the words of Peter Dobereiner, the widely respected English journalist and a passionate believer in the bigger hole, 'the 4¼-inch hole has proved to be a diabolically enduring feature of golf.'

That we should find the R & A handing down judgements and delivering verdicts on what is to be or not to be accepted in golf may appear surprising. After all, the Honourable Company at Edinburgh was in existence beforehand, and its members set down the first Rules of Golf, which were copied with only one minor amendment when 22 'Noblemen and Gentlemen, being admirers of the ancient and healthful exercise of the Golf' banded together at St Andrews in 1754. The usurpers even nicked the Silver Club idea; the members of the new society each subscribing five shillings to purchase the prize, claimed in its inaugural year by one Bailie William Landale.

But it did not take long for St Andrews to display its influence. In 1764, William St Clair covered the 22 holes of the Old Course in 121 strokes. It was decided, in the face of this contemptuous treatment of the links, to amalgamate the first four holes into two. Since the shared fairways and double greens which today distinguish St Andrews from any other course were already an integral feature of the design, that involved reducing the round to 18 holes. From small acorns. . . .

As we have already seen, Leith had only five holes at this time. For that matter, the North Inch course at Perth – which is considered by some experts to be the first golf course in Scotland which was recognizable as such – had just six; while Montrose, on the east coast between Dundee and Aberdeen, had 25. It wasn't until 1858 that the R & A stipulated 'one round of the Links or 18 Holes is reckoned a match'. There had previously been a distinct trend towards 18 holes being the norm, and the edict merely gave legal effect to popular practice. It meant that golfers

Sir George Chalmers's painting of William St Clair of Roslin, the man who reduced the length of a round. It was his scoring exploits in 1764 which caused the Old Course at St Andrews to become an 18-hole layout, thus setting a standard which endures today. Note his firm grip and exaggeratedly closed stance, the preferred method of striking the feathery ball.

Golf on the Old Course in 1798. Though times have changed, in many respects the scene has hardly altered at all. Anyone familiar with golf would immediately recognize St Andrews from this illustration of players on the first green.

confronted by a six-hole course played it three times while a nine-holer was toured twice.

By 1858, there had been other considerable changes in the upper echelons of golf and in the overall development of the game. In the struggle for supremacy, St Andrews had dealt the Honourable Company a mortal bow. In 1834, Murray Belshes, soon to become Captain of the St Andrews Society of Golfers, approached King William IV, asking him to agree to be their patron. He not only acquiesced to that but permitted the society to rename itself The Royal and Ancient Golf Club of St Andrews. Since the Honourable Company had left Leith, which was soon to deteriorate, and had not yet re-established itself at Musselburgh, its members were in no position to challenge the concurrent claim made on St Andrews' behalf by the R & A to the title 'home of golf'. From that moment, the authority and eminence of the R & A has been undisputed (except in the United States) and St Andrews has become the most revered golf course in the world, the inspiration to countless others everywhere.

At a humbler level, too, things were stirring. More clubs and societies sprang up along Scotland's east coast: at Aberdeen, Crail, Bruntsfield, Burntisland, and into the 19th century at Perth, North Berwick and, in 1851, at Prestwick, home of the first dozen Open Championships. One William Mitchell formed the Old Manchester Club at Kersal Moor in 1818, making it the second oldest club outside Scotland after Royal Blackheath.

It wasn't long before the British Empire began to feel the impact. A club was founded at Calcutta, later to become Royal Calcutta, in 1829. This was the first golf club outside the British Isles, and it was followed in 1842 by another course on the opposite side of India, at Bombay. Appropriately enough, the Indian Amateur Championship, which began in 1892, is also the world's oldest national tournament apart from the British Open (1860) and Amateur (1885), but before then golf had also taken root on the continent, at Pau in the French Pyrenees.

That occurred in 1856, eight years after the invention of the gutta percha ball (more commonly known as the 'gutty') had helped to revolutionize the game. It flew further than its predecessor, the 'feathery', rolled truer and was more durable. Its influence was vital. From this point on, golf became increasingly contagious.

Despite the events I have already mentioned, golf was not terribly popular until after 1850. Certainly, it had attracted a loyal band of devotees but they were, in terms of the entire population, small in number and were predominantly a wealthy minority, giving golf a reputation as a rich man's game which it still finds hard to shrug off in some quarters. Compared to the boom that golf was to enjoy in the second half of the 19th century, the growth of the game was almost stunted. Van Hengel went as far as to say: 'It is in fact a miracle that golf . . . survived the 18th century at all.'

He congratulated the masonic societies for keeping the flame burning, though golf itself was often simply regarded as an excuse for gluttony: 'a good exercise before sitting down for their sumptuous meals'. Those readers who have had the good fortune to experience the clubhouse fare laid out at the Berkshire Golf Club near London will know something of what he meant, but even the most eager Bordeaux buff might draw the line at following the example set by golfers of the 1770s, as described by Tobias Smollett: 'they never went to bed without having each the best part of a gallon of claret in his belly.'

Some 120 years later, golf had become distinctly more than a gourmand's delight, and for rather more people. Figures indicate that in 1850, around the time of the birth of the gutty, there were 17 golf clubs and societies in the United Kingdom; by 1890 this had leapt to 387, playing over an approximate 140 different courses. The inauguration of the Open Championship in 1860 helped to publicize the

'Golf at Blackheath' by F. P. Hopkins, 1875. Royal Blackheath is England's oldest golf club. In centuries past it typified the pomp and ritual of the masons who founded the early great clubs in the British Isles. Note the formal dress – in this case red jackets for playing in – which was *de rigueur* in those days.

game and within the ensuing decade three major English clubs were founded: Westward Ho! (now Royal North Devon) in the south-west, formed in 1864 and the oldest English club still using its original course; the London Scottish Club at Wimbledon, London (1865); and the Liverpool Golf Club (today also honoured with the Royal prefix) at Hoylake in 1869. The latter hosted the first Amateur Championship in 1885.

The first and third of these were, like the majority of early Scottish clubs, built on linksland; that is, the sandy strips of otherwise useless ground which were left along the coast when the seas withdrew after the last Ice Age. It was considered (indeed, still is by some purists) sacrilege to refer to any other type of course as a 'links', and eventually the term 'golf course' was coined to describe non-links golfing grounds. If now St Andrews would just as readily be described as a 'golf course' as a 'links', that's a state of affairs guaranteed to be disturbing a few graves; as must the tendency to describe as a links any course with a view over salt water.

But our forebears would doubtless be amazed rather than appalled at the way golf has developed in so many ways, and not just in the modern extent of its geographical base. For example, fewer than 20 golf books had been written 100 years ago but today golf has an enviable collection of literature devoted to it. In 1890, the world's oldest extant golf magazine, imaginatively named

Below left A 19th-century engraving of golf on Wimbledon Common, where the London Scottish Club was formed in 1865. Today it shares its course with Wimbledon Golf Club, which recalls a bygone age with its insistence that golfers must wear red clothing on their upper body.

Below The 10th green of the Royal North Devon Golf Club at Westward Ho! The photograph was taken in 1905, 41 years after the course was opened. It was a pioneering club in the cause of women's golf and it boasts the oldest links in England. The course itself now looks much as it did then.

Golf, was published in London. It is now known as *Golf Illustrated*, the title it changed to in 1899.

It was also in 1890 that the first edition of *The Badminton Library – Golf* appeared, edited by Horace Hutchinson. This volume contains a great deal of fascinating material, such as Hutchinson's comments on the mores of the contemporary professional.

'Especially to be reprobated is the practice at some clubs of offering a "drink" to a professional at the close of a round. If you leave him to himself there is no danger of his damaging his health by drinking too little. No golf professional is recorded to have died of thirst. On the other hand, the lives of many have been shortened and degraded by thirst too often satiated. . . .

'On the whole, the professional is not a bad fellow. He has little morality; but he has good, reckless spirits, a ready wit and humour. . . . He is apt to be insolent in order to show you that he imagines himself to have some self-respect – which is a self-delusion – but if you can endure a certain measure of this, he is a good companion. Never, however, bet with him; for so will it be best for him and best for you, as he is unlikely to pay you if he loses. This he is apt to do, for he is a bad judge of the merits of a golf match, a point which requires a delicacy of estimate usually beyond his powers.'

Hutchinson was a golfer of no mean ability: four times a finalist in the Amateur Championship and twice a winner but, as that brief pedigree demonstrates, he was an amateur – in cricketing parlance, a 'gentleman' as opposed to a 'player'.

If he believed the professional to be beneath him, the *Punch* cartoons of the era depicted the pro as a tyrant blessed with an acerbic wit, as exemplified by exchanges like:

Pupil: 'What am I doing wrong now?'
Pro: 'Standing too near the ball – after you've hit it.'

And again by this one:

Pupil: 'I say, d'you think I can go?'
Pro: 'Go? Why not? There's no-one in the bunker.'

Sometimes the instructor's advice was countered with a logical retort from his luckless charge:

Pro: 'The secret of putting is never to lift your head until you hear the ball rattle in the tin.'
Pupil: 'That's silly. You can't keep gazing at the ground for the rest of your life.'

But generally the last word was left to the crusty tutor, who emerges as a man with the

Professional golfers in 1867 were far from feted in the way they are now but this group assembled at Leith included some famous names. From left to right: Andrew Strath, Davie Park, Bob Kirk, Jamie Anderson, Jamie Dunn, Willie Dow, Willie Dunn, Alexander Greig, Old Tom Morris, Young Tom Morris and George Morris.

compassion of Genghis Khan and the brain of George Bernard Shaw.

This was the age when professionals were not permitted to enter clubhouses. It was enough that they breathed. Privilege was a word outside their dictionary – Hutchinson would doubtless have said outside their vocabulary. It is only relatively recently that the club pro has been regarded as a human being, and indeed even the stars between the wars, such as Walter Hagen and Henry Cotton, caused numerous ructions with their demands to be treated civilly. Hagen declined to enter the clubhouse at Troon for the presentation ceremony after the 1923 Open, where he had finished runner-up to Arthur Havers, because he and his colleagues had been refused admission during the championship.

Attitudes at the turn of the century especially were a far cry from the way Messrs Palmer, Nicklaus, Ballesteros, Norman & Co are feted and chased today. Then the pro was good for a few lessons and maybe the odd round. He could win tournaments or perhaps design a new course, but think of him as an equal? Really!

And then there were the caddies. It is one of golf's most repeated truisms that many of its finest exponents have graduated through the caddie ranks. That is hardly surprising. When Hutchinson was writing, the caddies would often be professionals who did not have an 'engagement'.

The word 'caddie' is derived from the French *cadet*: the son of a gentleman. The Scots mischievously traduced its meaning by using it to refer to those who carried the bags of the gentlemen who played golf in the earliest days of the game's history. In the strict Scottish vernacular, 'caddie' meant 'scrounger', and that is hardly the severest criticism to which caddies have been subjected down the ages. Their popular image has been recently upgraded into a kind of pseudo-profession by their regular attachment to the leading tournament players, as seen on television, but previously tour caddies were commonly dismissed as dirty, drunk or – in circumstances of extreme politeness – eccentric.

So much for the elite. The caddie most of us get on a visit to a strange club may be a thoroughly pleasant young chap, a boy or youth in between school or university terms, but the quaint image is of the gnarled old figure who says of one's good shots 'we hit a beauty there' and of the bad 'you made a right mess of that'. This is another mode of behaviour suggested by *Punch* and other

periodicals and books of around 100 years ago. The impression handed down the generations is of a unique band of men with a religious respect for the game, as in:

Player (after bad shot): 'Golf's a funny game, isn't it?'
Caddie: 'Aye, but it's no' meant to be';

a marvellous gift for diplomacy:

Player (after another bad shot): 'What are you looking there for? Why, I must have driven it fifty yards further!'
Caddie: 'But sometimes they hit a stone, sir, and bounce back a terrible distance';

and a severe lack of patience:

Lady golfer (who has missed the ball six times with various clubs): 'And which am I to use now?'
Caddie: 'Gie it a knock wi' the bag!'

Whatever the caddie may have thought, golf is in fact a funny game. Go back a century and the pro and the caddie were frequently the same person, but if not, united anyway in being a target of disrespect for the well-to-do golfer; a necessary evil for playing the sport. They were also comrades in displaying derision at the efforts of those who were their social betters but golfing inferiors. *Punch* intimated, probably erroneously, that their minds shared a sublime sense of sarcasm and, more correctly, that their shoulders bore the burden of an intolerable weight of chips.

How times have changed. They have long since gone their separate ways. The top tour

Above left 'Old Alick' Brotherston, hole-cutter to the Royal Blackheath Golf Club, as painted by R. S. E. Gallen. Alick was also a relatively distinguished member of the humblest profession – the caddies.
Above right Dave Musgrove, Sandy Lyle's constant companion of the fairways, is at the top of his profession too, but the tournament caddies of the 1980s are socially worlds apart from their generally despised early predecessors.
Below The Spy cartoon of Horace Hutchinson, a talented amateur golfer who wielded a witty if sometimes acerbic pen with the same dexterity as he did his clubs.

For many years North Berwick, near Edinburgh, was the most fashionable golf resort in Britain. Fifth from the left in this turn-of-the-century photograph is the diminutive figure of Ben Sayers, the club's professional, who became a master clubmaker.

The opening of Gorebridge golf course, south of Edinburgh, in 1897. The Edinburgh-Carlisle railway line in the background is relevant in that it was the railways which helped golf to grow away from the cities during golf's boom years in the 1880s and 1890s.

professionals are sporting heroes now. They can afford to buy clubhouses. The club pro, too, is welcome within and has become a respected member of golf club life: a skilled craftsman, club repairer, teacher, salesman, even a friend.

The caddie? Well, signs ordering 'No caddies' are to be seen all over Britain and elsewhere around the world. Maybe next century his time will come, but don't bet on it.

One century back, while the professionals and caddies were struggling along, golf was flourishing. Many famous golf clubs which now bear the proud title 'Royal' were created in the last two decades of the 19th century: Lytham & St Annes (1886), St George's (1887), Ashdown Forest and Birkdale (1889) in England; Belfast (1881), Dublin (1885), Portrush (1888) and County Down at Newcastle (1889) in Ireland; Porthcawl (1891) and St David's (1894) in Wales.

These are just the tip, albeit a distinguished one, of the iceberg. Scotland, of course, was already well endowed with important clubs and there was ample room and demand for more, such as Gullane (1882), Nairn (1887), Luffness New (1894) and Western Gailes (1897). Throughout this century golf has expanded to the point where there are over 2000 clubs in the British Isles, while the latter part of the 1800s is particularly significant as the time the game departed for the rest of the world.

India was its first proper outpost abroad, in 1829, but it was 60 years before the rest of Asia began to pick up the thread. From 1888 to 1890, courses were built at Taiping in Malaya, Bangkok in Thailand, and in Hong Kong. It was British expatriates who took the game to Asia and it was almost exclusively their domain, though the Asian nation which today is most associated with golf – Japan – has no history of colonial rule. The first Japanese golf course was opened in 1901 on the slopes of Mount Rokko, near Kobe, but it wasn't until the gap between the wars that the game exploded to the extent dealt with elsewhere in this book (see Chapter 16).

The 1920s and 1930s were the years of consolidation everywhere; a period when the seeds planted 50 years beforehand germinated with spectacular results.

Golf got off to a stuttering start in Australia and New Zealand. Royal Melbourne, dating from 1891 and now the owner of what is univerally recognized to be one of the world's truly great courses, can boast the longest continuous existence of an Australian club, though earlier attempts to import golf had met with limited success in Adelaide and Sydney and in New Zealand at Dunedin and Christchurch. South Africa led the way on the Dark Continent; the Royal Cape Golf Club at Cape Town celebrated its centenary in 1985 and the country now has several outstanding layouts. Other countries, dotted all over the vast land mass, have taken to the sport, often in a climate which taxes the ingenuity of the best greenkeepers. In South America, the game took off because of the railways; to be specific, because of the British golf enthusiasts who were employed to lay down the railway lines as part of a huge investment programme in Argentina. In their spare time they founded the Buenos Aires Golf Club in 1878. Trains were also the catalyst by which golf was introduced in similar circumstances to Brazil, at Sao Paulo in 1890. It was a fitting way of reaching the unconverted since in Britain the railways were partly responsible for encouraging the game to prosper away from the major cities and towns. They provided a speedy and convenient means of transport to the seaside and other holiday areas suitable for the building of golf courses.

It is evident that Britain spread the word either via the Commonwealth or through the independent activities of small groups of its nationals. The latter took golf to Pau in 1856, although it was largely in northern and central Europe – Germany, Sweden, Denmark, Czechoslovakia (well before the days of Stalin, Yalta and the Warsaw Pact) and, inevitably, Holland – that it received the greatest nourishment on the continent. Its development along the Mediterranean, notably in Spain, was a response to the wishes of sun-seeking northerners. Despite the tournament exploits of Severiano Ballesteros and others, and some gradual signs for optimism, the game in Spain is still mainly the preserve of the Spanish rich and foreigners.

The growth of golf in all these places between the two World Wars – often dubbed the 'Golden Age' – and subsequently is covered in Chapter 16, but in the last century there was, literally, a new world to conquer too.

The British shipped golf to North America in 1873, when a club was established at Montreal – now Royal Montreal – in Canada. An emigrant Scotsman, Alexander Dennistoun, takes the credit, and within 10 years there were further courses at Quebec, Toronto, Ottawa and Niagara. Another Scotsman, John Reid, is lauded, though more controversially, as the man who instigated the biggest breakthrough of all – the taking of golf to the United States.

Intriguingly, though golf is generally acknowledged to have taken root in the United States only 100 years ago, one has to go all the way back to 1650 to discover the first mention of *colf*; in the court records of the justices at Fort Orange in New York State. They dealt with perhaps the first documented instance of a brawl over who was to pay for the after-round drinks. One Jacob Stol was fined 20 guilders or 2½ beaver skins for his part in the fight: an unusual penalty, the currency being explained by Stol's nationality and the fact that the Dutch West India Company had based a settlement there, and the skins being appropriate since that was the prime commodity in which it did business. But the Dutch obviously took *colf* to America with them as well, and it was hardly their fault if the natives were reluctant to take it up in earnest, albeit as golf, for over another two centuries.

A holiday scene on the clifftop course at Scarborough, Yorkshire, prior to the First World War. The golf rush did not pass women by completely, although they have seldom been treated as golfing equals in Britain.

The continental breakthrough proved something of a false dawn. Pau Golf Club in France was founded in 1856, the first course on mainland Europe. Depicted here are golfers at Pau in 1887, but it is only 100 years later that the game in France is taking off with a vengeance.

In between times, there were desultory indications of golf making inroads into American society. Henderson and Stirk, in another remarkably researched book, *Golf In The Making*, uncovered a reference in the Port of Leith records to a consignment of 96 clubs and 432 balls being sent to Charleston, South Carolina, in 1743. There are documents showing that a golf club was formed there later, in 1786, and around that time there was also a golf club at Savannah in the same state. The source of that evidence – an invitation to the club's members to attend a ball – is all the material that bears testimony to Savannah's existence and it may be that it was really a social club which just fancied the word 'golf' included in its name; a kind of legacy from the masons.

Whatever the substance of these stories, the early clubs of the south-east perished during the Civil War. Several other courses claim to have had a life prior to 1888, including Douglas Field at Chicago (1875), Oakhurst Golf Links (*sic*) in the Allegheny Mountains of West Virginia (1882), the Dorset Field Club in Vermont (1886) and the Foxburg Country Club in Pennsylvania (1887). Their advocates may have a good case or not, but – as with St Andrews' somewhat dubious claim to be the home of golf – John Reid seems destined to be regarded as the man who introduced golf to the United States, thereby lighting a candle that has burned ever-stronger ever since.

Reid was born in Dunfermline in 1840 and had learned the game at Musselburgh. He was living in Yonkers, New York, when he requested a friend, Robert Lockhart, to purchase a few clubs and balls for him while on a visit to Scotland. This Lockhart duly did, from the shop of Old Tom Morris at St Andrews, and after Morris had shipped them across the Atlantic as ordered, Lockhart dispatched them on to Reid. On 22 February 1888, Reid and a few friends used the recently arrived equipment to negotiate a rudimentary three holes he had cut in a field close to his house. The date was the anniversary of Washington's birth. As the American writer, Charles Price, remarks in his book, *The World of Golf*: 'Thus, on the birthday of a man who is alleged never to have told a lie in his life, was played the round which presaged a pastime that has since created more lying Americans than any other save fishing.' The same is true the world over! On 14 November, Reid and his cronies formally drew up a constitution for their golf club. They called it – surprise, surprise – St Andrew's, although they had the grace to insert an apostrophe.

Reid's reputation as the Father of American golf is frankly undeserved. He did nothing to foster the infant game. He resisted uprooting to a more suitable site until the local authorities of Yonkers drove a road through his course, forcing the club

John Reid, who has posthumously – and by default – assumed the title of 'The Father of American Golf'. He formed the first golf club in the United States.

The site for Reid's rudimentary course was a field near his home in New York. Reid is on the extreme right of this 1888 group, the earliest known photograph of golf in America. He called his club St Andrew's and the Scottish connection was not confined to the name. The four players and two caddies here are clad in the fashion of their British counterparts, the caddies being the sons of Harry Holbrook, the man on the left. The other two gentlemen are A. Kinnan and John B. Upham.

to shift to a 30-acre orchard (from which his group derived the sobriquet 'The Old Apple Tree Gang') where they played over six holes. Eventually, and with some unwillingness on their founder's part, the club moved again to find room for a nine-hole course. Not until 1897 did they have a full 18, and that was only after further peregrinations.

By then, golf had progressed rapidly. In 1891, 'Young Willie' Dunn from Musselburgh had laid out 12 holes at Shinnecock Hills on Long Island to the east of New York city. The course, built on genuinely links-type turf, was a masterpiece of design, particularly for its day. Dunn later added a nine-holer for ladies and the two courses were amalgamated so that Shinnecock could host the second US Open Championship in 1896. It didn't get it back again until 1986.

The attraction of Shinnecock was not confined to its course or its views over Peconic Bay. Atop the hill overlooking the holes was erected an elegant clubhouse designed by the famous American architect, Stanford White: a man of the style, time and place so compellingly evoked by J. Scott Fitzgerald in *The Great Gatsby*.

All these facets conspired to make Shinnecock the first American golf course that looked like one. Not that it was widely known. One marvellous cameo scene was enacted in 1892 when John C. Ten Eyck, a leading figure at Reid's St Andrew's club, met Samuel Parrish, a founder member of Shinnecock, at the latter's Broadway offices. Ten Eyck commented that he'd heard people were playing golf on Long Island, a situation he presumably considered odd in view of Reid's stubborn stance not to have anything to do with popularizing the sport. Parrish's matchless reply shows that both men were equally startled by the truth. 'Why, yes,' he said. 'Does anyone else play golf in this country?'

Willie Dunn's going to America had hinged upon a happy coincidence. The three pioneers behind Shinnecock were vacationing at Biarritz, a classy resort on France's south-western Atlantic coast, in the winter of 1890 when they saw Dunn playing golf on the town's new course which he was in the process of completing, then the second in the country. They were captivated by this strange pursuit, convinced Dunn to follow them to the United States as soon as he could, and the rest – as they say – is history.

Hundreds of Scotsmen, and some Englishmen, took the trail blazed by Dunn. Some arrived in America as teaching professionals, others as

Stanford White's elegantly designed clubhouse at Shinnecock Hills on Long Island, New York. Shinnecock is the most venerable great course in North America and the club has hosted two US Opens in different centuries. The women golfers seen here are sporting the sort of clothing which adorned their opposite numbers in Britain, although ladies were accepted into American golfing circles far more readily than they were across the Atlantic.

greenkeepers, architects, ballmakers – anything. A Scottish accent was a passport to a job. It was a great opportunity for the emigrants and it was the reason why the United States was so overwhelmed by golf in such a short space of time.

Golf course construction provides the best barometer. In 1890, Reid's cow pasture was the country's only golf course. By 1896, the figure had risen appreciably to over 80. Four years later, there were 982. This phenomenal explosion meant that by 1900 there were more American courses than British ones, though, with very few exceptions, none worthy of being mentioned in the same breath as the famous existing links of Britain or the magnificent inland courses among the pine trees and on the heaths which would soon be built in England. This was primarily due to the prevailing philosophy, 'quantity, not quality'. One Tom Bendelow in particular has been heavily castigated by many writers for the number of 'quickie' courses he laid out, apparently without care or scruple, but it is likely that he was merely fulfilling the wishes of his paymasters within the budget he was allocated. The golden days of American architecture lay ahead and will be examined in appropriate detail in Chapter 14. For now, suffice it to say that though Dunn set a trend by working in America, most of those who came behind him either ignored, couldn't afford or couldn't be bothered to trek out to Long Island and learn from Shinnecock how it should be done.

Golf was a perfect sport for America in the Gay Nineties. Its upper-class genteel image fitted perfectly the thriving economy and the rise of that most American of symbols, the motor car. The United States was ready for golf; whether golf was prepared for Charles Blair Macdonald is more questionable.

Macdonald was an American whose grandfather lived in St Andrews (Scottish version). Young Charlie went to St Andrews University, met the great men of the game and assiduously studied the great British golf courses. His labours in the latter respect bore fruit when in

The American Amateur Championship that never was. Charles Blair Macdonald (centre) was expected to win this event at St Andrew's, New York, in 1894 but when he was defeated in the final he had the championship annulled. He was happier in 1895 when he won the first official US Amateur. Macdonald gave a lot to golf, particularly in the field of course architecture, but he immodestly exemplified the philosophy 'Show me a good loser and I'll show you a loser'.

The Scots wasted few opportunities to capitalize on their nationality in America. This aristocratic looking gallery were gathered for an exhibition match in 1896 between Willie Park and Willie Dunn (standing together with their clubs to the right of centre). The group includes Samuel Parrish, a founder-member of Shinnecock Hills (fourth from left), and Theodore Havemeyer, the first president of the USGA (eighth from left).

1909 he unveiled his pride and joy, the National Golf Links, right next door to Shinnecock Hills. Every hole on it was directly inspired by those he had seen and most admired on his travels throughout England and Scotland. Earlier he had designed the Chicago Golf Club, the country's first purpose-built 18-hole course.

Macdonald was a tremendous traditionalist, adamant that American golf should maintain close links with the game's founders. He was also an overpowering bull of a man. In 1894, the Newport Golf Club on Rhode Island, also on the eastern seaboard, staged what was intended to be America's first national amateur championship, over 36 holes of strokeplay. All was well until Macdonald collapsed in the second round with a score of 100 to lose by a stroke. He protested that he had been unjustly penalized by a controversial ruling, and that in any case no self-respecting national competition could be held at strokeplay, as manifested by the fact that he, the best golfer in the land, hadn't won it. Duly cowed, the members of St Andrew's agreed to hold a matchplay event a month later. This too was denied a place in the annals of the sport when Macdonald lost in the final after narrowly failing to overcome the combined effects of a late-night party thrown by Stanford White on the eve (and indeed the morn) of the last day, plus a bottle of champagne quaffed at lunchtime in a bid to drown his hangover.

Call it charisma, nerve, bombast or something ruder, but Macdonald's sharp criticisms of the calibre of the victor were upheld again. The championship did not count. Mr Stoddard went the way of the hapless Mr Lawrence before him and out of the record books. Macdonald bequeathed many things to the generations that followed but sportsmanship and good manners were not among them.

The 1895 US Amateur was more successful. It was the first run under the auspices of the United States Golf Association (USGA) and its first president, Theodore Havemeyer. To quote Charles Price again: 'It became clear to some of the level-headed players that American golf was fast on its way to becoming nothing more than an offshoot of Charlie Macdonald's mercurial personality.'

Accordingly, Havemeyer and two colleagues invited representatives from the nation's five most prominent clubs – St Andrew's, Shinnecock Hills, Chicago, Newport and The Country Club at Brookline, Massachusetts – to join them. John Reid and Macdonald were among these men, and out of this organization has grown the USGA, the American equivalent of the R & A.

The first 'official' US Amateur at Newport was also a success because it was won by Macdonald, though there were a few glum faces at the outcome. He pasted Charlie Sands, a Newport member, by 12 & 11 in the final, but Macdonald didn't suffer from an economy-sized ego and he wasn't satisfied at that. He was determined to set a new course record. He had the local pro hauled out to partner him for the remaining holes,

Another influential figure in the birth of American golf was Henry Tallmadge, one of the founders of St Andrew's and the first secretary of the USGA.

apparently unaware that it wouldn't have counted anyway as the contest had been at matchplay and not everything had been holed out. Having said that, who's to say he wouldn't have bullied the newly-founded authority round to his opinion had he managed to set a new 'record'?

On the day after the Amateur, the first US Open was played on the same course and won by Horace Rawlins, an Englishman, by two strokes from Willie Dunn. There were no complaints as

to the validity of this 36-hole event because Macdonald didn't bother to enter.

From 1895 onwards, golf caught hold in America. It blossomed in the Roaring Twenties as it had in the Gay Nineties and for similar reasons: an economic boom. It survived the Great Depression and the Second World War to be revitalized in the 1960s by Arnold Palmer, President Eisenhower and television, though not necessarily in that order. The impact of these

When Bobby Jones won
the 1930 US Open here at
Interlachen it gave him
the third leg of the
Impregnable
Quadrilateral, or Grand
Slam. His phenomenal
achievements, and the
modest manner in which
he accepted the rewards
of his genius, gave golf
an immense fillip in the
United States in the
Roaring Twenties and
beyond.

factors and others – Walter Travis being the first American-based player to win the British Amateur in 1904; Johnny McDermott being the first native-born American to win his national Open; Francis Ouimet's improbable and romantic triumph over the best of British, Harry Vardon and Ted Ray, at the 1913 US Open; Walter Hagen's domination of the British Open in the 1920s and then Bobby Jones's domination of the whole game – are best dealt with in more appropriate sections of this book. So too, in the next chapter, is the way in which America quickly cornered the equipment market, with the arrival of the A. G. Spalding Company on the scene in 1894 and the invention of the rubber-cored ball by a Cleveland chemist, Coburn Haskell, in 1901.

But it is apposite to note here how the east coast influence was gradually diluted in the face of a comprehensive conversion to the faith. If by 1900 there was at least one course in each of the then 45 states of the Union, the Golden Age between the wars saw a staggering increase along the Pacific shoreline and the creation of fabulous and luxurious resort courses on the mainland, especially in Florida, and on the glorious off-shore islands of the Caribbean. The boundaries of agronomy have been relentlessly pushed back. New strains of grass have been nurtured to cope with the enormous range of climatic conditions encountered across the United States. Even the inhospitable desert is today home to verdant golf courses which present an unbelievable contrast to their bleak, rugged surroundings.

Golf in the United States has never been a seaside game in the strict sense in which it began in Scotland, but the Americans have patented a new set of hallmarks typified by lavish clubhouses; country clubs where golf is but one of several amenities; and real-estate development funding the cost of building a neighbouring resort course. As Peter Dobereiner has written of the early 1900s: 'The game which had started as an informal knock-about on the sandy turf of a Scottish fishing town 450 years previously was now full grown and under new management.'

The American clubs of the early 1900s were so new that in the main they welcomed women members, which would certainly have distressed the old masons in Britain who championed male chauvinism. The rare men-only clubs in the United States became known as 'Eveless Edens', but that early precedent hasn't stopped many exclusive American clubs of the modern era doing more to keep women out than the most rabid anti-feminists have ever done in the United Kingdom.

Different strokes for different folks, ran an old hippie cliché, but throughout the world golf is about the same strokes for different folks. It's even the same away from this earth.

In February 1971, Captain Alan Shepard, commander of the Apollo 14 space mission, hit two shots with a 6-iron while on the surface of the moon. The R & A, jestingly exerting its authority over the game outside the USA, sent him a telegram of congratulations but reminded him that 'before leaving a bunker, a player should carefully fill up and smooth over all holes and footprints made by him.' In 1974, suitably rebuked no doubt, Shepard donated the historic club to the USGA for display in its museum.

Honours even, one might say.

Changing Fashions

Plus ça change, plus c'est la même chose. 'The more things change, the more they're the same.' Golf is still intrinsically the pastime it was centuries ago but there have been major changes to the way we play the sport and what we play it with and in. Some of these developments may be regrettable – the six-hour round and the growth in the use of golf carts and in the size of the rule book – but most are inevitable and have added to our enjoyment of the game.

First, consider the fundamental implements of golf – the ball and the club. Without wishing to reiterate the preamble to the last chapter, it is axiomatic, given what has gone before, that there are earlier references to the clubs and balls of golf – or *colf* – in the Low Countries than exist in Scotland. In the revised second edition of *Early Golf*, published in 1985, the year of his death,

Steven van Hengel discloses several 15th-century references to both club and ballmakers in Holland, and notes that the Scots imported balls from across the North Sea, literally by the barrel-load, as long ago as 1486.

The Dutch *colfers* originally played with wooden balls, generally of elm or beech, which had negligible aerodynamic properties. They gradually adopted a ball made of white leather and filled with cow's hair which was used in the local game of *kaatsen* (hand tennis). Although Roman soldiers had played *paganica* in Britain with a leather ball stuffed with feathers over a millenium before this, it almost certainly died out with their departure. It is therefore likely that it was the *kaatsen* ball which inspired the Scots to invent the feathery sometime in the 17th or early 18th century as a substitute for the wooden ball which, despite a lack of hard evidence, was probably the popular ball of the day.

The feathery consisted of a leather casing, usually bull's hide, soaked in alum and crammed with goose feathers which had been softened by boiling. This was then knocked into shape (round, of course!) and painted white to make it more visible and more resistant to the elements. On drying it became tighter and firmer. It weighed about the same as the modern ball (1.62 ounces) and was usually a similar size, though in those days there was no uniform diameter.

The feathery had two diverse effects. First the good news. Whereas the cumbersome wooden ball could seldom be propelled more than 100 yards, distances of twice that and more were regularly achieved with the feathery. Samuel Messieux, a Swiss schoolteacher based at St Andrews, boomed a measured drive of 361 yards over the Old Course in 1836. Conditions were slightly favourable – a frosty ground and a helping breeze – but the prodigious blow emphasized the qualities of the feathery. In wet weather, when it became rather soggy, its advantage over the wooden ball was not so marked. It is worth

Making a feathery. Each ball required a top hat full of feathers, usually from a goose although chicken feathers were also suitable. After the manufacturing process was complete a feathery cost up to four shillings, making golf an expensive game for those who wished to use the best equipment.

noting that the very act of stitching up the finished product inadvertently assisted its flight because the seams fulfilled a similar, if cruder, role to that played by the dimples which help the modern ball get airborne.

But the feathery had a downside too. It made golf far too expensive for the ordinary man. One feathery cost twelve times the price of the old boxwood ball and, astonishingly, about the same as a wooden club. Even the most skilled craftsman struggled to produce more than four a day, which accounted for its apparently exorbitant price, and the average player may have used that many balls a round due to the feathery's tendency to split or get too damp. It could also, of course, in the time-honoured manner, be lost.

The less wealthy no doubt had to make do with wooden balls for decades after the coming of the feathery, and it is from this era that golf's unwanted and unjustified image as a rich man's preserve still lingers; as no doubt does the equally unwelcome tag of being an old man's pursuit. In Scotland it has managed to retain a name as a game for the common man, even though that has not always been the case, but from the moment that the Stuart kings took the game south to England with them golf has always been exported with an up-market designer label. The introduction of the gutta percha ball in 1848 may not have eradicated golf's snobby reputation but it did an enormous amount to restore it as a genuinely popular game.

Gutta percha is like sap, a gum which can be tapped from trees indigenous to Malaya. The substance is malleable when boiled in water and becomes hard on cooling. Equally important for the 19th-century golfer, it had enough 'give' to be a suitable material for a ball.

There are mixed accounts as to how gutta percha came to find its niche in golf, but there is no disputing that disputes were what it caused in the 1850s as rival ballmakers like the Gourlays, Allan Robertson and Old Tom Morris wrestled with their consciences as to whether they should switch from featheries to gutties. Eventually they did, though not without intermittent acrimony, and even the Honourable Company of Edinburgh Golfers made the great transition for their Silver Club competition in 1865. With that, the last feathery had flown.

Its demise was not so much due to the greater distance that could be attained with the gutty as the difference in cost. Because the process involved in the manufacture of the latter was a great deal simpler, it was approximately a quarter

of the price of a feathery. At a shilling a ball, with clubs at 3s 6d (17½p) each and the highest subscription in the land standing at three guineas (£3.15), this was the age when golf in Britain became a game for everyone. The increased leisure time created by the prosperity of the Industrial Revolution was another vital ingredient that enabled the sport to catch the imagination of the nation.

The gutty could be remoulded if badly damaged, which was just as well since in the early days it was prone to break up in mid-air, thus forcing the Rules to accommodate this tendency by allowing the golfer to play a fresh ball from the point where the largest fragment had come to rest. This would be by no means the last occasion on which the Rules of Golf had to be amended to

Old Tom Morris (left) and Allan Robertson combining their considerable talents in a match at St Andrews in 1849. These two were not only outstanding golfers but skilled craftsmen, and around this time they were anxiously considering and vehemently arguing about the respective merits of the feathery and gutty balls. In this match they are using a feathery; note also the wooden putters.

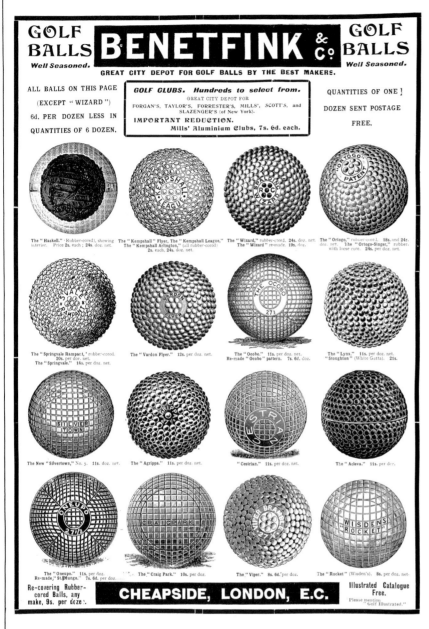

was wound around a rubber core under extreme tension and then encased in a patterned outer cover of gutta percha. Though there were a few initial teething troubles not unlike those that beset the gutty, it had the inestimable advantage of covering a reasonable amount of ground when mis-hit, whereas the less lively gutty went nowhere and left a stinging sensation in the fingers if topped.

The Haskell ball was dubbed as being fit only for hackers by the great Harry Vardon – largely, one suspects, because he could see that it would scupper the prospects of the Vardon Flyer, a Spalding-made gutty ball, which he had launched in America on a mammoth promotional tour in 1900 – and derided by others as a 'Bounding Billy' that would ruin the finer arts of shotmaking. If the ostriches could not see that a ball capable of compensating for a mis-hit was a gift from heaven to most golfers, in 1902 they were shown what a difference it made to the best players when Sandy Herd played four rounds at Royal Liverpool in 307 to beat Vardon and James Braid by one shot for the Open. Herd used the same ball for all 72 holes. It was a Haskell, and he was the only man in the field to play with one. Goodbye gutty.

From that moment, the Haskell ball has been improved to such effect that it has spawned a host of dicta from the R & A and USGA, the dual arbiters of the integrity of the sport. In 1920 they agreed the ball should weigh no more than 1.62 ounces and have a diameter of not less than 1.62 inches, a radical move since until then there had been no restrictions whatsoever, although the earlier enforcement of a 4¼-inch hole obviously ruled out ridiculously large balls. Both bodies pledged to 'take whatever steps they think necessary to limit the powers of the ball with regard to distance should any ball of greater power be introduced'.

But, from January 1931, the USGA turned its back on collective responsibility and opted for independence regarding the ball. The 'big ball' was introduced, having a minimum size of 1.68 inches and a maximum weight of 1.55 ounces. A year later the weight stipulation was raised to 1.62 ounces and that remains the position today.

The idea behind the big ball had been to provide 'an easier and pleasanter ball for the average golfer' but, as with Haskell's invention, the big ball was soon perceived to be better for professionals as well. It sat up more invitingly on America's predominantly parkland courses (unlike the smaller ball which had evolved in the

legislate for the properties of the golf ball. For the remainder of the 19th century, the new ball was repeatedly modified to make it more durable, and its outer shell was indented with a hammer after it was observed that the ball flew better when it had been cut or marked than when in its smooth, pristine state.

As quickly as the gutty came onto the scene, it was superceded. In 1901, the rubber-cored ball made its British debut. It was the invention of the fledgling American golf equipment industry. The idea belonged to Coburn Haskell, an employee of the Goodrich Tyre and Rubber Company in Ohio, and it was developed by a colleague with the appropriate name of Mr Work. Elastic thread windy conditions and tight lies prevalent in British links golf) and was easier to chip and putt well with – all benefits for the club player. However, it was also less forgiving of bad shots. American professionals therefore had to improve their striking technique in order to master the big ball.

In 1951, the USGA rejected a proposal, advanced by a special committee of its own and R & A members, that each ball should ordinarily be legal on both sides of the Atlantic (the Canadians had sided with the United States in 1948), though they agreed to the suggestion for players in international team competitions. Subsequent attempts to settle for a uniform ball, perhaps of 1.66 inches, failed, but the American belief in the supremacy of their ball has since been acknowledged as justified. The Professional Golfers' Association in Britain, swayed by the persuasive voices of those who attributed the American dominance of golf to their employment of the big ball, announced in 1968 that it was to experiment with the 1.68-inch version in its tournaments. Soon it was mandatory. In 1974, the R & A made the big ball compulsory for the Open Championship.

In still more recent times, the ball has – literally – gone from strength to strength. The original gutta percha shell of the Haskell has given way to new and refined compounds; as a rough guide, balata for the pros, surlyn (discovered by a chemist named Richard Rees) for the rest of us. Millions have been spent researching the properties of various formations of dimples. Winding has got tighter. Ironically, wound balls now compete with solid balls for their share of the market, though the solid ball of today is far removed from the solid wooden ball of *colf's* dark past. It is a two-piece composition invented by Bob Molitor, a research and development executive for the Spalding company, which is ideal for club golfers.

In the modern era, that pledge of 1920 has become meaningful. The young lions, or gorillas, of professional tournament golf hit the ball so far that many experts are worried that hundreds of the world's best courses are in danger of becoming obsolete. The imposition of an Initial Velocity Standard (set at 250 feet per second under test conditions) and an Overall Distance Standard has not stopped players like Davis Love III of America, to cite the best current example, from reaching 500-yard-plus holes with a drive and a sand wedge. This sort of hitting, though more

powerful and prevalent among contemporary golfers, is not an entirely new phenomenon. Back in 1966 Henry Longhurst, the famous writer and broadcaster, recognizing that excessive distance is only undesirable when given to professionals and is actually the biggest boon of all for mere mortals, advocated 'a special and shorter "tournament ball" for "them" and another, the present one, for "us".'

That is a cry frequently echoed nowadays, but talk of a standard tournament ball is invariably resisted by the players and manufacturers. The only limit in existence is that a ball to be used in competition has to be on a list of 'conforming balls' published and revised annually by the R & A and the USGA. As scientists continue to discover ways to squeeze even more dimples on to that little sphere, they are surely sending the ball progressively further.

Opposite Golf ball advertisements around the turn of the century. Note the Vardon Flyer is included on Benetfink & Co.'s wide range.

Below The evolution of the golf ball. From back to front: feathery, unmarked gutty, marked gutty and two early rubber-cored balls. The latter formed the basis for the developments shown in the next five – the bramble pattern, lattice pattern, dimple pattern, refined dimple pattern, and the modern ball which exemplifies the way more (and more efficient) dimples are being used.

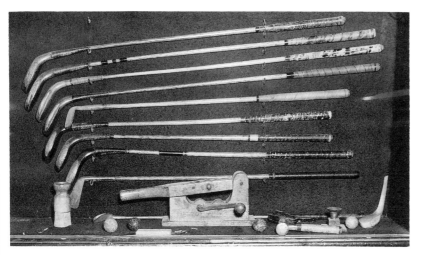

Old Tom Morris was perhaps golf's ultimate all-rounder – a great champion, ballmaker and clubmaker. This picture shows his own championship-winning clubs and some of the implements used in his St Andrews workshop to make the clubs and balls of his era.

A modern set of clubs. In the foreground are the blocks from which wooden heads are fashioned.

Further may be acceptable, but a few years ago the USGA drew the line at the no-hook, no-slice Polara ball because it was considered to undermine the integrity of the game. It was banned. The inventors engaged the USGA in bitter and expensive court proceedings which cost the governing body millions of dollars, but the prohibition was upheld. On the other hand, in 1984 the MacGregor company in America introduced the Cayman Ball, named after the Caribbean island where Jack Nicklaus was then building a resort course. It flies about 125 yards and is designed to make short 'executive' courses play like the real thing. No threat to the game's integrity there.

Golf ball manufacturing today is big business indeed, far removed from the age when Allan Robertson was stitching up his featheries and muttering darkly about the gutty. What would he have made of pink, yellow and orange balls?

The mass production of the ball throughout this century has brought golf within the pocket and reach of millions of people all over the world, and the improvement in its playing characteristics has perhaps been the single largest factor in enhancing our enjoyment of the game. It is for this reason that I have dwelt so long on the subject. However, a better ball would not be much use without better clubs with which to hit it.

It is man's primeval instinct to hit something with a stick. Clubs, whether they be for *paganica*, *cambuca*, *chole*, *colf* or golf, have been adapted for their specific purpose from this basic principle. Neither the Dutch nor the Scots can claim to have invented this innate desire, though the Scots can produce proof to show that they supplied wooden clubs to Holland around 1650.

Clubmaking came into its own with the advent of the feathery. Clubs no longer had to withstand the impact of striking a solid wooden ball, and artistry was given a free reign. Exquisite wooden clubs were fashioned from ash, thorn, apple and pearwood. The emphasis was on woods because irons would have inflicted untold damage on the delicate feathery and were generally used only for extricating the errant golfer from the awkward lies to be found in cart tracks and on railway lines.

But irons were ideally suited to the less yielding gutty when it appeared in 1848, whereas the wood-makers had to run to harder materials for the clubhead, which became more rounded and less banana-shaped. The period up to the end of the 19th century is a marvellous tale of the skills of Scotland's master clubmakers: the Dicksons, Henry Miln, Simon Cossar, Hugh Philp, Robert Forgan and others. It is admirably told by Henderson and Stirk in *Golf In The Making* but sadly there is no room for detail here.

By the turn of the century, the Americans had not only produced the Haskell ball but also begun to dominate the club market. They had unlimited natural resources available and wooden clubs were their forte, though for a while they still looked to Britain for iron heads. Persimmon and dogwood were employed in the making of these new woods, and hickory replaced ash in the shaft. From that time until the present day, the United States has led the equipment field.

When the Haskell ball made its controversial debut in Britain at around 2s (10p) a time, iron clubs cost just 3s 6d (17½p) and woods 5s (25p). That tiny margin between ball and club has since widened dramatically. A top-class ball today is anything up to £2; a club can cost from under £20 to hundreds.

As for clubs, forget the simple distinction between woods and irons. Now both can have a wide range of shafts – for example, steel, aluminium or carbon – with different swingweights, flexpoints, kickpoints, etc. to suit. (This whole area is a delight to jargon fans, with phrases like 'frequency matching' and 'peripheral weight distribution' littering the manufacturers' advertisements.) Woods don't necessarily have a wooden head. It could be metal, graphite, plastic or something more exotic; and might have a special section of yet another substance inserted in the clubface to fit the particular golfer's requirements. Irons may be hollowed out or solid or, again, have a super-compound head rather than steel.

Some of these developments are doomed to be regarded by posterity as mere fads; others will change the game forever, as did the arrival of steel shafts. Steel didn't have the problems of high torque, or twisting, inherent in hickory, and it enabled accurately matched sets of clubs to be mass produced, an invaluable aid to the average player.

Steel shafts were not allowed until 1924 when the USGA legalized them. At that time, the R & A ruled, 'it is much to be deplored that players, instead of trying to master the use of clubs, should endeavour to overcome the difficulties of the game by using implements which have never been associated with it', but by 1930 the R & A had acquiesced. Ironically, that was the year Bobby Jones won the Grand Slam, playing with hickory-shafted clubs. It was effectively their last hurrah, but what a way to go out.

Two years later, Gene Sarazen was practising his bunker play. He wasn't satisfied with the niblick he had been using so he had additional metal soldered on to it, creating a heavy, broad-flanged sole. Thus was born the sand wedge, and so efficacious was it that later in the summer Sarazen won both the British and US Opens.

Steel shafts and the sand wedge are an integral part of the modern game, but one does not need to be an unashamed romantic to mourn the passing of terms like niblick (9-iron), brassie (2-wood), spoon (3-wood), driving-iron (1-iron), mashie (5-iron) and mashie-niblick (7-iron). Even the 1-wood, which bears the universal name of 'driver', was formerly known as the play club since, in the days before the tee peg was invented, it was the club selected to drive the ball into play from a small mound of earth or sand. The putter, of course, has always been the putter. It is far too individual, too mercurial, to be known by an anonymous number.

Ever since there has been a hole to aim at, golfers have complained about their putter, often ignoring the obvious truth of the old proverb: 'It's a bad workman who blames his tools.' Putters used to be made of wood, but less so after the arrival of the gutty when iron heads came into fashion. They have come in all sorts of weird and wonderful shapes; with mirrors attached, on wheels, on rollers – you name it, it's been tried. These crazy-looking contraptions aren't just footnotes in the history books either: the Basakwerd putter, with its blade fixed to the shaft in reverse, was in vogue for a while on the US Senior Tour; former US and British Open

Left **Robert Forgan in his factory in 1880. He was one of the first to use hickory in making shafts, and he chose his materials with meticulous care. He was a pioneer in clubmaking technology and also in ball production.**

Below **The golf club business is big business – and so it was in the 1920s when Heath Robinson, that king of bizarre creations, was inspired to create 'An interesting new machine for testing the driving force of drivers in an up-to-date Golf Club Factory'.**

Putters have always been the most individual of golf clubs and have frequently aroused great controversy and debate. Walter Travis was caricatured with his Schenectady putter by *Golf Illustrated* after winning the Amateur Championship with it at Sandwich in 1904, thus causing the R & A to ban the centre-shafted putter. Bernhard Langer's unorthodox weapon reflects the contemporary professional's ceaseless search for the secret of the greens.

champion Johnny Miller has had success with a 48-inch putter which demands that the shaft be locked under the left armpit; 1985 Masters champion Bernhard Langer has wielded one with three plastic balls attached in line behind the head; and Jack Nicklaus won the 1986 Masters with a weapon which resembled a vacuum cleaner.

These have all stayed within the laws of the game, unlike the notorious Schenectady (centre-shafted) putter with which Walter Travis broke the British stranglehold on their own Amateur Championship in 1904. There was a good deal of ill-feeling all that week at Sandwich between Travis and the officials. When the R & A outlawed the instrument shortly thereafter, in what was widely seen as a fit of pique, they exported the unsavoury atmosphere across the Atlantic. Relations with the USGA were strained for a long time afterwards, perhaps accounting for the lack of agreement over the legalization of steel shafts and the breakaway over the ball. It was to be nearly half a century before the centre-shafted putter was given the R & A's blessing, and when that happened it paved the way for Ben Hogan – who used one – to make his solitary but successful pilgrimage to the Open Championship, at Carnoustie in 1953.

Clubs have had about as big an impact on the Rules of Golf as the ball. In 1938, the USGA restricted a player to a maximum of 14 clubs in his bag, a decision ratified by the R & A in 1939. The situation was getting badly out of hand. Caddies were having to lug round 30 clubs or more.

Club technology has repeatedly come under the microscope. Take grooves for instance. In 1949 the Americans protested that the grooves on the British players' irons for the Ryder Cup match at Ganton in Yorkshire were too deep. Ben Hogan, the US captain, requested that the clubfaces be filed down. His wish was granted. In 1977 Tom Watson was at the centre of a controversy when it was disclosed that the grooves on the clubs with which he had won so many championships were in contravention of the regulations. Should he retrospectively be disqualified for obtaining an unfair, if inadvertent, advantage, some purists asked. The answer was, rightfully, 'no'. At the time of writing, several of the world's best players are praising the latest (and currently legal) grooves on certain pitching clubs which allegedly enable them to impart greater control over the ball.

Some scientists say that such talk is nonsense; that no grooves are just as good as deep grooves, square-shaped grooves, or whatever. Try telling that to the players. The debate is reminiscent of the received wisdom that says weather conditions cannot affect the flight of a cricket ball. There isn't a man who's played on a heavy, overcast morning at Headingley who would agree with that.

The Rules of Golf have been amended considerably since the original 13 were enacted by the Honourable Company of Edinburgh Golfers in 1744 (see panel). That's hardly surprising; indeed, to pursue the cricketing analogy for a moment longer, that very same year the number of balls to be delivered in an over was set at four, and was not to reach six until 1900. The passage of time involves the passing of customs.

The first golf Rules were devised for matchplay and the one that was to cause the greatest argument was the original Rule 6, concerning touching balls. In 1775, 'touching' was redefined to mean within six inches of each other. The stymie had arrived.

The effect of the stymie rule was that the player furthest from the hole *had* to putt first. If his opponent's ball was dead on his line to the hole – assuming they were over six inches apart – it was too bad. He had to negotiate the obstacle as best he could. Some thought the stymie an abomination, an evil without merit since it could not be negated by the sporting gesture of putting out first. Others felt it was simply part of the strategy of golf, and this view was expressed with such ferocity that when the St Andrews' Society abolished the stymie in 1833 they felt compelled to restore it in 1834.

It was in 1834 that the Royal and Ancient Golf Club was created and soon its version of the Rules were accepted throughout Britain and beyond in preference to those of the Honourable Company, the latter body gracefully acceding to the inevitable decline in its influence. The R & A presided over an increase to 22 Rules in 1854, when St Andrews celebrated its centenary as a golf society.

In 1897 the R & A appointed its first Rules of Golf Committee but, as we have seen, its relationship with the USGA for over half a century was not entirely cordial – at best uncertain, at worst frosty. Differences in the formal Decisions each body handed down meant that the understanding of the Rules varied.

Accordingly, in 1951 a bid was made to heal the breach for the good of the game. A series of conferences was organized and the R & A and USGA arranged to meet regularly to review the Rules in unison. They could not reach a

---

Articles and Laws in Playing at Golf 1744

1 You must Tee your Ball, within a Club's length of the Hole.
2 Your Tee must be upon the Ground.
3 You are not to change the Ball which you Strike off the Tee.
4 You are not to remove Stones, Bones or any Break Club, for the sake of playing your Ball, Except upon the fair Green, and that only within a Club's length of your Ball.
5 If your Ball comes among Watter, or any wattery filth, you are at liberty to take out your Ball and bringing it behind the hazard and Teeing it, you may play it with any Club and allow your Adversary a Stroke, for so getting out your Ball.
6 If your Balls be found anywhere touching one another you are to lift the first Ball, till you play the last.
7 At Holling, you are to play your Ball honestly for the Hole, and not to play upon your Adversary's Ball, not lying in your way to the Hole.
8 If you should lose your Ball, by its being taken up, or any other way you are to go back to the Spot, where you struck last, and drop another Ball, And allow your Adversary a Stroke for the Misfortune.
9 No man at Holling his Ball, is to be allowed, to mark his way to the Hole with his Club or any thing else.
10 If a Ball be stopp'd by any person, Horse, Dog, or any thing else, the Ball so stopp'd must be played where it lyes.
11 If you draw your Club, in order to Strike and proceed so far in the Stroke, as to be bringing down your Club; if then, your Club shall break, in any way, it is to be accounted a Stroke.
12 He whose Ball lyes farthest from the Hole is obliged to play first.
13 Neither Trench, Ditch or Dyke, made for the preservation of the Links, nor the Scholar's Holes or the Soldier's Lines, Shall be accounted a Hazard. But the Ball is to be taken out Teed and play'd with any Iron Club.

John Rattray, Capt

The title of the print says it all – 'Stymied'. The stymie was finally abolished in 1951, but not before it had helped Bobby Jones defeat Cyril Tolley at the 19th hole in the fourth round of the Amateur in his Grand Slam year of 1930, a circumstance which the sporting American always regretted.

satisfactory compromise on the size of the ball but they did agree to jettison the stymie, thereby killing off a unique facet of matchplay.

Subsequently a Joint Decisions Committee has been set up to ensure uniformity of interpretation and even now the Rules are changing. As recently as 1984 the old method of dropping the ball, behind one's shoulder, was altered so that now the player 'shall stand erect, hold the ball at shoulder height and arm's length and drop it' (Rule 20–2a).

Golf has changed in so many other ways too. For example, nearly 100 years ago Harry Vardon came to prominence, and he may be said to have revolutionized the golf swing.

Vardon, who won the first of his record six Open Championships in 1896, not only gave his name to the overlapping grip which he popularized – although at least one leading player, Johnny Laidlay, a Scot who won the Amateur in 1889 and 1891, had used it before Vardon – but also used a swing which was then decidedly unorthodox. He stood slightly open to the ball at address whereas his rivals were closed; and he took the club away in an upright arc rather than with a long, low backswing. The consequences of these two moves enabled him to hit the ball from left to right, thereby reducing the risk of hooking. He could also hit the ball higher if required.

Throughout this century the best players have allied their own, individual actions to the improvements in equipment and worked on creating a swing to stand up under the rigours and pressures of tournament golf. Nobody has ever done it with such flowing grace, rhythm and style as Bobby Jones; no one has toiled so long on the range or hit so many perfect shots as Ben Hogan; no man has practised with such reward as Jack Nicklaus.

These three, together with Vardon, may well be the finest golfers in history. It is beyond dispute that there have been none better, but the secret of golf does not lie in copying them since even these four had, or have, idiosyncratic quirks which worked for them but wouldn't for others. It is a fact that fashions in golf swings will continue to come and go as the fortunes of the disciples of a particular method wax and wane. One year upright is in, the next sees the emergence of the low, slinging action. Does the left or right hand dominate? Does one try to fade or draw the ball? Would the interlocking, overlapping or 10-finger grip be best? And what about putting cack-handed, with the left hand below the right?

These and similar questions have been asked for the past 100 years and will be repeated for as long as golf is played. It is impossible to identify a certain style with a particular time, but we can be sure than when Harry Vardon began seriously to tinker with the fundamentals of the golf swing, he was setting a precedent that has fascinated millions of less gifted practitioners ever since.

In a chapter entitled 'Changing Fashions', it

Johnny Laidlay (left) and Harry Vardon, respectively a top amateur and the best professional of their days. These pictures have several similarities – such as the wide stance and the required, not to say restrictive, clothing worn on the course then – but chief among them is the grip. Vardon gave his name to the overlapping grip but it is reckoned that, in fact, Laidlay employed it successfully to win his two Amateur titles before Vardon won the first of his six Opens in 1896. Note too how Vardon proved generations before the birth of English professional Brian Barnes that it was possible to play well with a pipe in the mouth.

A detail from an engraving after Charles Lees's 'The Golfers – A Grand Match Played Over St Andrews Links', published in 1850. The illustration reinforces the points about golf fashions made hitherto. The swallow-tail coats and the top hats sported by the players were the regular dress of the gentry. The caddies have no bags. Of special interest is the little girl dispensing Ginger Beer, the drink which gives its name to the fourth hole of the Old Course.

would be remiss not to consider briefly how fashion itself has changed. It won't come as a total shock to learn that the most radical revisions in the mode of attire have concerned lady golfers, and due attention will be devoted to the sartorial aspects of the female game in Chapter 12, but a few words are in order here about the men.

If one was playing golf in the hearty days of the masons, formal dress was as much a part of the ceremony as it is today at a grand dinner or official function. A red or scarlet jacket was *de rigueur*, to be changed for a blue or grey one when it was time to sit down to the real business of eating and drinking. This splendid idea of a uniform was enthusiastically taken up by golf's early exponents in the New World. Around the same time the likes of Vardon played championship-winning golf while sporting a buttoned, ventless jacket. Indeed, Vardon felt the constraints this imposed on the body were an asset in maintaining a good, repetitive swing.

Climate was, inevitably, a major factor in the deregulation of clothing. Wearing a jacket to play golf in the August heat of central United States made no sense at all, yet that is exactly what Vardon and Ted Ray elected to do during the 1920 US Open at Inverness in Ohio. What's more, Vardon should have won the tournament and Ray did. Even the American competitors that week, although dispensing with jackets, wore a shirt and tie, and plus-fours (with trousers tucked into knee-length socks or stockings) were heavily favoured. From this time onward, conservative casual wear came into vogue. Ties were on the decline, but the vivid colours that adorn the modern tour pro were not spotted on the golf course until Jimmy Demaret and Max Faulkner arrived on the scene.

Demaret won the Masters three times either side of the Second World War, but his clothes did not always meet with the same approval as his golf. Pink and violet, lemon and peach – he tried

Casually smart attire in 1924 for a £500 international challenge match at Weybridge. From left to right: Macdonald Smith (USA), George Duncan (GB), Walter Hagen (USA) and Abe Mitchell (GB).

Sartorial elegance and shotmaking eloquence: Jimmy Demaret (left), three-time Masters champion and a pioneer of flashy golf gear; and Payne Stewart, one of the new breed of young professionals who flamboyantly revel in the opportunity to recall the pre-war era.

The golf cart *reductio ad absurdum* – comedian Bob Hope's $12,000 custom-built vehicle, with an instant replay machine for Hope to check his swing.

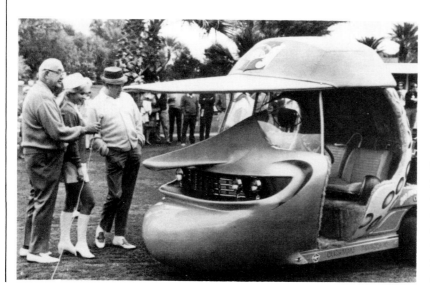

all sorts of combinations. At the 1949 Ryder Cup match he unsettled his opponent by stepping on to the first tee clad in a scarlet cap, salmon pink sweater and cherry red trousers. Faulkner, the 1951 Open champion, was similarly inclined to resemble a rainbow. Doug Sanders, who carried a vivid purple colour to disaster at the 1970 Open, continued the tradition and since then flamboyant dress has had to be pretty outrageous to be worthy of comment.

Rodger Davis from Australia and the American Payne Stewart recall the old days with their abbreviated plus-four socks (known as 'plus-twos' in Britain and 'knickers' in America, with sometimes embarrassing consequences in the UK). Conventional contemporary golf gear – brightly coloured or patterned V-neck sweaters

and wide-collared shirts – are now, despite the efforts of men like Greg Norman who shone like a beacon as he bestrode Turnberry's gloomy fairways *en route* to winning the 1986 Open, challenged by casual apparel straight out of the boutiques and fashion stores. Somewhere up above, Vardon is probably looking down in disgust, Demaret with delight.

This chapter started with a reference to my personal *bête noire* of post-war golf and it will end in the same manner. The golf cart has, on the whole, been one of America's less glorious contributions to the game. It has simultaneously managed to reduce a healthy exercise into a motorized recipe for bad backs, weak hips and flabby bellies; slowed it down by up to two hours when logic dictates it should have speeded matters up; and spoiled golf's visual appeal with ugly tarmac roads which regularly produce the following kind of absurd and infuriating spectacle.

Two men drive off from the tee in their cart and proceed 125 yards down the path on the left side of the fairway. One then climbs out, selects three clubs from his bag and saunters 150 yards across to the right rough where he's hit his sixth slice of the day. Meanwhile, his companion is in the trees to the left after exchanging his normal top for one out of the heel. Suddenly, action. The first player realizes he can get a wood at his shot. He makes his way back to the cart a little faster than he left it, leaving his three clubs by the ball. He then spots the group behind angrily stalking the tee, so he races back across the fairway with his wood and, by now totally flustered and disconcerted, hits another low slice even further right and only about 50 yards ahead. A cursory inspection reveals that he has no choice but to play his sand wedge, but of course that is back at the cart. He tears over for it (but not before forgetting his original three clubs) and there finds his mate, who has lost his ball but realizes that his partner's predicament has left him a chance of saving the hole. He's now contemplating driving back to play three off the tee. So it can go on, *ad nauseam*.

Golf carts are not all bad. They are marvellous for infirm or elderly golfers, they can be desirable in extreme heat, and they make a lot of money for clubs that operate them, thus helping to keep other expenses down. But, on the whole, the golf cart is confirmation that change is not always for the better and proof that progress does not necessarily take us forward – especially if the damned thing is stuck in reverse.

CHAPTER THREE

Household Names

The most widely accepted test of a golfer's greatness is his performance in the game's major championships. In the modern era, these comprise the Open Championship (or 'British Open' as it is sometimes referred to in this book in order to avoid confusion, though often so-called in error elsewhere), the US Open, the Masters (held in America each April) and the USPGA Championship. If one sets a minimum requirement of four major victories for inclusion in a ranking of great golfers, there are 23 qualifiers, but such a strict stipulation ignores so many other important attributes which deserve to be reflected in the list of 30 published here. Therefore, in an admittedly arbitrary manner, three of the 23 have been omitted and 10 'outsiders' brought. At least that leaves 20 beyond dispute.

The reluctant recipients of the bullet are Willie Park, winner of the first Open Championship and subsequently three more; Willie Anderson, four times winner of the US Open in five years at the turn of the century; and Jim Barnes, the emigrant Cornishman who in 10 seasons from 1916 won two PGAs and an Open on either side of the Atlantic. The achievements of all three are duly chronicled in the ensuing pages which deal with the history of each of the majors, but for the time being my excuse is that to include them would mean over-emphasizing the early years of championship golf and failing to give due recognition to the current stars.

Two of the 10 'outsiders' span the centuries: John Ball and Harold Hilton, great British amateurs from the era when amateurs could compete successfully against the professionals, and when the British and American Amateur Championships ranked only a notch below the two Opens. The remaining eight are professionals. In order, with the number of majors each has won, they are: Henry Cotton (3); Tony Jacklin and Johnny Miller (2); Roberto de Vicenzo, Bernhard Langer, Sandy Lyle and Greg Norman (1); and Isao Aoki (none).

Cotton was the outstanding non-American golfer of the 1930s and 1940s and three times Open champion. Several rivals of his time and later have won three majors – Tommy Armour, Denny Shute, Ralph Guldahl, Jimmy Demaret, Cary Middlecoff, Julius Boros and Billy Casper – but they were, as individuals, just one of many fine, or even finer, American players. Cotton, on the other hand, was an inspiration to future generations of Britons, like Jacklin and Lyle. The former's place in history is merited for similar reasons as Cotton's, whereas Lyle, like Langer and Norman, is a top player of the contemporary breed who could well have added to his total by the time you read this.

Miller may be a contentious pick too. Six other Americans (Dave Stockton, Hale Irwin, Larry Nelson, Fuzzy Zoeller, Andy North and Hubert Green), plus the American-based Australian David Graham, have won two of golf's big four in the last two decades, but none have dazzled the public as much as Miller did with the brilliance of his golf. Finally, de Vicenzo and Aoki are international choices, men who have done untold good in enhancing the game respectively in South America and Japan.

Apart from Ball and Hilton – and, of course, the incomparable Bobby Jones – the selection contains no amateurs: no Walter Travis, Jerome Travers, Francis Ouimet, Lawson Little or Michael Bonallack, all indubitably worthy of the label 'great'. There are no women, though Joyce Wethered (Lady Heathcoat-Amory), 'Babe' Zaharias, Mickey Wright and arguably one or two more would have a strong claim if the criteria were different.

These golfers and more are to be found within the relevant Chapters 11 and 12. In the meantime, I trust this list is thought-provoking. It certainly has not been devoid of thought.

The order in which the golfers are featured is chronological by the year in which they won their first major championship.

THE MORRISES In the last century the two Tom Morrises (Old and Young as they have inevitably been dubbed by history) created a little golfing dynasty that has never been known before or since. Aged 40, Old Tom won his first Open Championship – only the second ever held – in 1861, defended the title successfully 12 months later (by a margin of 13 strokes, still a record) and then won it twice more, in 1864 and 1867. On the first three occasions he was based at Prestwick, the Ayrshire club which hosted the first 12 Opens from 1860 to 1872. By the time of his fourth triumph he had returned to St Andrews as Custodian of the Links (effectively greenkeeper to the R & A), a position he retained until 1903, five years prior to his death.

Old Tom played in the Open until 1896, but by then his even more brilliant son was 21 years dead. Young Tom was born in 1851 and by 1868 he had won his first Open. He repeated the victory in 1869 – with his father in second place – and 1870. The completion of this incredible hat-trick by a man still a teenager earned him outright possession of the Championship Belt and caused a hiatus of one year before the Open was resumed in 1872. Young Tom then became the first winner of the replacement trophy, the coveted claret jug

OLD AND YOUNG TOM MORRIS

which is still contested today. No other golfer has ever won four consecutive Opens. His winning scores of 149 in 1870 and 154 in 1869 were never matched by anyone between 1860 and 1891, after when the championship began to be held over 72 rather than 36 holes. Young Tom died on Christmas Day 1875 of a ruptured lung, just three months after learning of the sudden death of his wife and baby son while he was playing an exhibition match with his father. He never recovered from the shock.

JOHN BALL AND HAROLD HILTON
Both from Liverpool, Ball and Hilton share with Bobby Jones the proud distinction of being the only amateurs to win the Open Championship. Ball, the son of a Hoylake hotelier, grew up on the Royal Liverpool links and as a 14-year-old in 1878 he finished fourth in the Open. He won it in 1890, thus breaking the Scottish monopoly on the title and presaging a period of English domination. Hilton, eight years younger than Ball, was triumphant in 1892, the year it was extended to 72 holes, and 1897.

But it was their perfomances in the Amateur Championship which were so consistently brilliant. From 1888 to 1912 Ball won it eight times, a tally which one can state categorically

HAROLD HILTON

JOHN BALL

will never be equalled. His record would probably have been even more formidable had he not taken a three-year sabbatical from golf to fight in the Boer War.

The first of these years was 1900 and that was also the occasion when Hilton (already three times a beaten finalist, once – in 1892 – at Ball's hands) took his first Amateur Championship. He was to be successful thrice more before the First World War, most notably in 1911 when he paired his win at Prestwick with the US Amateur at Apawamis, New York. This made him the first man, and still the only Briton, to achieve that double, but he had to survive a tremendous scare in the latter as Fred Herreshoff recovered from 6 down at one stage to take him to the 37th.

THE GREAT TRIUMVIRATE James Braid (1870), Harry Vardon (1870), and J. H. – John Henry – Taylor (1871) were born within 14 months of each other and they remained such close contemporaries that, from 1894 until the outbreak of the First World War, they won 16 Open Championships between them. They dominated the Open so overwhelmingly that on the five occasions another man was able to win, one of the three – who have since been hailed as 'The Great Triumvirate' – was second.

Taylor was quickest off the mark. In 1894, Royal St George's at Sandwich became the first English club to host the championship. Taylor made it a double-Anglo celebration by being the first English professional to win it. Any Scottish hopes that this was a mere geographical aberration were dispelled when he retained the title at St Andrews the next year. In later life Taylor assumed the mantle of champion for the lowly artisan golfers and he was a prime mover in the foundation of the British PGA, but in 1896 his bid for a hat-trick of Opens was thwarted after a play-off with Vardon.

Vardon, whose advancement of golf technique was referred to in the previous chapter, won again in 1898 and 1899, and in between an endless stream of tournament victories and lucrative exhibition matches he found time to go to America for more of the same in 1900. While there, he became the first transatlantic traveller to win either Open when he captured the title at Chicago. Taylor was runner-up. Vardon took his fourth Open in 1903 but shortly afterwards he contracted tuberculosis. This weakened him considerably (some say irreparably), but he recovered sufficiently to win for a fifth and then a

J. H. TAYLOR, JAMES BRAID AND HARRY VARDON

record sixth time in 1911 and 1914. In 1913 he failed to collect a second US Open when he and Ted Ray were defeated by Francis Ouimet in a momentous play-off; and only a terrible storm and fatigue denied him the 1920 US Open.

Whereas Taylor was from Devon and Vardon a native of the Channel Islands, the traditionalists could rejoice that Braid at least was a Scotsman. He was from Fife; a powerful golfer blessed with a serene disposition. When he won his first Open in 1901, Taylor and Vardon already had three victories apiece. By 1910 Braid had beaten both of them to five. He won all of them in Scotland, which was slightly ironic since he served most of his professional career in England, notably and latterly at Walton Heath.

including four in a row. These last nine majors were all gained in the 1920s, his halcyon days. The occasions when his customary tee-to-green brilliance deserted him were usually saved by a deft short game and a fabulous putting touch. Though past his prime towards the end, Hagen captained the first six US Ryder Cup teams, testimony to his eagerness to cement the relationship between British and American golf.

GENE SARAZEN Going into the 1922 season, 20-year-old Gene Sarazen (christened Eugenio Saraceni, the son of a New York-Italian carpenter) was the archetypal 'unknown'. His anonymity survived only a matter of months. By July he was US Open champion, making a birdie on the 72nd hole for a closing 68 (the first winner to break 70 on the last round) and a one shot margin over John Black and the as yet unfulfilled Bobby Jones. The following month he added the USPGA title to it, the second of the seven majors he would win.

In 1923, 'the Squire' beat 'the Haig' at the second extra hole of the PGA after 36 holes had failed to separate them, but his career then went into comparative decline until he enjoyed a marvellous renaissance in 1932 – after 'discovering' the sand wedge – with victory in both Opens. He took a third PGA the next year and in 1935 won the Masters, thus becoming the first player to win all four professional major championships. He did it with the invaluable assistance of probably the most famous golf shot in history when he holed out a 4-wood approach

WALTER HAGEN

WALTER HAGEN Walter Hagen was golf's first genuine superstar. He was not only capable of outstanding golf but also played the game with dash and elegance, and, off the course, champagne was a regular companion. In truth, 'the Haig' didn't consume half the drinks his reputation suggests but that didn't stop phrases like 'Don't forget to smell the flowers along the way' and 'I don't want to be a millionaire, just live like one' coming to represent his outlook on life. It was this philosophy which helped to lift his fellow-professionals to the level of esteem in which they are regarded today.

But Walter Hagen wasn't all playboy. He was the consummate competitor. 'Who's gonna be second?' he would ask on the first tee, and his bravado was regularly justified. He was born in 1892. He won the US Open twice, the Open four times and the USPGA Championship five times,

GENE SARAZEN

to Augusta's 15th green in the last round for an albatross two (three under on a par-5 hole). That was the most important single stroke of his life but not the only memorable one. At the age of 71, on the 50th anniversary of his first appearance in Britain, he holed-in-one at the 'Postage Stamp' 8th hole in the 1973 Open Championship at Troon. Half a century after dominating the headlines, Sarazen was still making news.

ROBERT TYRE JONES A few hundred words can as adequately sum up Bobby Jones's contribution to golf as can a few thousand. In anything less than a complete book there is insufficient space to do justice to the golfer or the man.

As a golfer, Jones was the greatest amateur ever; a convincing case can be put for regarding him as the greatest, period. A few facts make the point. From 1922 to 1930, he finished first four times and second four times in the US Open and won on each of his three appearances in the British Open. Outstanding athletes as they were, Hagen and Sarazen only got the better of him once in either Open from the time that Jones broke through by winning the 1923 American title. In addition to his four US and three British Opens, he won five US Amateurs and one British Amateur in the eight seasons to 1930. The pinnacle of his achievements came in that year, when he won all four – the 'Impregnable Quadrilateral'. Aged 28, and having no worlds left to conquer, he retired from competitive golf. Jones's feat was the original Grand Slam. It was the realization that nobody could emulate him that led to the modern Slam bringing in the Masters (founded by Jones) and the USPGA Championship in place of the two Amateurs.

But there was more to Jones than golf. He was a true amateur. For example, in 1923, 1924 and 1929, the US Open and Amateur were the only events he entered. 'My wife and children came first, then my profession [law]. Finally, and never in a life by itself, came golf,' he once said. While winning all these championships, he was studying and ultimately obtaining first-class degrees in mechanical engineering, English literature and law. He was so gifted that such a wealth of talent in one individual might have been a cause for envy had Jones not been the epitome of modesty. His name became such a byword for perfect behaviour that the USGA dedicated its sportsmanship award to him. He was adored on both sides of the Atlantic, where only his nick-

BOBBY JONES

name differed – Bob in America, Bobby in Britain. In 1948, Jones played his last 18 holes. He was suffering from syringomyelia, a terrible wasting disease which afflicts the spine. He died in 1971, after years of bravely endured agony. The most fitting epitaph has already been written, by the superb American author and golf writer, Herbert Warren Wind: 'As a young man, he was able to stand up to just about the best that life can offer, which is not easy, and later he stood up with equal grace to just about the worst.'

HENRY COTTON Henry Cotton, 'the Maestro', demonstrated convincingly that the Americans were not invincible when, as a 22-year-old, he secured the critical singles point in Great Britain's victory in the 1929 Ryder Cup contest at Leeds. He went on to win three Open Championships. His first Open was captured at Sandwich in 1934 and was based on opening rounds of 67 and 65, which permitted him to stumble home in 79 on the last afternoon and still win by five shots. Three years later he fired a closing 71 in atrocious weather at Carnoustie to defy the entire US Ryder Cup team, and in 1948 he recorded his third Open victory at Muirfield.

Like Hagen, Cotton refused to accept that the club pro should be treated no better than a servant. He demanded to be accorded privileges and he got them. He was largely responsible for raising the level of tuition fees and, with his erudite and controversial comments in newspaper columns, magazines and books, he increased public awareness and appreciation of the skills of the golf professional. In later life he has been involved in course architecture and his building of Penina did much to popularize Portugal's Algarve coastline as a golfing holiday destination.

HENRY COTTON

BYRON NELSON If Ball's total of eight Amateur titles and Jones's remarkable Grand Slam will never be matched, then surely neither will the phenomenal exploits of Byron Nelson in 1945. He won 18 of the 30 US Tour events he entered, was second in another seven and was never worse than ninth. Included in this *annus mirabilis* was a streak of 11 consecutive tournament victories. He smashed all the circuit's scoring records, set a stroke average of 68.33 shots and was 320 under par for the season.

It was golf of this calibre that established Nelson's reputation as a superlative striker of the ball, a fact which has been confirmed by the USGA naming its repetitive ball-testing machine 'Iron Byron'. Such an unbelievably high standard of sustained performance also explains why Nelson's two Masters, two USPGA and one US Open Championship are comparatively ignored. Had the Second World War not intervened, many more majors would surely have fallen to 'Lord Byron', yet, ironically, he was only free to do what he did in 1945 because he was exempted from National Service as a haemophiliac.

SAM SNEAD Sam Snead won the Masters and USPGA Championship three times each and the Open Championship – at St Andrews in 1946 – once, yet he never won the US Open. That latter fact is one that is eternally recalled in any evaluation of Snead's record, largely because he quite often contrived to squander his chances of

BYRON NELSON

victory, and often quite spectacularly. However, it is unfair to dwell on the one blemish in a career which features a record 84 official US Tour victories, a figure that the man himself reckons should be doubled to take account of regional events.

Raised in the backwoods of West Virginia, Snead has the most 'natural', fluid swing the game has seen. The physical ease with which he generated his immense power enabled him to become the first golfer to break 60 in a significant competition (a 59 at his home course, The Greenbrier, in 1959); to be the oldest winner of a US tournament (52 years 10 months at Greensboro in 1965); to finish tied third when aged 62 in the 1974 USPGA Championship; and to be the first man to beat his age on the US Tour (scoring 66 when he was 67 at the Quad Cities Open in 1979).

BEN HOGAN In many ways, Ben Hogan might be said to have completed an American version of The Great Triumvirate. He, Nelson and Snead were all born in 1912. Like Nelson, Hogan was introduced to golf as a caddie – both at Fort Worth, Texas. Like Snead, he developed terrible putting problems – the 'yips' – in the twilight of his career. But unlike either of them, Hogan had to wait until after the Second World War to win his first major, the 1946 USPGA Championship. He won it again in 1948, and won

his first US Open that summer too. Eight months later, he was lucky to be alive.

Hogan was fortunate to survive an appalling car crash in February 1949. He might never walk again, said the doctors, much less play golf. They reckoned without their patient's indomitable spirit, the iron strength that in better times branded him as cold and aloof. Sixteen months later, sentimentally, improbably, he was US Open champion again. He retained the title in 1951, after winning his first Masters. In 1953, he won five of the six tournaments he entered, including the Masters for a second time, the US Open for a record-equalling fourth time, and the Open at Carnoustie in his only bid for golf's oldest title. He couldn't play in the PGA because it clashed with the Open.

The concept of the professional Grand Slam didn't exist at the time. It remains elusive, but it was Hogan's performance in 1953 that made it a 'live' subject. That year he won the three majors he could enter and nobody can ask for more. The hours on the practice range – no man has so relentlessly and methodically searched for the perfect swing – paid off to the extent that Hogan is the only 20th-century professional who can claim for a substantial period to have beaten the field more than it beat him. The early 1950s belonged to him and 1953 was effectively his swansong, though he came agonizingly close to more championships.

SAM SNEAD

BEN HOGAN

BOBBY LOCKE Christened Arthur D'Arcy Locke but called Bobby throughout his career, this singular South African provided one of the classic examples of 'it's not how but how many'. His swing was not the most graceful ever seen but his repetitive hook kept putting the ball on the fairway and then on the green. Once there 'Ol' Muffin Face', as the Americans rather unkindly dubbed him, was in his element. He was one of the truly great putters.

Locke even played his putts with a draw, and more often than not that last right-to-left roll took the ball into the cup. His record emphasized that: four times Open champion and twice runner-up, five times in the top five at the US Open, nine times South African Open champion – his first win being in 1935 as a 17-year-old amateur – and so on. Apart from those four Open titles, perhaps his most astonishing feat was winning 11 US Tour events from 1947 to 1950; indeed, he won four tournaments in five weeks in 1947 and ended the season second on the US Money List. His success was received with a sad lack of manners by some Americans but their ill-humour only served to underline his achievements there.

PETER THOMSON Peter Thomson hardly conforms to type. He is a professional golfer with wide cultural interests outside golf. He is an Australian who prefers discussing politics or

BOBBY LOCKE

listening to music than drinking beer or surfing. He is a sportsman who has made a successful transition from competitor to writer.

In fact, Thomson is still a formidable competitor. On the burgeoning US Senior Tour, which has proved such a money-spinning boom for people like Sam Snead too, Thomson has earned hundreds of thousands of US dollars: a belated but appropriate retort to those Americans who doubted his ability to play the game in the 1950s. Despite winning the British Open four times in five years, including a hat-trick from 1954 to 1956, it was not until all the top Americans played in the 1965 championship that Thomson, aged 35, had the chance to prove to them that he was the master of anyone when it came to controlling the small British ball over a demanding links in difficult conditions. The sceptics had to concede he had some talent, but Thomson was not bothered anyway. He has always been concerned with more cerebral matters than receiving grudging praise.

ARNOLD PALMER Cometh the hour, cometh the man. Arnold Palmer was the symbol that sold golf to the American public in the television age of the late 1950s and 1960s. He

PETER THOMSON

made it exciting for millions of people who knew nothing about it by making birdies from impossible positions and charging to victory from absolutely nowhere. His rugged all-American good looks, magnetic personality and ready smile made him a hero when he birdied the last two holes to win the 1960 Masters and, two months later, shot a closing 65 to win the US Open; they made him the object of national sympathy when he lost play-offs for three more US Opens and struggled in vain to win the PGA, which eluded him just as the US Open eluded Snead.

Palmer's era ran from 1958 to 1964, even though his influence in bringing millions of dollars into the sport lingers on. In those seven seasons he won seven majors to add to his 1954 US Amateur title: four Masters, one US Open and two Opens. He also resurrected the fortunes of the latter championship by persuading his compatriots to make the pilgrimage to Britain. His best golf probably came at the 1964 Masters when he was 34; he was remorselessly accurate with his irons and deadly on the greens. Nobody would have believed it was to be his last major.

GARY PLAYER This tenacious South African played piggy-in-the-middle to Palmer and Jack Nicklaus. That is not a flippant or derisory comment but a recognition of how Player, the physically small guy (5ft 7in) sandwiched between two American giants, came to be regarded as their peer. He was the third link in golf's 'Big Three', a position he reaffirmed with admirable regularity. He won the first of his three Opens in 1959, the first of his three Masters in 1961, the first of two PGAs in 1962 and his one US Open in 1965. Between 1965 and 1973, he also won five World Matchplay Championships.

Player overcame not only his short stature but also the logistical problems imposed by regularly commuting to tournaments from his family home in Johannesburg. That golfing rarity, an overseas success in the United States, he has been the international golfer *par excellence*. In 1974, he became the first man to break 60 in a national championship when he had a 59 in the Brazilian Open, and that same season he notched up his 100th professional title worldwide. Player owes much to an unquenchable spirit allied to a strict fitness regime and, of course, tremendous skill. These are qualities that enabled him, at 42, to shoot a 64 on the last day to snatch victory at the 1978 Masters; and have given him, like Palmer, a new competitive life on the US Senior Tour.

ARNOLD PALMER

GARY PLAYER

JACK NICKLAUS If one simply looks at the record books, Jack Nicklaus is the greatest golfer of all time. Maybe he is anyway. He is certainly the most successful, in no small part due to the intense thoroughness with which he always prepares himself and the sheer strength which in his prime enabled him to strike the ball as if it was fired from a bazooka. He hit the ball further than his contemporaries and higher than anyone ever has, especially with the irons. His controlled power meant Nicklaus could carry all the trouble he ever encountered, both for distance and height – an awesome advantage.

One could fill a whole chapter merely by listing Nicklaus's incredible achievements, but pride of place goes to his surely unbeatable tally of 20 major championships: two US Amateurs, a record six Masters, a record-equalling four US Opens and five USPGA Championships, and three British Opens. He has thus collected at least three each of professional golf's most important titles. Just three other men – Ben Hogan, Gary Player and Gene Sarazen – have won all four and they have only one complete set each.

It could be that the 20th of his 20 majors was Nicklaus's finest hour because when he won the 1986 Masters by playing the last 10 holes in seven under par he was, at 46, regarded by many as 'over the hill'. As remarkable as the number of tournaments the 'Golden Bear' has won is the frequency with which he has been second or third; and, perhaps above all, the way in which he has always put his wife and family first, while simultaneously managing to maintain a balance between his golf on the one hand and business commitments in club and clothing manufacturing and golf course design on the other. Therein lies part of the reason for his phenomenal longevity in championship golf.

Nicklaus is today regarded with universal affection and respect. It was not always so. As an overweight, crew-cut kid who ousted Palmer before the hero's reign had hardly begun, he was subjected to ridicule and venom by overly partisan spectators. The stoical manner in which he accepted all that stamped him as a man apart, a worthy heir to Jones's reputation for graciousness and sportsmanship.

JACK NICKLAUS

ROBERTO DE VICENZO

ROBERTO DE VICENZO To borrow that clumsy but accurate American euphemism, Roberto de Vicenzo is the 'winningest' golfer in history. It is estimated, for that is the best that can be done when dealing with such a huge total, that he has received the winner's cheque at a minimum of 240 tournaments. Forty of these were national Opens, mostly in his native South America or in Europe.

Notwithstanding his successful career, de Vicenzo's place in golfing lore is primarily due to events at championships less than 12 months apart. At Hoylake in 1967, in one of the most popular triumphs ever, he at last won the Open after several heartbreaking near-misses. Then, on his 45th birthday, he appeared to have tied Bob Goalby for the Masters the following spring only to discover that he had inadvertently signed for a four on the 17th when he had actually taken three. There was to be no play-off; de Vicenzo's mistake meant he was beaten by a shot. His reaction was typical – he attributed his awful mistake to the pressure put on him by Goalby's superb golf. De Vicenzo lost that Masters, but sportsmanship, as on some 240 other occasions, was a winner.

LEE TREVINO Lee Trevino's is a classic story of poor boy made good. Brought up on the United States/Mexico border, this 'Texican'

learned his golf with a bottle in hand – to hit the ball with, not to drink from. He developed what was termed an 'agricultural' swing, but whatever it looked like then and now, it has earned Trevino a fortune. He is a magical shot-maker and has a fast wit with which he has entertained crowds all over the globe.

Trevino's first significant victory could hardly have been more auspicious: the 1968 US Open at the age of 28. Three years later he collected the 'Triple Crown' – the US, Canadian and British Opens – within 20 days, and he retained his British Open title the following summer when he holed from off the green three times in the last 21 holes to crush the spirit of Tony Jacklin. Since then he has twice won the USPGA Championship, in 1974 and 1984, but he has never been enamoured with the course at Augusta so the Masters is likely to elude him forever. One also wonders whether his magnificent career would have been still more glittering had he not been struck by lightning during a tournament in 1975, an incident which has caused him recurring and severe back problems.

LEE TREVINO

TONY JACKLIN

TONY JACKLIN For four seasons – from 1969 to 1972 – there was no brighter star in golf's firmament than Tony Jacklin. He accomplished a great deal. The only regret is that it could have been much more. Aged 25, he won the Open at Lytham in 1969, the first British champion for 18 years. Watching from the grandstands was a young boy called Sandy Lyle who would succeed Jacklin as the next home winner. Within a year, Jacklin had added the US Open with no less than seven shots to spare, thus becoming the first Briton for 50 years to win America's national title.

Jacklin revitalized British, and ultimately European, golf with these exploits, but in the ensuing two years he was to suffer cruelly. A month after his US Open triumph he opened his defence of the British Open in such blistering fashion that he stood eight under par after 13 holes. Suddenly, a torrential storm halted play. The spell was broken and ultimately he finished fifth. Two summers on, Trevino wickedly chipped him into forlorn submission at Muirfield. Jacklin was never the same again, but 13 years later he was the inspirational non-playing captain as Europe secured a rare and memorable Ryder Cup victory. His opposite number on the American side was, fittingly and ironically, Lee Trevino.

RAYMOND FLOYD Just a month after Jacklin burst on to the scene, so did Raymond Floyd. The latter has proved rather more durable. The 1986 US Open champion has matured with age. When he won his first major, the 1969 USPGA Championship, he was known as Ray in most of the bars and nightclubs where the US Tour called a weekly halt. Now he's Raymond and married with a family, and also – at 43 – the oldest winner of the US Open, a remarkable effort achieved with what must frankly be described as an ungainly swing, a laboured affair which has nevertheless made him one of the sport's biggest ever dollar earners.

In between these two triumphs Floyd won both the 1976 Masters and the 1982 PGA the way he loves best – from the front. He opened with 65–66 at Augusta and eventually equalled the lowest 72–hole score in the tournament's history. Six years later he started 63–69 at Southern Hills and his rivals knew after just 36 holes that as hardened a pro as Raymond Floyd had wrapped up another major championship. Not for nothing is he regarded as the best front-runner on the US Tour, and at Southern Hills he proved exactly why.

RAYMOND FLOYD

JOHNNY MILLER Like Tony Jacklin, Johnny Miller spent four years in the limelight. His time immediately followed Jacklin's and has to be acknowledged as even more brilliant. Miller set the US Tour on fire. In 1974 he won eight events, including the first three of the season. The next January he won the first two tournaments, with a 61 in each, and in 1976 he confirmed himself as the 'Desert King' of American golf by winning the tour's opener for the third consecutive year.

But Miller didn't just leave his best golf for ordinary tournaments. His closing eight-under-par 63 at Oakmont in 1973 broke the US Open single-round record and it gave Miller a fantastic victory. It was, simply, one of the greatest rounds ever played. In the 1975 Masters, he shot 65–66 over the last 36 holes but was pipped by Jack Nicklaus in a tremendous tournament. His finishing 66 at Royal Birkdale in 1976 was of the highest class too, and it earned him, at 29, the Open Championship. It seemed then as if that would signal further glories but instead Miller appeared to lose interest. He has since won intermittently but never so thrillingly. Miller at his best was as good as golf can be.

TOM WATSON In July 1975, Tom Watson was considered a 'choker', a cruel label applied to this charming and articulate Kansan because of the manner in which he had wasted opportunities to win both the 1974 and 1975 US Opens. Subsequently, nobody could have more vehemently made the point that he was a champion rather than a chicken. Watson won his first Open Championship at Carnoustie that month, and by 1983 he had won his fifth. Only Harry Vardon has bettered that. Furthermore, Watson had by then also won the Masters, twice, and the US Open. He became the unanimously acclaimed heir apparent to Jack Nicklaus as the world's best golfer until a slump, hopefully temporary, bedevilled him in the mid-1980s.

Two of Watson's triumphs will be remembered forever. His head-to-head confrontation with Nicklaus at Turnberry for the 1977 Open may have been the greatest major championship in history. The Young Pretender, then aged 27, prevailed with a final two rounds of 65–65 to Nicklaus's 65–66. In 1982 he denied Nicklaus again at the US Open, largely thanks to holing an outrageous chip shot on the 71st hole. Watson's short game has always been his strongest suit, and never did he show it off to better effect than on the last nine holes that day at Pebble Beach.

JOHNNY MILLER

TOM WATSON

SEVERIANO BALLESTEROS If Arnold Palmer had not already made golf fans aware of the word 'charisma', Seve Ballesteros would have done it for them. The Spaniard is surely the best European golfer since Vardon and he makes golf as exciting to watch as did Palmer – with big hitting, occasional wildness, unbelievable powers of recovery and a nerveless putting touch. Ballesteros has also 'invented' more shots than any other contemporary golfer. His unique ability to imagine and execute improbable strokes is an invaluable legacy of learning to play golf with just one club and of receiving a golfing education through the caddie ranks.

Ballesteros is the successor to Gary Player's position as the game's foremost international competitor, having already been victorious in a dozen different national Opens. He has won four majors to date: the Open Championship in 1979 (the youngest winner this century) and 1984, and the Masters in 1980 (the youngest ever winner at 23 years 4 days) and 1983. His second Open title, at St Andrews, when he overcame the challenge of his great adversary, Watson, was a classic encounter. Ballesteros has been Europe's leading golfer for 10 years and he has proved to other Europeans that the Americans are not invincible, even on their home soil and in their most cherished championships. It has been said that

Ballesteros was born to golf because his right arm is an inch longer than his left, thus making it easier for him to adopt the ideal stance at address. If so, it is a gift from God that he hasn't wasted.

BERNHARD LANGER AND SANDY LYLE These were the first two obvious beneficiaries of the Severiano Ballesteros factor: the immediate inheritors of the belief that European golfers could beat the best of the rest in the world, including the Americans, in the 1980s.

Bernhard Langer of West Germany donned the traditional green jacket of the US Masters champion when he outplayed the Spaniard, his great continental rival, down the stretch at Augusta in April 1985. Langer had twice previously topped the European Order of Merit and twice been runner-up in the Open Championship. The 27-year-old's win at the Masters confirmed his status as one of the modern stars and proved to be an emphatic case of third time lucky when in contention at a major championship. It also demonstrated, at one of the world's most searching examinations of putting, that a formerly jabbering wreck on the greens could conquer the dreaded 'yips'.

Sandy Lyle lifted the Open Championship trophy at Royal St George's, Sandwich, just three months later; ironically after Langer had shared

SEVERIANO BALLESTEROS

SANDY LYLE   **BERNHARD LANGER**

the lead and been hot favourite going into the final round. At 27, Lyle was the first British winner of the title since Tony Jacklin in 1969 and, though he too was a former double-winner of Europe's Order of Merit – an honour he collected for a third time in 1985 – many so-called experts outside Europe previously doubted the ability of this massively strong and immensely pleasant man. They should have known better. He, like Langer, is a multiple-tournament winner in the United States and seems destined for more great deeds.

GREG NORMAN The experts had been waiting a long time to hang the label 'champion' around Greg Norman's neck, but going into the 1986 Open Championship at Turnberry it seemed possible that the prodigiously powerful 31-year-old Australian would keep them waiting forever. He had led both the Masters and the US Open after 54 holes earlier in the season and yet let both slip. Two years previously he had been demolished by Fuzzy Zoeller in a play-off for the US Open. Norman badly needed that first major championship to make up lost ground on younger rivals like Ballesteros, Langer and Lyle.

At Turnberry, he got it – convincingly, by five strokes. In a week in which the conditions and the course humbled the greats, Norman was the only man to match par for the four rounds. Not before

time, Greg Norman had arrived, and with every likelihood of staying, as indicated by his sensational run of six consecutive tournament victories later that autumn and subsequent topping of the 1986 US Money List.

ISAO AOKI Although Isao Aoki has been upstaged in the last two or three years by his Japanese compatriot, Tsuneyuki (Tommy) Nakajima, he was the first player from that golf-mad nation to make a significant impact outside the Far East. For that reason he has been chiefly responsible for proving that Japan is a serious force in golf, with every prospect of becoming more serious.

At six feet, he is tall by Japanese standards. By any standards he is an outstanding putter, but it takes more than wizardry on the greens to win over 40 tournaments, including the Japan Open, on the tough and lucrative Japanese circuit. Aoki has, in addition, won the World Matchplay Championship and European Open in Britain, and provided a stunning climax to the 1983 Hawaiian Open on the US Tour – he holed a full wedge shot for an eagle at the last to win by a stroke. His best effort in a major was in 1980 when, aged 37, he recorded the third-lowest score in US Open history. Sadly for him, Jack Nicklaus returned the lowest.

GREG NORMAN

ISAO AOKI

The Oldest of Opens

'Typically British,' many overseas golf enthusiasts will say. 'They call it "The Open Championship" as if it was the only Open in the world.'

When it began in 1860, it was. Today it is regularly referred to as the 'British Open' to distinguish it from the Opens of every other golf-playing nation, and especially from the United States Open which is held in as high esteem as the original, but 'British' is technically a superfluous addition to the name. It gained currency in the 1960s, when the fortunes of the championship were revived by Arnold Palmer

Allan Robertson, who was considered to be the finest golfer of his day. When he died in 1859 it was decided to hold a tournament to find his successor. Thus was born the Open Championship.

and other Americans who, understandably, used the single word 'Open' to mean the national championship of their country. Ironically, in the 1980s, the simple, unencumbered title 'Open Championship' is more justified than it has ever been. No golf tournament in the world can match if for the quality of its international field. By comparison, either due to circumstances or design, other Opens appear to be 'closed'.

To be fair, so was the first Open itself. Only professionals were permitted to enter and only eight of them did. Willie Park won by two strokes from Old Tom Morris with a score of 174 for three circuits of Prestwick's 12-hole layout on Wednesday 17 October 1860. He received a red Moroccan leather belt, an unusual memento of victory in the days when a medal was invariably the prize. Park was to win the title three more times. His son, Willie Jnr, won it twice and his brother, Mungo, once.

Park's total in 1860 did not represent good scoring, even in the early days of the gutty, and there was discontent among several leading amateurs that they had been excluded. Accordingly, Major J. O. Fairlie, the Prestwick member who proposed the competition in the first place, acceded to their wishes. He was initially inclined to restrict the invitation to the 'gentlemen' of eight prominent clubs but, after being persuaded at the eleventh hour to be more generous and extend the offer, on the eve of the competition he declared that the 'Belt to be played for tomorrow and on all other occasions until it be otherwise resolved shall be open to all the world.' Seldom can the intentions of such a grandiose statement have been so impressively fulfilled.

The championship had been inaugurated in 1860 to determine who was Scotland's – and perforce the world's – best golfer following the death the previous year of Allan Robertson, who was recognized to be supreme. Robertson had covered the Old Course at St Andrews in 79 strokes in 1858. It was the first time 80 had been broken and, given the equipment of the day and the unkempt condition of the links, it has to be considered a more formidable feat than many a 62 in a modern tournament. It was golf of that quality that led to one R & A member commenting, after Robertson had succumbed to hepatitis at the age of 44: 'They may shut up their shops and toll their bells, for the greatest among them is gone.'

In fact, Old Tom Morris was such a keen rival and near-equal that Robertson had shied away from further matches against him after two defeats, taking him on instead as his foursomes partner. With Robertson's death, Morris came into his own and, like Willie Park, he won the Open four times. When Morris won for the last time in 1867, aged 46 years and 99 days, he became, and still remains, the oldest winner. The next year his son was, and is ever likely to be, the youngest champion at 17 years and 161 days.

Prize money had been introduced in 1863 but by 1870 there was no belt left to dispute. Young Tom had claimed ownership of it by completing a hat-trick of victories. His winning totals in 1869 and 1870 added up to 303 for 72 holes: not until Harry Vardon shot 300 round the same course, Prestwick, in 1903 was that bettered. Obviously, such comparisons are invidious and take no account of different conditions, but it has to be pointed out that Vardon's score was achieved after the demise of the gutty in favour of the rubber-cored ball. To play Prestwick's first hole of over 500 yards in three, as Morris did in 1870, was remarkable, but then Young Tom was a prodigy, an aggressive player who is said to have been such a vigorous waggler of the club at address that the head would sometimes come off the shaft even before he had hit the ball. Morris is also assured of one other footnote in Open history. In 1868 he recorded the championship's first hole-in-one.

With Young Tom perhaps fondly gazing at the belt resting on his mantelpiece, there was no tournament in 1871. When hostilities were resumed in 1872, the Championship Trophy had replaced it: a silver claret jug which had been jointly donated by the Prestwick Club, the R & A at St Andrews and the Honourable Company, then at Musselburgh. The three agreed to host the Open on a rota basis, a system which in essence still exists, although it now involves more clubs and has a much less strict order of rotation. There was no renewal of the clause about three wins in succession earning the victor outright possession

of the trophy, and just as well. Jamie Anderson (1877–1879) and Bob Ferguson (1880–1882) both accomplished the hat-trick, though not before Young Tom had emulated his father and won a fourth championship in 1872. He finished third and second respectively in the next two years before dying suddenly in 1875. He was posthumously accorded this tribute to his genius by his father: 'I could cope wi' Allan [Robertson] myself', but never wi' Tommy.'

The following year, 1876, Bob Martin tied with David Strath, but the latter refused to enter a play-off after a protracted and acrimonious debate following allegations that he had contravened the conventions of etiquette by hitting to the infamous 17th green at St Andrews before it was clear, thus ensuring that his ball was prevented from going on to the dreaded road. Overtime was actually contested for the first time in 1883 – over 36 holes – and Willie Fernie made a two at the last to beat Bob Ferguson by a stroke and thereby deny him the chance to equal Young Tom's four consecutive triumphs.

The Open has always been a byword for constancy, but in the 1890s several of the earliest traditions were cast aside and barriers were broken. John Ball won at Prestwick in 1890 – the first English champion, the first amateur winner. Victories by amateurs have not become commonplace (just Ball once, Hilton twice and

Above left Charlie Hunter (left) watches the style of Old Tom Morris during the first Open at Prestwick. Hunter finished sixth and Morris second.

Above right Young Tom Morris with the Morocco leather belt which became his personal property when he achieved a hat-trick of Open victories between 1868 and 1870.

The best players in the world. A group of Scottish professionals at Troon in 1887. Among them are Open champions Jamie Anderson (back row, second from left), Willie Park Jnr (third from left), Old Tom Morris (standing with the white beard), Jack Simpson (front row, third from left), David Brown (sixth from left), Bob Ferguson (second from right) and Bob Martin (lying down).

Jones three times) but Ball's success did signal the end of the Scottish stranglehold on the Open and, coincidentally, soon ushered in the era of the Great Triumvirate of Vardon, Taylor and Braid. They would dominate matters at the expense of the artisans – the plasterers, slaters, stonemasons, bakers – who had prevailed as part-time professional golfers for the preceding 15 years or so.

A veritable revolution occured in 1892. Prize money soared, from £28 10s to £110. An entry fee was imposed. The championship was doubled to 72 holes and played over two days. The Honourable Company had just quit Musselburgh and settled in at Muirfield, so the Open broke fresh ground since it was their turn to stage it. With a distinct echo of the old feud between the R & A and the Honourable Company, a disgusted Andrew Kirkaldy from St Andrews opined of the new course: 'It's an auld water meadie. I'm glad I'm gaun home.' His temper was not improved by

J. H. Taylor was the first of the Great Triumvirate to get his name on the Championship Trophy. He is seen at St Andrews in 1895 holing the putt which enabled him to retain the title he had won for the first time at Sandwich.

the victory of Harold Hilton, Ball's amateur colleague from the Royal Liverpool Club at Hoylake; and no doubt his humour got no better 12 months later when that course and Royal St George's at Sandwich were added to the rota. First the English won the Open, now they were staging it.

In the subsequent years more courses have come on to the roster while others have fallen from favour. Royal Cinque Ports at Deal (1909), Troon (1923), Royal Lytham & St Annes (1926), Carnoustie (1931), Prince's (1932) and Royal Portrush (1951) – the two latter playing host just once – Royal Birkdale (1954) and Turnberry (1977) have joined the list of courses which have enjoyed the highest accolade in British golf. All are links (some, it must be admitted, bearing a greater resemblance to the original meaning of the word than others) and it is probably the most revered element of Open tradition that the championship should retain this connection with its roots. The truth is rather more prosaic, or at least rather more commercial, in that the wide open spaces adjoining links courses are perfect for erecting the vast tented village and the rest of the paraphernalia associated with the Open today. Few, if any, inland courses could cope with these extensive trimmings, and indeed venues like Hoylake and Carnoustie have been rendered redundant by the importance of essential frills such as hotel accommodation, road access and other commercial considerations. Whether their absence from Open duty will be temporary or permanent is hard to say, especially in view of Sandwich's successful resurrection in 1981 after 32 years in the metaphorical wilderness. At present, St Andrews, Muirfield, Troon and Turnberry in Scotland, plus Birkdale, Lytham

and St George's in England, are the only seven courses to have hosted the Open since 1975 or scheduled to do so before 1992. Prestwick, incidentally, was retired in 1925. The course, now regarded as a delightful anachronism, was even by then outdated as a genuine test of ability. The Open was held there 24 times in all, a tally which St Andrews will match in 1990.

But back to the past. The 20 years preceding the First World War were monopolized by the Great Triumvirate, which explains why Sandy Herd's one-shot triumph over Braid and Vardon in the 1902 Open was such a potent advertisement for the Haskell ball (see page 28).

Standards were improving rapidly. Vardon's win at Prestwick in 1898 represented the first occasion 80 had been beaten in all four rounds. When the Open returned there in 1903, Vardon

James Braid's first of five Open Championships, at Muirfield in 1901. It is obvious from this scene around the final green, as the crowds watch Braid hole out for victory, that the tented village isn't entirely a modern phenomenon.

At the turn of the century Harry Vardon was supreme. Here he is addressing the ball on the first tee at St Andrews, with Sandy Herd – who was to win the Open in 1902 – looking on. Vardon won the Open a record six times but not in 1900, when this was taken.

Arnaud Massy. His win in 1907 at Hoylake made him the first overseas winner. Stories of foreign successes have been the rule rather than the exception since the Second World War, but not until Severiano Ballesteros won in 1979 did another continental golfer lift the coveted trophy.

won again with a record total of 300, beating his brother Tom by six shots in a unique family double that will surely never be repeated. At St George's the following season, a number of new marks were set as Jack White shot 296 and three players (White, Braid and Vardon) became the first Open competitors to shoot a round in the 60s. In 1907, the year that qualifying rounds were introduced, Arnaud Massy of France became the first overseas player to receive the trophy.

Vardon edged ahead of Braid and Taylor in the immortality stakes with his record sixth and last victory in 1914, and the war in Europe meant it was 1920 before he had to relinquish the trophy to George Duncan. At Deal, Duncan opened with consecutive rounds of 80 (the last champion to return a score over 79) and was 13 shots adrift, but by closing with 71–72 he made up the deficit with two shots to spare.

That was the first championship held under the auspices of the R & A, the result of an accord between the six hosting clubs of the time who decided it was good for golf, as well as for the Open, for there to be just one ruling body. The R & A has since instigated a massive increase in the popularity and scope of the championship. The number of entrants has multiplied hugely, but nothing makes the point more clearly than a glance at the rising prize fund over the years. In 1920, the purse was £225, of which the winner received £75. The former didn't breach the four-figure barrier until 1946, the latter until 1955. As recently as 1975, total prize money was a modest £75,000 and Tom Watson collected 10 per cent of that. Twelve years later, the champion's cheque was as much as the whole fund at Carnoustie, and a total of £650,000 was on offer. Even allowing for inflation, these statistics are nothing short of astonishing. In financial terms, the Open used to be the poor relation. Today, despite the vagaries of the pound's international value, it is invariably among the 10 richest tournaments in the world, and surely the richest in terms of prestige.

If traditionalists of the 1920s were hoping the formal acknowledgement of St Andrews' pre-eminence would coincide with a return to the days of Scottish domination, they were in for a devastating shock. The 1921 champion was Jock Hutchison, a Scotsman by birth but an American by residence. The trophy went across the Atlantic for the first time. It was a journey with which the silver jug was to become very familiar, for until 1934 only Arthur Havers (in 1923) was able to stem the inexorable shift of power to the west.

Opposite Sealed with a kiss – Hagen celebrating his triumph of 1924 with his wife.

In the vanguard of the transatlantic assault was Walter Hagen. He pioneered the idea of Americans contesting golf's oldest honour, much as Arnold Palmer was to resuscitate the notion in the 1960s. Hagen made his first appearance in the Open in 1920 when, to quote Herb Wind, 'he had been press-agented as the golfer who would show British golf a thing or two. Walter showed them four rounds in the 80s and finished a lurid 55th.'

But the Haig turned the tables on George Duncan in 1922, and won for a second time in 1924, having to hole from eight feet at the last to beat Ernie Whitcombe. He sank it with aplomb. 'You seemed to treat that putt very casually,' somebody remarked afterwards. 'Did you know you had it to win?' Hagen's response was typical. 'Sure, I knew I had it to win, but no man ever beat me in a play-off.'

The answer wasn't an example of cool confidence but of an outright lie. Sarazen had nipped him in a play-off for the USPGA Championship less than a year beforehand, but Hagen was never inclined to let a small matter of fact bother him. He was content in the knowledge of his own capabilities, which were such that Bernard Darwin, the doyen of all golf writers,

Bobby Jones putting on the final green at Lytham in 1926. His victory there, the first of his three Open wins, was preceded by one of the most famous rounds in history when he qualified with a 66 at Sunningdale.

was moved to comment of Whitcombe's gallant but ultimately futile challenge: 'there is this difference between the two, as so often between Hagen and the other man. Hagen just won and the other man just didn't.'

Hagen stories are always good value. They are even better for being true rather than apocryphal. He was audacious – in 1926 he ordered the flagstick to be removed while he attempted to hole out from 150 yards to tie Bobby Jones at Lytham. He was generous – he presented his winner's cheque in 1928 to his caddie. He was arrogant – while out partying the night before the final two rounds at Muirfield in 1929, he was reminded that the leader, Leo Diegel, was already in bed. 'Yeh, but he ain't sleeping,' was the snappy riposte. Hagen won, Diegel was third. There will never be another Hagen.

The other American stars of this glorious, vintage stretch were Gene Sarazen and Bobby Jones. Sarazen arrived at Troon in 1923 as the reigning US Open champion but he left without

striking a blow in the championship proper. Like everybody in those days, however mighty or humble, he had to play two qualifying rounds to get in (a situation not remedied until 1963 when specified categories of leading players were exempted from the ordeal). Sarazen drew the worst of some atrocious weather and failed to qualify. Nine years later he was triumphant at Prince's, and he might well have won in 1928 and 1933 as well.

Jones was the winner in 1926, 1927 and 1930. In the first, victory at Royal Lytham was rescued from apparent defeat in the final round when he struck a tremendous long iron shot from a sand bunker to find the heart of the 17th green. Jones later called it the greatest shot he ever hit when it really mattered. It so startled his closest rival, Al Watrous, that he three-putted. The Lytham members later erected a plaque to commemorate the spot from where Jones played the stroke. His win in 1930, of course, led to the Impregnable Quadrilateral.

A happy homecoming for the Silver Scot. Tommy Armour, a native Scotsman who emigrated to the United States, accepts the congratulations of kilted Lord Airlie after his narrow win at Carnoustie in 1931.

In between times, two more exiled Britons – Jim Barnes (1925) and Tommy Armour (1931) – emulated Jock Hutchison, and in 1933 Denny Shute was consistency personified with four 73s. That got him into a play-off with another American, Craig Wood, which he won comfortably.

Shute and his compatriots only took part at St Andrews because they had been in Britain anyway for the fourth Ryder Cup match at Southport. From 1934 until Palmer took up Hagen's cause in 1960, a lot of the gloss was stripped from the Open. The Americans came in force just once more, in 1937 when the Ryder Cup was again scheduled close to the Open.

It isn't hard to discover the reasons for the championship being discarded like last year's fashions. In the 1930s, the United States was suffering from the Great Depression and travel was prohibitively expensive. The Second World War came next, which depressed everybody. When that ended in 1945, the British economy was hopelessly ravaged while happy American golfers were finding themselves deluged by dollars at home. There was simply insufficient incentive to make a long sea journey, at colossal cost which even the first prize could not cover, on the off-chance of winning a trophy, however important. And until Palmer arrived the importance of the Open was greatly diminished in American eyes.

That is not to suggest there were no worthy winners for 25 years. In 1934 Henry Cotton began a sequence of six successive British victories, against largely domestic opposition, with a stylish triumph at Sandwich. His record 65 in the second round was used to name the famous Dunlop 65 ball and it was not bettered until Mark Hayes shot

Cotton at the Maiden. This is the sixth green in the final round of the 1934 Open at Sandwich and the gallery is watching anxiously as Henry Cotton fritters away a big lead. In the end it didn't matter that he closed with a 79. His golf had been so brilliant for three days that he could afford a poor performance and still have five shots in hand. Cotton is seen chipping, with his playing partner, Charlie Whitcombe, in attendance.

63 at Turnberry in 1977. Three years later, in 1937, Cotton, in his finest hour, repulsed the heavy American threat in terrible conditions at Carnoustie.

The immediate post-war years were dominated by Bobby Locke and Peter Thomson with four wins each. Locke's first is invariably remembered for a bizarre incident during the second round when Harry Bradshaw's ball got lodged in a broken bottle. The genial Irishman had to play the ball as it lay and he bogeyed the hole. That the episode led to a change in the Rules was scant consolation to Bradshaw. He ended the tournament tied with Locke and lost the play-off. It has often been argued that the bottle cost him the championship, but that is to ignore the truth that one cannot alter one fact in a sequence and assume all the others would have remained constant.

Locke's farewell appearance on the victory rostrum in 1957 was also touched by controversy. It was an odd week anyway. The venue had been switched from Muirfield to St Andrews at short notice because of the petrol shortage afflicting Britain in the wake of the Suez crisis. Locke

caused something of a crisis within the R & A when it was realized after he had received the trophy and his cheque that he had not replaced his ball properly before holing out on the last green. He had marked it a putter-head away from its spot in order not to interfere with his partner's line, but had then forgotten to allow for that when putting it back. Since he had won by three strokes, the championship committee felt it safe to deduct a theoretical two-shot penalty (but didn't actually do so) without affecting the outcome. Locke might, indeed, have been disqualified, but such a decision would have been a travesty.

There were three British winners, an increasingly endangered species, in this period: Fred Daly (1947), Cotton (1948) and Max Faulkner (1951), the latter on the only occasion the Open has been held in Ireland. The hard-luck stories of the other leading home players of the 1940s and 1950s are legion. Charlie Ward, Dai Rees, Eric Brown, Dave Thomas, Christy O'Connor and many more were near-miss experts.

Not so the top American professionals. Snead won in 1946 on the second of only three attempts.

Above left **Bobby Locke about to win the 1957 Open with the three-footer that he neglected to replace correctly on the 18th green at St Andrews. The R & A subsequently decided that his transgression was not material and the result was unaltered. This was Locke's fourth Open title.**

Above right **Peter Thomson sinks this short putt to claim the last and sweetest of his five Opens, at Royal Birkdale in 1965. On this occasion he beat the cream of American golf.**

Above left Ben Hogan – the 'Wee Ice Mon' as he was dubbed by the Scots – on the way to glory in his one and only appearance in the Open, at Carnoustie in 1953.

Above right Arnold Palmer has always received and will always deserve the credit for elevating the status of the Open in the 1960s by encouraging his fellow-Americans to make the journey to Britain. The great man is seen doing what he did best – extricating himself from trouble – *en route* to the first of his two Open titles, at Birkdale in 1961.

In 1953, Hogan – chasing a third major of the year – memorably came, saw and conquered Carnoustie. He hadn't been before and he never returned. Otherwise it was Locke or Thomson (whose hat-trick from 1954 to 1956 is unique this century), until a young South African called Gary Player survived a double-bogey at the 72nd hole in a final round of 68 to win at Muirfield in 1959. Then came Palmer.

The great man lost by a shot to Kel Nagle on his debut appearance in 1960. In 1961 and 1962 he won it. That he did so impressed his fellow-Americans; that he could be bothered to make the trip influenced them. Suddenly, the Open was back in business. Soon it was to be big business.

In 1966 Jack Nicklaus completed his collection of the four majors with a victory at a rough-strewn Muirfield. This proved conclusively to himself and to his dwindling band of doubters that he could cope with the wind and the fast-running turf of British links golf. That same year, the traditional Friday double-round was abandoned. Instead the Open was played over four days and ended on Saturday, a belated acknowledgement that there were regular tournament professionals who did not have to be

back behind the counter of their pro shops for the weekend. Saturday play obviously made commercial sense, as did the earlier decision to replace the 36-hole play-off with one of just 18 holes in the event of a tie. (This move followed the one-sided battle between Bob Charles and Phil Rodgers in 1963 when the former, the best putter in the world for a decade, became the only left-hander to win a major championship.)

In 1967 the ABC TV company bought the American television rights for the championship, and in 1968 Keith Mackenzie, who was to be a marvellous salesman and entrepreneur for the Open, was appointed secretary of the R & A. These two apparently diverse occurrences were linked by subsequent developments.

The television deal presaged the broadcasting of the Open to Japan, Australia and all points of the compass. It is reckoned that tens of millions of fans now watch it from their armchairs. The coverage in Britain, in the extremely capable hands of the BBC, has been extended to over eight hours 'live' each day for the first two rounds and to all 18 holes on the weekend (since 1980, the championship has started on Thursday and concluded on Sunday), and that's not counting

THE OPEN CHAMPIONSHIP – WINNERS

Year	Venue	Winner	Score	Year	Venue	Winner	Score	Year	Venue	Winner	Score
1860	Prestwick	Willie Park	174	1900	St Andrews	J. H. Taylor	309	1949	Sandwich	†Bobby Locke (SA)	283
1861	Prestwick	Tom Morris Snr	163	1901	Muirfield	James Braid	309	1950	Troon	Bobby Locke (SA)	279
1862	Prestwick	Tom Morris Snr	163	1902	Hoylake	Sandy Herd	307	1951	Portrush	Max Faulkner	285
1863	Prestwick	Willie Park	168	1903	Prestwick	Harry Vardon	300	1952	Lytham	Bobby Locke (SA)	287
1864	Prestwick	Tom Morris Snr	167	1904	Sandwich	Jack White	296	1953	Carnoustie	Ben Hogan (USA)	282
1865	Prestwick	Andrew Strath	162	1905	St Andrews	James Braid	318	1954	Birkdale	Peter Thomson (Aus)	283
1866	Prestwick	Willie Park	169	1906	Muirfield	James Braid	300	1955	St Andrews	Peter Thomson (Aus)	281
1867	Prestwick	Tom Morris Snr	170	1907	Hoylake	Arnaud Massy (Fr)	312	1956	Hoylake	Peter Thomson (Aus)	286
1868	Prestwick	Tom Morris Jnr	157	1908	Prestwick	James Braid	291	1957	St Andrews	Bobby Locke (SA)	279
1869	Prestwick	Tom Morris Jnr	154	1909	Deal	J. H. Taylor	295	1958	Lytham	†Peter Thomson (Aus)	278
1870	Prestwick	Tom Morris Jnr	149	1910	St Andrews	James Braid	299	1959	Muirfield	Gary Player (SA)	284
1871	No competition			1911	Sandwich	†Harry Vardon	303	1960	St Andrews	Kel Nagle (Aus)	278
1872	Prestwick	Tom Morris Jnr	166	1912	Muirfield	Ted Ray	295	1961	Birkdale	Arnold Palmer (USA)	284
1873	St Andrews	Tom Kidd	179	1913	Hoylake	J. H. Taylor	304	1962	Troon	Arnold Palmer (USA)	276
1874	Musselburgh	Mungo Park	159	1914	Prestwick	Harry Vardon	306	1963	Lytham	†Bob Charles (NZ)	277
1875	Prestwick	Willie Park	166	1915–9	No competition			1964	St Andrews	Tony Lema (USA)	279
1876	St Andrews	Bob Martin	176	1920	Deal	George Duncan	303	1965	Birkdale	Peter Thomson (Aus)	285
1877	Musselburgh	Jamie Anderson	160	1921	St Andrews	†Jock Hutchison (USA)	296	1966	Muirfield	Jack Nicklaus (USA)	282
1878	Prestwick	Jamie Anderson	157	1922	Sandwich	Walter Hagen (USA)	300	1967	Hoylake	Roberto de Vicenzo (Arg)	278
1879	St Andrews	Jamie Anderson	169	1923	Troon	Arthur Havers	295				
1880	Musselburgh	Bob Ferguson	162	1924	Hoylake	Walter Hagen (USA)	301	1968	Carnoustie	Gary Player (SA)	289
1881	Prestwick	Bob Ferguson	170	1925	Prestwick	Jim Barnes (USA)	300	1969	Lytham	Tony Jacklin	280
1882	St Andrews	Bob Ferguson	171	1926	Lytham	*Bobby Jones (USA)	291	1970	St Andrews	†Jack Nicklaus (USA)	283
1883	Musselburgh	†Willie Fernie	159	1927	St Andrews	*Bobby Jones (USA)	285	1971	Birkdale	Lee Trevino (USA)	278
1884	Prestwick	Jack Simpson	160	1928	Sandwich	Walter Hagen (USA)	292	1972	Muirfield	Lee Trevino (USA)	278
1885	St Andrews	Bob Martin	171	1929	Muirfield	Walter Hagen (USA)	292	1973	Troon	Tom Weiskopf (USA)	276
1886	Musselburgh	David Brown	157	1930	Hoylake	*Bobby Jones (USA)	291	1974	Lytham	Gary Player (SA)	282
1887	Prestwick	Willie Park Jnr	161	1931	Carnoustie	Tommy Armour (USA)	296	1975	Carnoustie	†Tom Watson (USA)	279
1888	St Andrews	Jack Burns	171	1932	Prince's	Gene Sarazen (USA)	283	1976	Birkdale	Johnny Miller (USA)	279
1889	Musselburgh	†Willie Park Jnr	155	1933	St Andrews	†Densmore Shute (USA)	292	1977	Turnberry	Tom Watson (USA)	268
1890	Prestwick	*John Ball	164	1934	Sandwich	Henry Cotton	283	1978	St Andrews	Jack Nicklaus (USA)	281
1891	St Andrews	Hugh Kirkaldy	166	1935	Muirfield	Alf Perry	283	1979	Lytham	Seve Ballesteros (Sp)	283
1892	Muirfield	*Harold Hilton	305	1936	Hoylake	Alf Padgham	287	1980	Muirfield	Tom Watson (USA)	271
1893	Prestwick	Willie Auchterlonie	322	1937	Carnoustie	Henry Cotton	290	1981	Sandwich	Bill Rogers (USA)	276
1894	Sandwich	J. H. Taylor	326	1938	Sandwich	Reg Whitcombe	295	1982	Troon	Tom Watson (USA)	284
1895	St Andrews	J. H. Taylor	322	1939	St Andrews	Dick Burton	290	1983	Birkdale	Tom Watson (USA)	275
1896	Muirfield	†Harry Vardon	316	1940–5	No competition			1984	St Andrews	Seve Ballesteros (Sp)	276
1897	Hoylake	*Harold Hilton	314	1946	St Andrews	Sam Snead (USA)	290	1985	Sandwich	Sandy Lyle	282
1898	Prestwick	Harry Vardon	307	1947	Hoylake	Fred Daly	293	1986	Turnberry	Greg Norman (Aus)	280
1899	Sandwich	Harry Vardon	310	1948	Muirfield	Henry Cotton	284	* amateur	† won play-off		

Here is another man doing what he did best. Bob Charles, the only left-hander to win a major championship, putted Lytham and Phil Rodgers into submission in 1963.

Right The making of a nickname. Tony Lema only managed to play 27 holes in practice for the 1964 Open yet he mastered the Old Course at St Andrews like a veteran to beat Jack Nicklaus by five strokes. His victory toast to the press earned him the sobriquet 'Champagne Tony'. Two years later he was dead.

Below There has never been a fiercer competitor than Gary Player, winner of the Open in three different decades – in 1959, 1968 and 1974.

highlights programmes. Before Palmer, an hour and a half's transmission of a few holes on the final day was considered sufficient and the BBC paid a meagre £450 for the privilege.

Mackenzie presided over the physical and financial flourishing of the Open – unquestionably assisted by the enthusiasm generated by Tony Jacklin's exhilarating triumph at Lytham in 1969 – before retiring to make way for Michael Bonallack in 1983. Mackenzie made endless visits to the United States to cajole the country's leading players into competing. He encouraged the creation of the tented village complex containing banks, bars, champagne tents, eating facilities, hospitality units, golf equipment and merchandise stalls, and an enormous press centre. On the course he arranged dozens of fixed and mobile scoreboards, and huge grandstands around the final hole and at other strategic locations to cope with the crowds. And all this is forgetting necessities like course preparation, administration, officers' wages, salaries and subsistence, and ancillary services like drainage and electricity.

Bonallack has maintained the trend. Around £2 million is spent on providing these amenities. On the credit side, 193,126 golf enthusiasts paid to watch the 1984 Open at St Andrews, a record on either side of the Atlantic. They poured over £1 million into the R & A's coffers in gate receipts alone; on top of that were players' entry fees, spectator car parking and a cut from the tented village. Twenty years previously, when Tony Lema (soon to be killed in an aeroplane crash) won at St Andrews on his first trip to Britain, 35,954 devotees handed over just £14,704 to get in.

It seems odd, even ironic, that, in the marketing of its championship, an august British institution like the R & A should have been an inspiration to, rather than the pupil of, the Americans at the USGA. Critics allege it's not so much 'marketing' as 'manipulation'; witness the late starting times on the last day of the Open and the decision, taken in 1984, to hold any future play-offs over just four or five selected holes, even though the USGA has retained the 18-hole play-off. These steps by the R & A are seen in some quarters as acts of appeasement to the great god TV, though that is not to suggest that the R & A has wantonly forsaken its grand traditions and heritage, and indeed there are many players as well as officials who welcome the demise of the 18-hole play-off.

Whatever the merits of that debate, just as its saviour Palmer produced some dramatic golf in the

Britain's first Open champion for 18 years. Tony Jacklin acknowledges the thunderous applause as he clinches the title in 1969. It was not only a great moment for Jacklin and British golf but also a further boost to the fortunes of the championship itself.

Below left One of golf's most heartbreaking moments, and perhaps its saddest miss. Doug Sanders had this putt for the 1970 Open; Jack Nicklaus benefited from his profligacy.

Below right Lee Trevino celebrates as another long putt disappears in the last round of the 1971 Open at Royal Birkdale. It was just as well for the American that his putter was so hot that day because in the end he had only one shot to spare over Mr Lu from Taiwan.

1960s, the Open has followed suit in the 1970s and 1980s.

If the losing of a golf tournament can ever justify being called a tragedy, then that is what happened to Doug Sanders at St Andrews in 1970. He needed only to par the 18th, surely the most straightforward closing hole in championship golf, to win the Open. Horribly, he three-putted, missing from three feet for the title, and he had to return the next morning to face Jack Nicklaus. That he put up a brave fight was commendable; that he would lose the play-off was inevitable. Nicklaus drove the ball over 380 yards at the final hole, beyond the green where poor Sanders had endured his mental torture the previous afternoon. Nicklaus chipped back to eight feet and, as the putt for a birdie toppled in, he hurled his putter towards the heavens in exultation.

At Muirfield in 1972, Tony Jacklin suffered as badly as Sanders. He had to watch while his playing partner and rival, the defending champion Lee Trevino, thinned a bunker shot against the flagstick and then into the hole for a

From 1975 to 1983 Tom Watson won the Open Championship five times, four of his triumphs coming in Scotland and the other at Birkdale, where he is seen (below) emerging from the vast crowds as he salutes his win of 1983. The crowds were no less enthusiastic in 1977, but the photograph above captures a rare moment of apparent solitude as Watson putts on the 10th green during his fantastic final round battle with Jack Nicklaus at Turnberry.

birdie at the 16th in the third round, and then trump that by chipping in for another on the 18th. Yet, with two holes of the championship remaining on the Saturday, Jacklin's star seemed to be in the ascendancy. Trevino volubly conceded he had lost his chance when he lay four over the back of the 17th green. Instead, his 'give-up' chip went into the hole. Jacklin, shocked into misguided aggression, charged his birdie putt, missed the short one back and took six. The glory was Trevino's, the sorrow Jacklin's. He would never again have the chance to repeat his triumph of 1969.

Turnberry made its championship debut in 1977 and instantly produced an epic, arguably the greatest golf tournament ever played. Only two men were involved: Tom Watson and Jack Nicklaus. Watson played the last 36 holes in 130 strokes, Nicklaus in 131. It was virtually matchplay. So emphatically did they trounce the pack that third place went to Hubert Green, who was 11 shots off the pace. Watson birdied four of the last six holes in the most breathtaking fashion to make up three shots on Nicklaus and win by one. So marvellous was their golf that their scores (respectively 268 and 269) are the only sub-270 totals in major championship history. At least Nicklaus had consolation a year later with another St Andrews victory, his third Open in all. When Watson won at Birkdale in 1983, it was his fifth.

At Turnberry, the leading non-American was Tommy Horton of England, who tied for ninth.

That represented the nadir for international golf. Within 10 years, the rest of the world had demonstrated to the Americans that they could play too.

Three recent championships amply underline the point. Severiano Ballesteros of Spain, the champion in 1979, collected his second title at St Andrews in 1984. This was the best Open since Turnberry and more thrilling than most of those before it. Ballesteros birdied the last hole to beat his greatest rival, Watson, and his most dangerous European challenger, Bernhard Langer, by two strokes. His celebrations as the winning putt disappeared were the most exuberant displays of pleasure the Old Course has ever seen.

Sandy Lyle succeeded Ballesteros in 1985. Lyle is a phlegmatic and powerful Anglo-Scot, his precise nationality being the subject of occasional but heated late night discussion between the English and the Scots. (The former say, with some truth, that when Sandy plays well he is termed 'the Super-Scot' north of the border. If he's had an indifferent round, those same folk will dub him 'English-based Lyle'. The perfect compromise has unwittingly been reached by the US Tour which, in its handbook, describes Lyle's birthplace as Shrewsbury, Scotland.)

The 1986 Open was won by Greg Norman of Australia after a formidably impressive performance in terribly tough weather and over a Turnberry set up to play as hard as it possibly could. The authorities evidently didn't want a repetition of the humiliation to which the course was subjected in 1977, but even the best endeavours of the R & A could not prevent Norman returning a fantastic seven-under-par 63 on the Friday.

The modern international nature of the Open sets it apart from its contemporaries. It is an aspect not confined to the nationality of the winners. Of the 17 golfers who finished tied for fifth or higher from 1984 to 1986, only five were American: an unthinkable ratio a decade ago. Others came from Spain, West Germany, Great Britain, the Republic of Ireland and Australia. Furthermore, the 1986 Open was contested by participants from 15 different countries as well as the four of the United Kingdom.

The oldest of Opens; the most cosmopolitan of Opens. From Tom Morris to Tom Watson, Sandy Herd to Sandy Lyle, all its champions have felt, for 12 months at least, that they have followed in the footsteps of Allan Robertson as 'the greatest among them'.

Royal Birkdale looks like a great links should look, and its appearance is not deceptive – it is a great golf course. Tom Watson, who won the 1983 Open Championship there, considered this hole – the par-3 12th – to be the best of the 18 and one of the finest short holes in the world. The magnificent duneland terrain is typical of Birkdale, and the siting of the green represents a marvellous example of man adapting the landscape to the maximum advantage.

The 'Postage Stamp'. The 8th at Royal Troon is the shortest hole on the Open Championship rota at 126 yards. It has witnessed many memorable moments, both heroic and tragic. In 1973 Gene Sarazen had a hole-in-one on the 50th anniversary of his first appearance in the Open. The next day he holed out from a bunker for a two. In sad contrast, a German amateur, Herman Tissies, needed 15 strokes to negotiate the hole in the 1950 Open.

Just down the Ayrshire coast from Troon lies Turnberry, host to two Opens. This photograph amply demonstrates why the great amateur golfer and now secretary of the R & A, Michael Bonallack, once said, 'If you're not playing well you can still admire the scenery.' The 8th green is in the lower right half of the picture, with the 9th and 10th holes stretching out either side of the lighthouse along the rugged shoreline.
This shows why Turnberry has been compared with Cypress Point and Pebble Beach.

Breaking the American mould in the Open.

Far left Severiano Ballesteros of Spain shows how much victory meant at St Andrews in 1984. He later described his winning putt as 'the happiest single shot of my career – the happiest for ever, I should think'.

Left Twelve months later Sandy Lyle of Britain did not know he had done enough to win as he left the last green at Sandwich. Instead, he feared a bogey there may have cost him the title. Shortly afterwards he discovered it hadn't.

Below There were no such doubts for Australia's Greg Norman at Turnberry in 1986. He is seen here acknowledging the cheers of the huge crowds which invariably pack the grandstands around the final hole, thereby creating a tremendous atmosphere in this open amphitheatre.

It is said that golf tournaments are never won until the last putt has gone down, but Jack Nicklaus (right) effectively wrapped up the 1980 US Open at Baltusrol with this birdie from 20 feet on the penultimate hole of the championship. Two years later, Tom Watson (left) was even more delirious when he chipped in on the second to last hole at Pebble Beach to deny Nicklaus a record fifth US Open.

Shinnecock Hills on Long Island, New York, the first great golf course in the United States. By staging its second US Open in 1986, 90 years after its first, Shinnecock proved that it remains as testing as it is beautiful. The windmill in the top-left corner of the photograph is on Charles Blair Macdonald's masterpiece, the National Golf Links, itself a revelation and inspiration in the field of golf course architecture.

CHAPTER FIVE

The US Open: from Shinnecock to Shinnecock

First, an admission. The United States Open Championship did not begin life at Shinnecock Hills in 1896 but at the Newport Golf Club on Rhode Island in 1895, the winner being Horace Rawlins. The excuse for the above title is that the brief facts of that inaugural tournament, which was a mere appendage to the main business of the US Amateur, have been dealt with in Chapter 1; and besides, one can't allow historical pedantry to override a neat headline.

For most of the 90-year span separating James Foulis's and Raymond Floyd's victories at Shinnecock, the US Open has been regarded – on average – as the equal of the Open Championship. It is important to add that rider because each has enjoyed periods of ascendancy. When Harry Vardon entered the US Open in 1900, it was partly as a break from a series of promotional outings and exhibitions he was conducting in the United States. Although exhibitions are regarded with some scorn these days, they used to be the professional's major means of making money. When Hagen won all his championships in the 1920s, he said they were welcome not only for the glory but also as invaluable meal tickets he could take on the road: he used to manage a gruelling schedule of anything up to 10 exhibition matches per week.

Thus it was that Vardon incidentally won the sixth US Open while in the country for some lucrative extra-curricular remuneration. His triumph was a fillip for his own golf days and also for American golf. By the time he returned in 1913, the championship was well established and had even been won by a home-bred player.

The early days of the US Open were dominated by displaced Britons. After Rawlins and Foulis came Joe Lloyd, Fred Herd, Willie Smith, Vardon, Willie Anderson, Laurie Auchterlonie, Alex Smith, Alec Ross, Fred McLeod and George Sargent. Vardon was the only champion to have made a transatlantic journey to win but, with the exception of Anderson, the rest had honed their games in the old country, usually Scotland, and brought their skills over to America with them.

Willie Anderson was exceptional in many ways. He won the title four times: in 1901 and then from 1903 to 1905. Nobody else has ever accomplished the hat-trick, and his record of four victories is shared by Bobby Jones, Ben Hogan and Jack Nicklaus but bettered by nobody. Those three are impressive company. In the 1950s, several people who saw Anderson, Jones and Hogan in their respective primes vouched that Anderson was superior. He was indeed a marvellous striker and a fearsome competitor (he won his first two Opens in play-offs) but one is tempted to suggest that the evidence of those eye-witnesses is flawed by nostalgia, frequently the enemy of truth. Jones and Hogan were the best players in the world in their eras, Anderson was the best in America in his. It is hard to believe that he would have been so successful had Vardon, Taylor and Braid bothered to compete

A trio of early US Open champions. In this group photo Horace Rawlins, the winner of the inaugural championship, sits in front of the great Willie Anderson, who has his arm around Alex Smith, victorious in 1906.

Johnny McDermott was the first American-born player to win his country's national title.

Above right and opposite One of golf's most momentous occasions. Francis Ouimet won the 1913 US Open in a play-off with Vardon and Ray. A virtually unknown American amateur had beaten the cream of British and professional golf, and the balance of power had decisively shifted from one side of the Atlantic to the other. Ouimet is seen here with his little caddie Eddie Lowery, whose tears of disappointment persuaded Ouimet to let him continue to carry his bag for the play-off after he had contemplated hiring another friend. Later, as the drenched crowds wait for the end, Ouimet lines up his final, short putt.

during the years of his brief reign. Whatever their comparative merits, it was a sad loss when Anderson, aged just 32, died of arteriosclerosis in 1910.

The US Open matured quickly, picking up the habits of its British cousin with alacrity. Prize money was instituted straight away rather than after a three-year wait. It took only four years rather than 32 to be extended to 72 holes. Standards of scoring soon caught up too. It was in 1898 that 80 was first broken on all four days of the Open; four years later Auchterlonie did it in the US Open. A total below 300 and a single round below 70 were not achieved in Britain until 1904; in the United States the first of those hurdles fell in 1906 and the second in 1909. The most emphatic margins of victory in both Opens were set in their formative years; in Britain it remains the 13 shots by which Old Tom Morris swamped the rest in 1862, in the United States the 11 by which Willie Smith prevailed in 1899. Neither is likely to be increased, not least because the fields these days are rather larger.

By 1911, the championship had been staged 16 times and a native had yet to win. It was all about to change. Johnny McDermott took the title at Chicago in 1911, at 19 the youngest-ever winner, thus ending the years of overseas domination. He won again in 1912, in the process becoming the first man to record a sub-par total, but the big breakthrough was a year away.

In 1913, the US Open was won by 20-year-old Francis Ouimet (pronounced, in cumbersome franglais, as 'We-met'). A good but hardly spectacular amateur, Ouimet nearly withdrew from the tournament a week beforehand and rather wished he had when he struggled to a pair of 88s in two late practice rounds. But play he did, and play himself into the history books.

The weather that week at The Country Club in Brookline, Massachusetts, was uniformly awful. It had either just rained, was doing so or was about to, but the conditions did not stop the cream of British golf, Harry Vardon and Ted Ray, rising to the top with the lowest totals of 304. Out on the course, an unknown pro called Walter Hagen needed to par the last five holes to tie them but nobody was surprised when he blew up with a seven. He had to wait 12 months to win the title, Ouimet just another 24 hours.

Ouimet was a regular caddie at The Country Club. Carrying his bag in the Open was a 10-year-old boy, Eddie Lowery, who repeatedly and tersely reminded his man: 'Keep your eye on

the ball.' Sound advice, but it didn't seem likely to be sufficient when Ouimet, having astonished and delighted the damp gallery by being in contention for so long, needed to birdie two of the last six holes to catch the Englishmen. He not only did it but then routed his rivals in the play-off, Vardon by five shots – though Ouimet led him by only one with two holes to play – and Ray by six.

It is often stated that, overnight, this phenomenal performance converted a hitherto arcane pastime derided as 'cow pasture pool' into the biggest thing since hash browns. It did not, but Ouimet's relatively humble social status and engaging, pleasant manner did help to diminish golf's upper-crust image and broaden its appeal. One may argue that after the First World War the United States would have taken to golf anyway, as it did to many other sports. Maybe, but the fact that Ouimet had convincingly and dramatically beaten the world's best player head-to-head did wonders for the confidence of American golfers. It is a reflection of the significance attached to the events of 20 September 1913 by the USGA that a few years ago The Country Club was awarded the 1988 US Open – the 75th anniversary of the occasion, the centenary celebration of John Reid's game in his cow pasture.

Just as John Ball had severed the Scots' grip on the game, so Ouimet broke that of the British. Coincidentally, both were the first amateurs to win their respective national Opens, but whereas Ball's success did not herald a decline in the influence of the professionals in Britain, Ouimet's victory was the precursor of two glorious decades

of amateur achievement. Nineteen US Opens took place between 1913 and 1933 (the war caused cancellations in 1917 and 1918) and amateurs won eight of them: Ouimet (1913), Jerome Travers (1915), Chick Evans (1916), Bobby Jones (1923, 1926, 1929 and 1930) and Johnny Goodman (1933), the last amateur to win one of the four major championships. In addition, Jones was second four times (twice losing play-offs), while Evans and George von Elm were each runner-up once. The latter was on the wrong end of the 144-hole Open (72 holes of regulation play plus two 36-hole play-offs) of 1931. He and Billy Burke tied on 292 for four rounds. They were still level on 149 after another day's battle, and Burke

finally nipped it 148–149 the next afternoon. With that the 36-hole play-off, which had been introduced in 1928 yet had already been used twice previously, was abolished in favour of a return to 18 holes. The USGA probably felt that while stamina is an integral part of any sport, the US Open is supposed to be a golf tournament rather than a training session for the 50-kilometre walk.

The period between the wars was crammed with marvellous championships. After Hagen had won his second, and surprisingly last, US Open in an ill-tempered play-off with Mike Brady in 1919, Ted Ray took the trophy back to Britain from Inverness, Ohio, in 1920.

Harry Vardon (left) and Ted Ray (right) on their last exhibition tour of the United States in 1920. Between them is the tour manager, Arthur Peterson. Vardon was by then aged 50 and Ray 43, but they were still good enough for Ray to win the US Open that year and for Vardon (who seemed to have it in the bag) to finish in a tie for second.

That was a watershed year. It was the first time the clubhouse had been completely opened up to the professionals. Once this giant step had been taken other clubs soon followed suit and the old prejudices were swept away; in the United States, it must be said, before Britain. The professionals, duly grateful, donated a grand clock, which still graces the clubhouse, in recognition of the members' emancipatory attitude.

Inverness also witnessed the Open debut of men like Bobby Jones, Gene Sarazen, Johnny Farrell, Tommy Armour and Leo Diegel, and the unhappy farewell of Harry Vardon. The great man, seeking a second US Open a full 20 years after his first, led by five shots after 11 holes of the final round but a sudden and severe storm off Lake Erie destroyed his game, especially his putting touch which was by then quite delicate anyway, and he stumbled home in level fives for the last seven holes. Ray beat Vardon and three others with a stroke to spare.

One anecdote from that week is priceless. Vardon was paired with Jones in a qualifying round when the latter thinned a shot terribly. 'Mr. Vardon,' he asked, 'did you ever see a worse shot than that?' 'No,' came the reply.

Opposite Great friends, great rivals. Bobby Jones (right) with Gene Sarazen after Jones had succeeded Sarazen as US Open champion in 1923.

But Vardon's day was done. The twenties roared for Bobby Jones. He won the first of his 13 majors at the 1923 US Open, despite a double-bogey on the 72nd hole which enabled Bobby

Cruickshank to catch him with a birdie. In what was to be the first of six US Open play-offs in nine years, Jones clinched the title by two strokes.

Jones was involved in four of those extended Opens, but curiously, in view of his superb matchplay record in amateur competition, he could claim only a 50 per cent success rate. He lost to Willie Macfarlane in 1925 and to Johnny Farrell in 1928, both times by one shot over 36 holes, though in the first instance that was because an extra 18 had not been enough to separate them.

The second round of normal play in 1925 threw up a famous incident. Jones called a shot penalty on himself when his ball moved fractionally as he was addressing it. Nobody else saw it happen but when Jones was later congratulated for his sportsmanship he responded: 'You might as well praise a man for not robbing a bank.' Jones knew only one way to play and it is golf's great good fortune that this mode of behaviour has been adopted by the vast majority of those who chase the rich rewards available in the contemporary professional game.

One cannot say that Jones would have won that Open had his ball not budged: one can say that he

Two of the championships won by Jones and Sarazen.

Left A large gallery watches Jones annihilate Al Espinosa by 141 strokes to 164 in their play-off in 1929. This was the third of Jones's four US Open titles.

Below Sarazen won the US Open twice, either side of Jones's period of domination. This was the last of the 100 shots he needed to cover the final 28 holes at Fresh Meadow to win in 1932, just over two weeks after he had brought home the British Open trophy.

would have beaten Macfarlane in their second play-off had he not frittered away a four-shot lead over the last nine holes. In any event, he only had to rue his mistake for a year. By winning the title at Scioto, Jones became the first player to hold simultaneously the British and US Opens (in those days the American event was held second of the two). He repeated the feat in his Grand Slam year of 1930, and to date just Sarazen (1932), Hogan (1953), Trevino (1971) and Watson (1982) have emulated him. Jones's third US Open victory, in 1929, is also noteworthy. He faced the most treacherous 12-footer conceivable on the last green at Winged Foot but he sank it to tie Al Espinosa. He demolished his opponent by 23 strokes in a 36-hole massacre the next day, but not before he had graciously asked the USGA to delay the play-off to allow his opponent, a devout Catholic, to attend Mass.

Bobby Jones was not the only man then playing decent golf in the US Open. Tommy Armour, a transplanted Scot like Cruickshank and Macfarlane, won in 1927 at Oakmont, with Jones down in 11th place. Armour knew he had to birdie the last hole, a formidable par-4, to catch Harry Cooper. As the 'Silver Scot' surveyed the 3-iron shot he had left, a club member, so the legend goes, called out: 'I've been reading that you're a great iron player. Let's see you hit one now.' Armour hit it 10 feet from the hole. 'Will that do?' he asked. He made the putt and defeated Cooper the following day.

In 1932, after Jones's retirement, Gene Sarazen played the last 28 holes at Fresh Meadow in exactly 100 strokes – the last 18 in 66, a record that stood until 1960 – to win by three. Two years later

he took a triple-bogey seven at Merion's 11th hole in the final round and lost to Olin Dutra by one. Such is tournament golf – win some, lose some. But for Sam Snead, there were to be no US Open wins to offset the losses, and some of those were horribly hard to bear.

Snead made his debut in 1937 and finished runner-up, two strokes adrift of Ralph Guldahl. It was surely just a matter of time, the sages said. In 1939, in one of the most infamous blow-ups in golf lore, Snead made an eight on the last hole at Philadelphia when a par-5 was all he needed to win. The wise men changed their minds. Snead is one of the game's great players but fate has treated him cruelly in the US Open.

Another man to be jinxed in the major championships was Craig Wood. Snead's munificence meant that Wood, Byron Nelson and Denny Shute played off for the title in 1939. Shute was eliminated on the first 18 while Nelson stayed alive by dint of a birdie at the last. On the fourth hole of the second play-off, Nelson holed a 1-iron for an eagle two and was never caught. Wood's luckless defeat gave him a unique niche in the record books and one of the most unwanted honours in golf: play-off losses in all four major championships. Happily, by all that's right, Wood eventually went on to win two majors: the Masters and US Open, both in 1941.

In 1940, yet another play-off was won by Lawson Little. (One wonders what modern union leaders would have made of all this overtime, though at least it was paid.) Poor 'Porky' Oliver returned a score of 287, which appeared to tie

Little and Sarazen until it was learned that he and five others had been disqualified for teeing off in advance of their starting times for the last round because they were worried about a brewing storm.

The war halted the golf action between 1942 and 1945. If anyone bothered to reflect on the respective status of the two Opens at this time there was only one conclusion to be drawn: the US Open had moved past its British counterpart in a very few years. The decline of the latter could be traced to the moment Jones quit the competitive arena. Apart from Cotton's victory in 1937, the Americans won it if they went over – Armour in 1931, Sarazen in 1932 and Shute in 1933 – but generally they were losing interest. They already knew they were the best players in the world; to them their national Open, as the premier tournament of the world's premier golfing nation, was *per se* the game's most prestigious title. Why waste time and money and ruin a good swing in the sea winds off the British coast?

This attitude hardened after the war when the Ryder Cup matches between the professionals of the two countries were seldom worthy of the name contest. It was reinforced when Snead won the Open at St Andrews in 1946 and Locke won it four times in eight years. Americans knew that Snead could win everything except the US Open and that Locke could win tour events but not the US Open. When Hogan decided to have one attempt at the British Open and won it in 1953, that settled it. A great champion like Hogan could

Ben Hogan playing the 17th at Oakland Hills in 1951 on the way to what he called 'the greatest round I have ever played', his 67 on the last afternoon. He added: 'I haven't played all the courses in the world but I don't want to if there are any tougher than this one.'

walk over and win in Britain at will, but even he couldn't win the US Open every year (though he wasn't far off for a time). The British Open was a nice link with history but the US Open was *the* championship. It was perhaps inevitable that it took an American – Palmer – to tip the scales back towards equilibrium, or even beyond as many would argue with some justification today in view of the heavy American bias in the composition of the fields for the US Open.

Back in 1946, Hitler and the Japanese had been seen off but the Americans were not rid of their penchant for play-offs. Lloyd Mangrum, Byron Nelson and Vic Ghezzi were in this one but, after another in the long chain of golf's bizarre occurrences, Nelson had every right to feel hard done by. His caddie had inadvertently trod on Byron's ball on the final hole of the championship proper, costing him a one-shot penalty and probably a second US Open. In another protracted drama, Mangrum took the play-off at the second attempt after all three had shot 72s for the first 18 holes. Even Snead got into the play-off act in 1947, thanks to a six-yard putt on the last hole. Just 24 hours later, he missed from a yard on the same green to lose to Lew Worsham. Snead's last chance had gone. Enter Ben Hogan.

From 1948 to 1953, Hogan won the US Open four times and was third once. He didn't play in 1949 because he couldn't walk, a legacy of his near-fatal car crash that February. In 1948 at Riviera he set an aggregate scoring record of 276, which was five better than anything before and lasted until 1967. At Merion in 1950 he was so pained by cramps in his still sore legs that with a few holes left he contemplated quitting, but he stoically soldiered on and tied Mangrum and George Fazio. It had been a whole three years since the last play-off and Hogan took this one by four strokes, a margin exaggerated because Mangrum literally blew away his chance on the 16th green by picking up his ball, without having first marked it, to blow off a bug.

The following year, Hogan manufactured a masterly winning last round of 67 at Oakland Hills, a course stringently doctored by Robert Trent Jones who was appointed by a committee which, in the words of one member, wanted a layout 'so tough that nobody can win'. At the prize-giving ceremony, Hogan remarked: 'I am glad to have brought this monster to its knees.' Two years later he won for a fourth time at Oakmont with a consummate display of shot-making that leant support to the apparently

absurd theory that what should have been a debilitating accident had actually been the catalyst which led to an improved technique. The runner-up, six shots in his wake, was the eternal bridesmaid, Sam Snead.

Hogan made three strong bids for an unprecedented fifth title, notably in 1955. He had finished with a total of 287 at Olympic and, though he refused to acknowledge victory in public, he was confident enough to proffer the ball with which he had holed out for display in the USGA's museum. His challengers wilted until only Jack Fleck remained, and he was hardly a known quantity, let alone a threat to Hogan. He needed two birdies in the last four holes to tie (leaders then did not necessarily go out last) and improbably – shades of Ouimet – he got them, in his case with a birdie at the last. Like Ouimet, he beat his fancied rival in the play-off too. Hogan was second again in 1956 but there were to be no more major championships for him after 1953.

Cary Middlecoff was the man who denied Hogan in 1956. It was Middlecoff's second Open (he had won in 1949) and he came as close as is possible to retaining the title in 1957 but was beaten – in a play-off, of course – by Dick Mayer. Hogan was also in the thick of things in 1960 until he uncharacteristically gambled everything on a nervy pitch shot over water to the 17th green in the final round. He felt his legs wouldn't carry him comfortably for the 18 holes of a play-off and he had to try to make a winning birdie. When the

The moment when Hogan lost his last chance of a record fifth US Open. He was a shot behind Jack Fleck as they stood on the 18th tee of their play-off in San Francisco in 1955 but his foot slipped as he hit his final drive and when the ball disappeared into this awful rough Hogan's hopes went with it. He eventually holed out for a double-bogey six and a three-shot defeat.

ball toppled back into the hazard, that chance had gone. It was all he could do to walk up the hill to the final green, hitting the ball seven times on his way to the clubhouse. Shortly afterwards, Arnold Palmer, who had begun the afternoon seven shots behind the leader, came home with a 65 to win in fantastic style.

The manner in which Palmer began that round is one of the most famous episodes in championship golf. He drove the first green, a par-4, and two-putted for a three. This kind of stuff – no holds barred, smash the course into submission – was typically Palmer. Never mind that the same aggressive policy on the first three rounds had led to him dropping three strokes to par on what was really an innocuous opening hole, this was Palmer's hallmark. After his perfect start, he birdied five of the next six holes and the foundations for one of the most memorable days' golf ever seen were solidly and spectacularly laid.

It was as well Palmer won that Open. He wasn't to win another. There were four play-offs in the 1960s (a good vintage) and Palmer lost three of them: in 1962 to Jack Nicklaus, the rookie pro who had been second to Palmer as an amateur in 1960 and was to bring Palmer's era to a premature close not long after it had begun; in 1963 to Julius Boros, who had also won in 1952; and in 1966 to Billy Casper (the 1959 champion) when he let slip a seven-shot lead with nine holes of regulation play remaining because he foolishly forgot about his rival and instead mounted a vain assault on Hogan's record total of 276. Ironically, the following summer Nicklaus produced a series of magnificent iron shots towards the finish at Baltusrol and, in relegating Palmer into second place, shot 275.

The third member of the Big Three, South African Gary Player, became the first overseas winner of the US Open since Ted Ray when he captured the 1965 championship in a play-off with Kel Nagle of Australia. The previous June the tournament had reached an emotional high not experienced since Ouimet's sensational win when Ken Venturi triumphed at Congressional.

Triumphed is the correct description. Venturi was a peerless iron player at his best, but he had lost three Masters in heartbreaking fashion and in

Arnold Palmer celebrates one of the greatest closing rounds in championship history, the 65 which earned him victory at Cherry Hills in Denver in 1960.

After his victory in 1960, Palmer never won another US Open. Heartbreakingly for him and his army of fans, though, he lost three play-offs for it.

Far left In 1962, 22-year-old Jack Nicklaus beat him 71–74 at Oakmont to achieve his first win as a professional.

Left In 1963 it was 43-year-old Julius Boros's turn to deny Palmer in a three-way play-off with Jacky Cupit. Ironically, Nicklaus missed the cut.

Palmer's hat-trick of play-off agonies was completed in 1966 when he threw away a big lead in the fourth round and Billy Casper made him pay the price. This is Casper exulting as a bunker shot turns out rather better than expected during the second round at Olympic that year.

THE US OPEN CHAMPIONSHIP – WINNERS

Year	Venue	Winner	Score	Year	Venue	Winner	Score	Year	Venue	Winner	Score
1895	Newport	Horace Rawlins	173	1926	Scioto	*BobbyJones	293	1960	Cherry Hills	Arnold Palmer	280
1896	Shinnecock Hills	James Foulis	152	1927	Oakmont	†Tommy Armour	301	1961	Oakland Hills	Gene Littler	281
1897	Chicago	Joe Lloyd	162	1928	Olympia Fields	†Johnny Farrell	294	1962	Oakmont	†Jack Nicklaus	283
1898	Myopia	Fred Herd	328	1929	Winged Foot	†*Bobby Jones	294	1963	Brookline	†Julius Boros	293
1899	Baltimore	Willie Smith	315	1930	Interlachen	*Bobby Jones	287	1964	Congressional	Ken Venturi	278
1900	Chicago	Harry Vardon (GB)	313	1931	Inverness	†Billy Burke	292	1965	Bellerive	†Gary Player (SA)	282
1901	Myopia	†Willie Anderson	331	1932	Fresh Meadow	Gene Sarazen	286	1966	Olympic	†Billy Casper	278
1902	Garden City	Laurie Auchterlonie	307	1933	North Shore	*Johnny Goodman	287	1967	Baltusrol	Jack Nicklaus	275
1903	Baltusrol	†Willie Anderson	307	1934	Merion	Olin Dutra	293	1968	Oak Hill	Lee Trevino	275
1904	Glen View	Willie Anderson	303	1935	Oakmont	Sam Parks	299	1969	Champions	Orville Moody	281
1905	Myopia	Willie Anderson	314	1936	Baltusrol	Tony Manero	282	1970	Hazeltine	Tony Jacklin (GB)	281
1906	Onwentsia	Alex Smith	295	1937	Oakland Hills	Ralph Guldahl	281	1971	Merion	†Lee Trevino	280
1907	Philadelphia	Alec Ross	302	1938	Cherry Hills	Ralph Guldahl	284	1972	Pebble Beach	Jack Nicklaus	290
1908	Myopia	†Fred McLeod	322	1939	Philadelphia	†Byron Nelson	284	1973	Oakmont	Johnny Miller	279
1909	Englewood	George Sargent	290	1940	Canterbury	†Lawson Little	287	1974	Winged Foot	Hale Irwin	287
1910	Philadelphia	†Alex Smith	298	1941	Colonial	Craig Wood	284	1975	Medinah	†Lou Graham	287
1911	Chicago	†Johnny McDermott	307	1942–5	No competition			1976	Atlanta	Jerry Pate	277
1912	Buffalo	Johnny McDermott	294	1946	Canterbury	†Lloyd Mangrum	284	1977	Southern Hills	Hubert Green	278
1913	Brookline	†*Francis Ouimet	304	1947	St Louis	†Lew Worsham	282	1978	Cherry Hills	Andy North	285
1914	Midlothian	Walter Hagen	290	1948	Riviera	Ben Hogan	276	1979	Inverness	Hale Irwin	284
1915	Baltusrol	*Jerome Travers	297	1949	Medinah	Cary Middlecoff	286	1980	Baltusrol	Jack Nicklaus	272
1916	Minikahda	*Chick Evans	286	1950	Merion	†Ben Hogan	287	1981	Merion	David Graham (Aus)	273
1917–8	No competition			1951	Oakland Hills	Ben Hogan	287	1982	Pebble Beach	Tom Watson	282
1919	Brae Burn	†Walter Hagen	301	1952	Northwood	Julius Boros	281	1983	Oakmont	Larry Nelson	280
1920	Inverness	Ted Ray (GB)	295	1953	Oakmont	Ben Hogan	283	1984	Winged Foot	†Fuzzy Zoeller	276
1921	Columbia	Jim Barnes	289	1954	Baltusrol	Ed Furgol	284	1985	Oakland Hills	Andy North	279
1922	Skokie	Gene Sarazen	288	1955	Olympic	†Jack Fleck	287	1986	Shinnecock Hills	Ray Floyd	279
1923	Inwood	†*Bobby Jones	296	1956	Oak Hill	Cary Middlecoff	281				
1924	Oakland Hills	Cyril Walker	297	1957	Inverness	†Dick Mayer	282				
1925	Worcester	†Willie Macfarlane	291	1958	Southern Hills	Tommy Bolt	283	* amateur	† won play-off		
				1959	Winged Foot	Billy Casper	282				

Ken Venturi's triumph in 1964 was one of championship golf's emotional highpoints. With a mixture of relief and almost disbelief, Venturi realizes he has at last quietened his doubters.

the preceding few years had been plagued by back injuries, pneumonia, and a circulatory problem in his hand which impaired his sense of feel. In the 1964 Open Venturi also suffered from heat exhaustion and intense dehydration caused by the oppressive humidity that hung over Washington that week; indeed, he was so badly affected that a doctor had to accompany him for the final round. In spite of it all, he made birdies and pars while those around him faltered. As he walked down the hill to the last green, with victory secure, he was cheered home a hero by the fans massed along the sides of the fairway, many of whom had tears in their eyes. When he holed the final putt to win by four strokes, he raised his eyes to the heavens and cried out: 'My God. I've won the Open.'

Even the Lord may have been surprised at some of those who succeeded him, such as Orville Moody (1969), Lou Graham (1975) and Andy North (1978 and 1985). Lee Trevino looked likely to be a freak winner when he won in 1968, but he has proved to be right out of the top drawer.

Trevino had first come to public attention in the 1967 championship, not so much for finishing fifth but because he wore scuba goggles in the dry

air of New Jersey. He explained that was how he dressed for golf in El Paso, Texas: goggles were essential to protect his eyes from the sand and dirt whipped up by the wind. But any suggestions that Trevino had been a fluke champion in 1968 were dispelled when he did it again in 1971, this time in a play-off. He quoted Hagen: 'Anyone can win the Open once. It takes a great player to win it twice.' Trevino's pedigree was further enhanced by the identity of the runner-up on both occasions – Jack Nicklaus.

Between Trevino's double act came Orville Moody and Tony Jacklin, the latter winning by seven strokes in 1970 and in so doing being the first Briton to steal the opposite Open since Ted Ray precisely 50 years before. Three years on, Johnny Miller set fire to a rain-sodden Oakmont with a 63, the lowest closing score in major championship history, to take the title by a shot. A further three years elapsed before Jerry Pate, needing a par for victory, struck a glorious 5-iron to within two feet of the last hole at Atlanta for an easy birdie and his first success as a pro. The Atlanta Athletic Club was the 47th different US Open venue but the first in the Deep South. The club was awarded the honour at the behest of Bobby Jones, who died in 1971, and the people of Georgia responded by setting new attendance records.

The roll-call of recent champions is impressive and each has an extraordinary tale to tell. Hubert

Green defied a death threat in 1977. Hale Irwin overcame the jitters in 1979 as effectively as he had in 1974. Jack Nicklaus turned back the years and a Japanese putting machine called Isao Aoki to receive that record-equalling fourth trophy in 1980. Twelve months later David Graham struck so many wonderful shots on the Sunday at Merion that even Hogan would have been envious.

Tom Watson won in 1982 at Pebble Beach, thwarting Jack Nicklaus as dramatically as he had done at Turnberry five years previously. He holed consecutive putts of 25 feet on the 10th and 11th holes in the final round, made a monster of 50 feet on the 14th, and then chipped in from a hanging lie for the crucial birdie at the 17th. 'Try to get it close,' his caddie Bruce Edwards had suggested, a trifle unnecessarily but also, it appeared, optimistically in view of the lie of the ball and the speed of the green between Watson and the hole, 20 feet away. 'Close?' replied Watson. 'I'm going to hole it.' When he did, he toured the green, arms aloft, in a lap of honour, before calming himself sufficiently to sink another putt of 20 feet at the last for a closing birdie which widened the gap between himself and Nicklaus to two shots. In the most devastating manner, Watson thus denied Nicklaus a fifth US Open and ensured that he

Opposite **Yet another birdie for Johnny Miller, one of nine that took him from 12th to first on an astonishing Sunday afternoon during the 1973 US Open at Oakmont.**

Walter Hagen said: 'Anyone can win the Open once. It takes a great player to win it twice.' Andy North has won the US Open twice, in 1978 and 1985, but he seems destined to be regarded as a lucky winner. He prevailed by a single stroke each time, having bogeyed the final hole on both occasions, and he had to get down in two from this bunker at Cherry Hills to do that in 1978.

If in this chapter the exploits of Byron Nelson and other names from the past have been accorded more space than those of Larry Nelson and other contemporary stars, that is not to denigrate the skills of the latter group. It is simply an acknowledgement that the deeds of the former are perhaps less familiar than the better chronicled occurrences of recent times. But however far back one goes, no tournament (let alone the US Open) has ever seen a man make three more miraculous pars than did Greg Norman on the last three holes at Winged Foot in 1984. The putt of 30 feet he holed at the 18th, as slippery as a snake, seemed well nigh impossible. As Norman exulted at yet another escape, Fuzzy Zoeller stood back down the fairway waving a white towel in mock surrender at his rival's unfailing ability to extricate himself from trouble. That gesture of supreme sportsmanship will be spoken of for as long as people care about the game.

Zoeller parred the hole in Norman's wake and went on to win an anti-climactic play-off (the 27th in all) by eight shots, a shattering defeat which Norman bore with laughter and grace. The following summer, Tze-Chung Chen of Taiwan demonstrated that Orientals are not necessarily inscrutable by smiling in adversity as Andy North

The pleasure of a putt. Larry Nelson (above) holes from 60 feet on the 70th green at Oakmont in 1983; Greg Norman (right) from 30 feet at Winged Foot the following year. Nelson won the title by a shot from Tom Watson, but Norman went down with a 75 to Fuzzy Zoeller's 67 in a play-off.

himself would not have to carry forever the stigma borne by Sam Snead. The US Open was already threatening to become a psychological hurdle. At Pebble Beach, Watson laid the bogey with a blitz of birdies.

He might well have won the next year too, but Larry Nelson played the last two rounds in 65–67 (10 under par), the best-ever aggregate for the second half of the championship. A thunderstorm delayed the finale until the Monday, when Nelson had three holes to play, but though the torrential rain had interrupted his flow it couldn't disrupt it. He holed a birdie putt of fully 60 feet on the 16th in the eerie atmosphere of the morning after and he was on his way again.

The joy of winning. Raymond Floyd with the US Open trophy after his success at Shinnecock Hills in 1986.

won for a second time, and adversity in golf does not come any tougher than taking an eight on a par-4 to lose a major championship by a stroke.

In June 1986 Shinnecock returned to the schedule. The USGA had interfered a little with the substantially revised layout William Flynn had moulded from Young Willie Dunn's original masterpiece, but not to any degree that made it unrecognizable. The major change was in the preparation of the course. Shinnecock underwent the kind of surgery which the USGA routinely performs on all Open venues these days. This operation creates narrow but immaculately groomed fairways lined with thick rough, and lightning-fast greens surrounded by lush, tufty grass; the speed of the greens themselves being determined by a ball-rolling device known as a Stimpmeter which enables a quick, uniform pace to be established and maintained for all 18 holes.

Critics complain these measures mean that the US Open isn't a test of driving (because no player dare use a driver off the tee) or chipping (because once in the heavy stuff it requires brute strength rather than finesse to get out). The USGA responds that its methods are designed to identify the best golfer in the world, not to penalize him, while simultaneously trying to protect the integrity of the course. The latter job was so well done in 1986 that Ray Floyd was the only man to break par, and his total of 279 was just one under.

Shinnecock proved itself to be old but not old fashioned. Already, authoritative voices are whispering that 90 years is too long to wait. Members permitting, a third visit to Shinnecock in 1995 – to celebrate 100 years of US Opens – is a distinct possibility.

The Magic of the Masters

Fruitlands Nursery, which Alister Mackenzie and Bobby Jones converted into the Augusta National golf course in the 1930s. This view of the property in its pristine state is taken from just behind and to the left of where the clubhouse stands today.

If the Open Championships of Great Britain and the United States are the two most important and prestigious tournaments in the world, the next in line is the Masters Championship, held at Augusta National Golf Club in Georgia each April. It is perhaps remarkable that a championship which was only inaugurated in 1934 is held in such high esteem, but the origins of that respect and affection can be identified with just one person: Bobby Jones.

Jones was the greatest amateur golfer in history: some would simply say the greatest golfer in history. He retired from competition in 1930 having, at the age of 28, completed the Impregnable Quadrilateral – or Grand Slam in modern parlance – by winning the Open and Amateur Championships of Britain and the United States in the same season. He quit because there was nothing left for him to prove and, it has to be confessed, because his constitution had been tormented by the strain of contending for major championships. He followed the advice of that popular sporting aphorism and got out when he was on top.

But Jones was not about to become totally divorced from the game to which he had given so much and derived such pleasure. He and Clifford Roberts, a New York banker who combined with Jones to establish Augusta National and the Masters and was later to rule the tournament with an iron hand, learned of an old horticultural nursery at Augusta, Georgia, which would make an ideal site for the golf course of their dreams. Jones called in an expatriate Scotsman, Dr Alister Mackenzie, who was responsible for the creation of fine British courses like Alwoodley and Moortown at Leeds and the spectacular Cypress Point in California. By 1934 the course was ready to host its 'First Annual Invitation Tournament'; a gathering of several of Jones's friends – the field comprised 72 players – who also happened to be the best golfers in the world. Jones actually played too, as he did on 12 occasions altogether, but it was always more out of a sense of politeness to his guests than with any hope or desire to win.

Horton Smith won the first event but the press and other admirers of Jones were not prepared to tolerate the modest and innocuous title he had bestowed upon his tournament. It became known as the Masters, despite Jones's initial protestations that such a name was pretentious, because the masters of golf were all in attendance. The label stuck more readily the following year when one of those masters, Gene Sarazen, holed a full 4-wood shot on the par-5 15th hole of the final round for an albatross, or double-eagle, two. It enabled him to catch Craig Wood and Sarazen won the ensuing play-off. Thus was the Masters endowed with what can only be termed 'instant tradition'.

It would not have been possible for Sarazen to make this devastating challenge to Wood at such a crucial moment in the round had Augusta National been set up the same way as it had been the previous year. Then the 15th was the 6th, but in 1935 the order of the two loops of nine was reversed and that is the way the course has

remained ever since, even though some holes have changed over the years. For example, Mackenzie would not recognize the famous 16th, a testing par-3 over water which has witnessed many dramatic moments in the closing stages of the Masters. It was built after the last war by Robert Trent Jones, the renowned American golf course architect, and it bears no resemblance to the original.

The golf course is an integral part of the Masters for the obvious reason that the tournament is the only one of golf's four major championships to be played at the same venue every year. That is one unique feature of the Masters. Another is the complete absence of billboards and advertising slogans which are to be found everywhere else in the increasingly commercial world of golf. Yet a third is the system of series badges operated by the club for the four days of competition. There is no admission to the course on a normal daily basis so these coveted season tickets are treated as family heirlooms, passed down through the generations.

The American commentators who describe the Masters as 'the toughest ticket in sport' are not exaggerating, but then nothing is easy to get into at Augusta.

It is one of the world's most exclusive clubs; not only are invitations to join precious and rare but it isn't even a simple matter to play the course as a member's guest. It has been suggested that the easiest way to join Augusta National is via the honorary membership given to all Masters champions, and that the easiest way to get a game over the hallowed fairways is to play in the championship. The latter remark is greeted with scepticism in some quarters because getting into the tournament is hard enough, even for good players.

One doesn't enter the Masters. To this day it remains a relatively small-field, select event. There are no pre-qualifying competitions as there are at the major Open Championships. Criteria are laid down which mean that a native player who fulfils a certain requirement knows he is in –

Jones was, of course, meticulous in ensuring that the dream he had should be realised in perfection. He is seen here in the process of driving a few balls to ascertain the best site for the 8th tee.

Seven early Masters champions. From left to right: Horton Smith (1934 and 1936), Byron Nelson (1937), Henry Picard (1938), Jimmy Demaret (1940, 1947 and 1950), Craig Wood (1941), Gene Sarazen (1935) – note how small he is, surely the greatest short golfer in history – and Herman Keiser (1946).

Opposite One of the great Masters traditions is that on the opening morning two old-timers should be honorary starters. They usually settle for playing nine holes. Sam Snead (left) and Gene Sarazen have recently assumed the responsibility that used to be shared by Jock Hutchison (1920 USPGA champion and 1921 British Open champion) and Fred McLeod (1908 US Open winner).

for instance, by finishing in the top 24 at the preceding Masters – but these only apply to Americans and represent their only avenue into the tournament. Some foreigners may happen to fall into one of the categories, such as being a past champion, but strictly they have to depend on an invitation.

There have been criticisms that the Masters officials are too parsimonious with these, and that they fail to take sufficient account of the rapidly rising standards of golfers elsewhere in the world. This is a fair point, one that the committee is slowly coming to terms with in the face of fine performances by those overseas competitors who do play in the Masters. However, another common complaint – that there are too many amateurs taking the spots of worthy professionals – demonstrates a failure to acknowledge and understand a tradition which owes its existence to Jones's roots. But tradition and controversy are no strangers to the Masters.

The traditions include the previous year's champion helping his successor into a club member's green jacket, a ritual performed once for the benefit of the TV audience in a closed room (Jones and Roberts were not unaware of the power of television) and then again at the prize-giving ceremony. Just once has the neatness of this formality been upset and that was in 1966

when Jack Nicklaus became the only man to retain the title. He had to help himself into the famous coat. There are formal pre-tournament dinners for the past champions (when the defending champion picks up the bill), international players and amateurs. To date only Gary Player, Severiano Ballesteros and Bernhard Langer have been eligible to attend the first two of these. On the eve of the championship, a nine-hole par-3 competition is held over the club's beautiful short course, but it isn't taken too seriously. All the entrants are aware that nobody has ever won the big event after winning the little one.

Controversy may seem an odd companion for such a smooth operation as the Masters but it is never easy to make everything look perfect. Both in public and behind the scenes there have been enough sensational stories to satisfy any soap opera buff.

In 1968, Roberto de Vicenzo and Bob Goalby appeared to tie for the championship after some scintillating golf on the final afternoon (65 by de

The former plantation mansion, now Augusta's clubhouse, fronted by a flower-arranged map of the United States, a flagstaff bearing the Stars & Stripes and the club flag, and a Pinkertons guard.

Far left This colourful gentleman is obviously a Masters regular, as indicated by the collection of series badges he has proudly attached to his hat.

Left A pair of double Masters champions. Tom Watson practises his bunker play under the supervision of his friend and mentor, Byron Nelson.

Augusta is a breathtakingly glorious place during Masters week. In the lower portion of the top photograph is Amen Corner, with the 11th and 12th holes clearly visible to the right and the curve of the 13th fairway evident on the left. The ponds adjoining the 15th and 16th greens are the focus of attention in the bottom photograph. Other holes in view include the demanding long par-4 5th in the foreground, the 6th green at lower left and the 7th and 17th stretching out towards the trees in the distance.

The 10th has been described as the most beautiful hole in the world. On a course of outstanding beauty, it stands out. The brilliant emerald fairways, bright white sand bunkers, dazzlingly coloured flowers, customarily azure skies and the magnificent cathedral of pines all conspire to create a seductive setting and a superb test of golfing skill.

Ben Crenshaw about to play one of the most crucial shots in his Masters triumph of 1984. He hit this 6-iron to 12 feet on the 12th hole in the final round and holed the putt for a birdie. The perils of Rae's Creek are obvious and daunting, and its waters accounted for Crenshaw's closest pursuers – Tom Kite and Larry Nelson – just as they have for so many other hapless contenders down the ages.

Right Another of Augusta's gorgeous but hazardous par-3s. Water and sand endanger the golfer on the 16th just as much as they do on the 12th.

Far right One of the Masters' great traditions: the old champion helps the new into the winner's green club jacket. Here Bernhard Langer of West Germany, victorious in 1985, lends a hand to Jack Nicklaus, who won for a record sixth time in 1986.

The scene around the 18th green late on the Sunday afternoon of Masters week is invariably one of golf's annual highlights. Never was the occasion more emotionally charged than in 1986, as Jack Nicklaus falls to his knees and his caddie, his son Jackie, uses 'body-English' in an attempt to coax the ball forward an extra few inches for yet another birdie. In the end it didn't matter. Nicklaus won by a shot from Tom Kite and Greg Norman.

Vicenzo, 66 for Goalby). The assembled multitude had barely gathered its collective breath when it was learned that de Vicenzo had mistakenly signed for a four on the 17th when he had actually taken a three. His 65 became a 66. He was 'beaten by the pencil' and there was to be no play-off. Under the rules, there was no choice. Goalby was declared the champion. Jones would have loved to have bent the laws of the game but he would have been the last man to do so.

Jones was inevitably involved in that sad decision but his crippling illness was annually taking a greater toll and Roberts – who in later life dispensed with the 'benevolent' bit before 'dictator', a label often applied behind his back – arranged for Jones to take no part in any of the post-tournament formalities. Such ruthless behaviour towards a sick man, an old friend, is indicative of the autocratic manner in which Roberts ordered affairs at Augusta. Television commentators were not allowed to mention prize money during the tournament: nor were the cameras permitted to show the usually immaculate course when it was flooded so severely in 1973 that the third day's play had to be postponed. The Masters has an enviable image of beauty, serenity and efficiency and Roberts would not allow anything to besmirch that. As someone once said: 'At Augusta, dogs do not bark and babies do not cry.'

But perfection had a high price. Roberts so distressed Jones with his authoritarian rebuff in 1968 that the two never spoke to each other again before Jones died in December 1971. By then the Masters was embroiled in a heated debate.

Georgia is in America's Deep South. By the beginning of the 1970s, no black golfer had ever qualified to play at Augusta. Civil rights campaigners called it a scandal and complained that the club was pursuing a racist policy. This was arrant nonsense. It was just that no black player had made the grade demanded of American golfers under the existing criteria. But rather than permit the issue to escalate, in 1971 Roberts expanded the qualification categories and announced that henceforth any winner of a US Tour event would automatically qualify for the Masters.

Two years later, no black golfer had yet fulfilled this new requirement and a deputation from Congress alleged that the Masters was still a discriminatory institution. Roberts was now on firmer ground and replied that having changed the rules he wasn't going to invite a player just

The master of the Masters, Cliff Roberts. He ruled with an iron hand until one night in 1977 when he wandered out to the club's par-3 course and committed suicide.

because he was black. He added: 'We are a little surprised as well as being flattered that 18 Congressmen should be able to take time out to help us operate a golf tournament.' The row ended 12 months later when Lee Elder won the Monsanto Open and thereby secured an invitation to the 1975 Masters.

Roberts, to the surprise of many expert Augusta-watchers, resigned as chairman in 1976 and handed over the reins to Bill Lane – but in name only. Roberts didn't actually relinquish power until one evening the next year he walked out into the club grounds and shot himself. No one knows for sure, but it is presumed that he knew he too was becoming increasingly ill and that, unlike Jones, he was not prepared to suffer the consequences.

Bill Lane died in 1980 and was succeeded by Hord Hardin. The controversies have abated but the traditions go on, and one of the traditions is that the shape of the course changes.

Some alterations have been major, such as the wholesale restructuring of the 16th hole, as mentioned previously; the relocating of the 10th

Two of Augusta's finest and most treacherous holes. The 15th (foreground) and 16th greens are both well defended by water.

green to create one of the most majestic par-4s in the world; and the moving of the tee on the 11th which, together with the building of a pond to the left of the green, converted a mundane drive-and-pitch hole into a formidable test which demands length and accuracy off the tee and considerable nerve with the approach shot. Ben Hogan, perhaps the most remorselessly accurate striker in history, once said: 'If you ever see me on the 11th green in two, you'll know I missed my second shot.' He always elected to play safe to the right with his iron, generally saving par with a chip and a putt.

Every year at Augusta something is added or altered: a new bunker on the 1st fairway, mounds inserted in the driving zone on the 3rd and 15th, more humps put in to protect the entrance to the 8th, a swale over the back of the 13th green, and so on. Some players at the Masters, usually after they have dropped a shot as a result of tangling with one of these modifications, protest that the course should be left alone. They are neglecting the fact that Augusta is a living memorial to Jones, not a

mausoleum. Jones approved many amendments to the design on which he and Mackenzie had collaborated, but that should not be allowed to convey the impression that their original plans were badly flawed. On the contrary, Augusta has been an inspiration to countless golf course architects since the very day it was unveiled.

Augusta was revolutionary. There were only 22 bunkers on the whole course in 1934 and there remain fewer than 50 today (it doesn't pay to be too dogmatic because one never knows when a couple more may be built). The rough is negligible, the fairways are massively wide, the greens huge. The philosophy was to make the course easy for club members to play to their handicaps while posing serious problems for the tournament golfers in search of birdies. Jones and Mackenzie achieved this by the judicious siting of tees and by cultivating extremely fast, contoured greens which set as tough an examination of putting as can be found anywhere. In 1980 the club decided to kill off the old Bermuda and rye grasses and reseed the greens with bent grass. The result has been to speed them up even more and, by cutting the holes in the trickiest places for Masters week, Augusta National can be turned from a gentle giant into a magnificent monster.

It is the magnificence of the scenery at Augusta which has, over the years, attracted and awed millions of golf fans, whether they be fortunate enough to have attended in person or been forced to settle for watching the Masters on television. To golfers, springtime is Masters time, when the legacy of the old Fruitlands nursery is in glorious evidence, with azalea, dogwood, redbud, wisteria and a score of other blooms in a host of vivid colours, all set against a marvellous backdrop of tall pines, emerald fairways and deep blue water hazards. Even the sand used to fill in the divots is dyed green, and the ponds and streams are given an artificial tint of blue.

There is nothing false about the water within, as hundreds of golfers have discovered during the Masters. From the 11th to the 16th holes at Augusta, only the 14th is devoid of water. The most notorious of these hazards is Rae's Creek, which takes the form of a pond in front of the 12th green. A meandering stream then takes over down the left-hand side of the fairway of the dog-leg 13th; almost the archetypal short par-5 at 465 yards, which on most courses would only rate as a par-4. It finishes its journey with a flourish by skirting the front edge and right side of the 13th green. As their balls have plummeted into either this creek or Rae's, or into the little lakes protecting the 15th and 16th greens, several notable names have waved a deep blue goodbye to their aspirations of winning that year's Masters.

In 1937, Ralph Guldahl sampled damp misery beside both the 12th and 13th greens in the final round. He took five on the 12th, a par-3 of only 155 yards but such a severe test of accuracy and temperament that Jack Nicklaus has called it 'the most demanding tournament hole in the world'; and six on the 13th. Byron Nelson came along behind him and played them in 2–3. Having made up six shots on the leader in just two holes, Nelson beat Guldahl for the title by two strokes. Two years later, Guldahl got his revenge. He eagled the 13th and jumped into a one-shot lead over Sam Snead which he carried to the end.

There have been many similar stories of heartache and happiness. In 1954, Billy Joe Patton, an eminent amateur golfer from North Carolina, had a hole-in-one at the 6th on the Sunday and led the field as he played the 13th. But then courage got the better of him. He went for

the green with his second shot, found the creek and walked off with a seven. He made the same decision on the 15th and took six. He finished a shot adrift of Hogan and Snead. Two subsequent horror stories graphically illustrate the perils of the water. Tsuneyuki (Tommy) Nakajima of Japan had a 13 on the 13th in 1978, while Tom Weiskopf carded the same score at the 12th in 1980.

The stretch from the 11th to the 13th at Augusta is known as 'Amen Corner', a nickname apparently derived from an old jazz song and justified by the number of times that golfers' prayers have been answered, kindly or otherwise, over that fiendish three-hole spell. Arnold Palmer got the nod in 1958 when he made a fortunate par on the 12th after being awarded a free drop from a plugged lie, and he followed that with an eagle on the 13th. An hour or so later, he had won the first of his four Masters by a stroke. One year later, Palmer got the thumbs down. He was cruising home until the sirens protecting the 12th green lured his ball into the pond. He took a triple-bogey six and was left floundering in the wake of Art Wall, who birdied five of the last six holes.

Tom Watson (1981) and George Archer (1969) both hung on to win despite last round flirtations with the waters of the 13th and 15th respectively.

Arnold Palmer's first major championship. Palmer (in the light shirt) is seen at a critical moment in the final round of the 1958 Masters, discussing a ruling with Masters officials. He had holed out for a double-bogey five on the 12th but had all along believed himself to be entitled to a free drop for an embedded ball. He had accordingly played another ball and made a par with it. As he was walking down the 15th he was told that he was indeed right and his score for the hole was duly recorded as a three. Listening to the debate in the white flat cap is Palmer's playing partner, Ken Venturi.

THE MASTERS – WINNERS

Year	Winner	Score	Year	Winner	Score
1934	Horton Smith	284	1962	†Arnold Palmer	280
1935	†Gene Sarazen	282	1963	Jack Nicklaus	286
1936	Horton Smith	285	1964	Arnold Palmer	276
1937	Byron Nelson	283	1965	Jack Nicklaus	271
1938	Henry Picard	285	1966	†Jack Nicklaus	288
1939	Ralph Guldahl	279	1967	Gay Brewer	280
1940	Jimmy Demaret	280	1968	Bob Goalby	277
1941	Craig Wood	280	1969	George Archer	281
1942	†Byron Nelson	280	1970	†Billy Casper	279
1943–5	No competition		1971	Charles Coody	279
1946	Herman Keiser	282	1972	Jack Nicklaus	286
1947	Jimmy Demaret	281	1973	Tommy Aaron	283
1948	Claude Harmon	279	1974	Gary Player (SA)	278
1949	Sam Snead	282	1975	Jack Nicklaus	276
1950	Jimmy Demaret	283	1976	Ray Floyd	271
1951	Ben Hogan	280	1977	Tom Watson	276
1952	Sam Snead	286	1978	Gary Player (SA)	277
1953	Ben Hogan	274	1979	†Fuzzy Zoeller	280
1954	†Sam Snead	289	1980	Seve Ballesteros (Sp)	275
1955	Cary Middlecoff	279	1981	Tom Watson	280
1956	Jack Burke	289	1982	†Craig Stadler	284
1957	Doug Ford	283	1983	Seve Ballesteros (Sp)	280
1958	Arnold Palmer	284	1984	Ben Crenshaw	277
1959	Art Wall	284	1985	Bernhard Langer (Ger)	282
1960	Arnold Palmer	282	1986	Jack Nicklaus	279
1961	Gary Player (SA)	280	† won play-off		

Nevertheless, proving that one's ball does not have amphibious properties tends to be extremely painful, and Augusta's water holes have never had more impact on the outcome of the Masters as on three Sundays in recent times.

In 1984, Ben Crenshaw struck a marvellous 6-iron to within four yards of the flag at the 12th and, as one expects of him, the putt went down for a two. Just before Crenshaw played the hole, Larry Nelson had found the pond there with a weak tee shot; a few minutes after Crenshaw left the green, Tom Kite did likewise. Nelson took five, Kite six. Crenshaw played the 13th and 15th conservatively, laying up short of each green in two, but he still birdied the latter. That, coming on top of the putts of 60 feet and 20 feet for birdie and par respectively that disappeared into the cup on the 10th and 14th, gave him a couple of shots to spare in one of the most popular major championship victories in history. Crenshaw is an exceptionally likeable man.

The next year, Curtis Strange seemed poised to overcome the burden of an 80 in the first round and earn an improbable triumph. Then he found

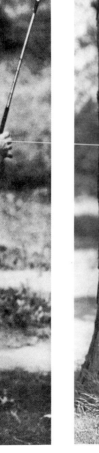

Jimmy Demaret, the first three-time Masters champion. His first victory came in 1940, the year that Lloyd Mangrum (right) established a course record of eight-under-par 64, a mark that was not beaten until Nick Price shot 63 in 1986.

Seve Ballesteros won the 1980 Masters despite his ball suffering a dunking in the creek in front of the 13th green. Six years later he was not so fortunate and his hopes of collecting his third title at Augusta drowned when his ball made a splash landing in the pond at the 15th.

the water on the 13th and 15th and bogeyed both holes. Bernhard Langer birdied them and won by two strokes. In 1986, for all Jack Nicklaus's glorious golf under pressure – birdies on 9, 10, 11, 13, 16 and 17 and an eagle on 15 – it was Seve Ballesteros who looked a certain champion until he hit what, in the circumstances, has to be considered the worst shot of his career when his 4-iron to the 15th fell feebly into the pond. He eventually holed out for a six and was thus hopelessly vulnerable to Nicklaus's late and heroic charge.

Nicklaus has won more Masters than anyone else. The 1986 victory was his sixth and made him, at 46, the oldest winner. His longevity is such that his successes have spanned 23 years, but before him several other players enjoyed brief spells of dominance in the Masters, even if these sometimes overlapped. From 1940 to 1954, for instance, Jimmy Demaret, Sam Snead and Ben Hogan won it eight of the 12 times it was played.

Demaret was the first three-time winner, his years being 1940, 1947 and 1950. The latter was gained at some psychological cost to the Australian Jim Ferrier, who bogeyed five of the last six holes to lose by two shots. Demaret was a nightclub singer turned pro golfer and to celebrate this third green jacket he treated the crowd to a rendition of 'How Lucky You Are' at the prize-giving ceremony.

Sam Snead was a natural golfer turned pro and he captured the title on three occasions in six years: in

1949 (with two 67s to close), 1952 and 1954 (when he beat Hogan 70–71 in a play-off).

Hogan had also been on the wrong end of a one-stroke margin in the 1942 play-off with Byron Nelson, who played the stretch from the 6th to the 16th in six under par. In 1946, Hogan faced a 12-footer to win on the last green but three-putted to hand the tournament to Herman Keiser. He had to wait until 1951 to break through at Augusta, before winning again in his unbeatable year of 1953. As late as 1967 he fired a third round of 66, with 30 on the inward half, to bring a glow to the hearts of his admirers and even a smile to his usually stern features. But by then Palmer and Nicklaus had taken over.

Palmer won the Masters in the four even-numbered years from 1958. His victories in 1960 and 1962 were classics from the mould that made him synonymous with the word 'charge'. In the first he birdied the last two holes, respectively from 30 and six feet, to pip Ken Venturi by a stroke (poor Venturi had, when still an amateur, lost the 1956 Masters by a single shot after a disastrous final round of 80). That magnificent finale, and the uproarious reaction of Palmer's gallery to it, led to his fans being christened 'Arnie's Army'. They cheered him home just as tumultuously in 1962 when he chipped in on the 16th and holed from 12 feet on the 17th to catch Gary Player and Dow Finsterwald. In the play-off, Palmer gave Player a three-shot start and then thrashed him with a devastating burst of birdies

A hug of congratulation from playing partner Seve Ballesteros for Gary Player after the South African had holed his final putt in 1978. Player was the first non-American Masters champion, Ballesteros the second and Bernhard Langer of West Germany the third.

early on the back nine. That gave Palmer special pleasure since the previous year he had ceded the championship to Player by contriving a six on the last hole, thus making the South African the first overseas winner.

Nicklaus won for the first time in 1963 but his *tour de force* came in 1965. He equalled the course record of eight-under-par 64 in the third round, a mark only bettered by Nick Price of South Africa with a 63 in 1986. Nicklaus's total of 271 left him nine shots ahead of his great adversaries, Palmer and Player, and has only been matched once, by Ray Floyd in 1976. At the presentation ceremony, Bobby Jones remarked of Nicklaus's stunning power golf: 'Jack is playing an entirely different game, one which I'm not even familiar with.'

In 1966 Nicklaus retained the title in a play-off with Gay Brewer (who was to win the next year) and Tommy Jacobs, and he regained it in a dull tournament in 1972. His fifth victory, in 1975, was a spectacular affair as he, Johnny Miller and Tom Weiskopf produced blazing golf to match the weather, ultimately being separated by a putt of fully 40 feet which Nicklaus sank on the 70th hole. Many experts claim 1975 to be at least the equal of any Masters. Nicklaus might have won

A dance for joy from Fuzzy Zoeller after clinching the first sudden death play-off in Masters history in 1979. Tom Watson has his back to the camera while Ed Sneed, who seemed a certain winner with just a few holes to play, ponders in anguish what might have been.

have lately provided Gary Player with foreign reinforcements. Ballesteros became, at 23 years and 4 days, the youngest-ever winner in 1980, but he had to settle for a four-shot triumph after dissipating a massive lead on visits to the water at the 12th and 13th. Three years later he opened the final round with a brilliant salvo of birdie-eagle-par-birdie which destroyed his immediate rivals, Watson, Floyd and Craig Stadler, the 1982 champion.

All these tales show that just as there is more than one way to skin a cat, so there is more than one way to win a golf tournament, and there is even more variety in the methods man can devise to lose one. In the Masters that has been repeatedly demonstrated, most frequently on that water-strewn back nine.

Left Jack Nicklaus salutes a birdie putt on the 2nd hole in the third round in 1965, a day which saw him shoot 64 to spreadeagle the field and all but seal his second Masters.

Below Twenty-one years older but more than 21 pounds slimmer, Nicklaus urges home his last birdie on the fantastic afternoon that he earned a record-breaking sixth green jacket. This putt on the 17th gave him a shot to spare over Tom Kite and Greg Norman and killed off the faltering Ballesteros.

again a number of times, such as in 1971 when he surprisingly let in Charles Coody and in 1977 when Tom Watson, as so often against the Golden Bear, got the upper hand in a keen duel.

Until 1980, Gary Player was the sole non-American Masters champion. He was victorious for a third time in 1978, capping a marvellous homeward nine of 30 with a birdie putt of 15 feet at the last for a round of 64, which proved to be good enough when Watson and Hubert Green fluffed excellent chances to force a play-off. There was overtime in 1979, however. The hapless Ed Sneed squandered a five-shot lead on the Sunday afternoon, a calamity climaxed with bogeys at the last three holes. Fuzzy Zoeller took advantage by stealing the first 'sudden death' Masters at the second extra hole with a birdie to beat Sneed and Watson, thereby becoming the first man since Sarazen in 1935 to win on his debut in the championship. Jack Nicklaus, incidentally, was left to rue a bogey at the penultimate hole which killed his chances of participating in the play-off. It is astonishing how his unsurpassable collection of major championships could have been even mightier had some of his near-misses been converted into yet more wins.

Severiano Ballesteros of Spain (1980 and 1983) and Bernhard Langer of West Germany (1985)

The USPGA Championship: the Cinderella of the Majors

Jim Barnes (driving) won the first two USPGA Championships. Jock Hutchison (in the checked plus-fours) won the third.

Although there have been some changes to the dates down the ages, golf's four major championships these days each occupy a different month. The Masters is in April, the US Open in June and the Open Championship in July, while the United States Professional Golfers' Association Championship (from hereon called the PGA) is held in August. The PGA is indisputably fourth of the four, bottom of an admittedly exalted class. It has been that way since . . . 1953, perhaps, when Ben Hogan chose to contest the Open at Carnoustie rather than play in

Michigan; or 1958, when the organizers ditched the matchplay format for strokeplay; or 1968, when the tour players broke away from the PGA – the body, that is, not the tournament – to form their own division and in 1974, in a logical consequence of the split, launched the Tournament Players' Championship (TPC) which undermined the original still further.

The political in-fighting involved in the dispute of 1968, an acrimonious affair, is best left until the next chapter, but it is pertinent to point out here that the PGA Championship is run by the PGA of America. This organization primarily represents the interests of club professionals, so it is no shock to learn that many tour pros value victory in their own TPC as much as one in the PGA. Some even feel that the TPC's popular nickname of 'the fifth major' should be upgraded by at least one position. Most other people do not.

In recent years the PGA Championship has recaptured something of its former glory. It might lack the kudos of the other three majors, but lately it has been able to boast great champions and memorable championships, two essential criteria which have come about through a combination of luck and improved management. The PGA of America realized that if the battered flagship of its operations was to improve its tarnished image it needed to be held on superior golf courses which were worthy of a major championship rather than on poorly maintained and averagely designed layouts which were sometimes selected for dubious motives. That is one significant factor which has helped the tournament to retain, if at times tenuously, its status. The other is something neither the TPC nor anything else can easily acquire – history.

The PGA goes back to 1916 and has champions of bygone generations like Hagen (five times), Sarazen and Snead (three times apiece), and Hogan and Nelson (twice each). In the modern era Jack Nicklaus has equalled Hagen's mark, while Gary Player and Lee Trevino both have two

Walter Hagen dominated the USPGA Championship to an extent which no other professional golfer this century has managed in any major championship. He won it four times in a row and five times in all, a total equalled by Jack Nicklaus in 1980.

wins to their credit. Arnold Palmer has never won it. That is a sad omission from his record because, if the idea of the professional Grand Slam grew out of Hogan's hat-trick year of 1953, it was Palmer who first made it seem feasible that a professional could come as close as is possible to emulating what Bobby Jones did in 1930 and win the four most important tournaments open to him. Palmer gave credence to the notion by winning the Masters and the US Open in 1960. The PGA, as the next most esteemed event on the American golf calendar, was to be the fourth leg of the Grand Slam after Palmer had popped over to St Andrews and brought back the British Open. Instead, Kel Nagle ruined everything when he foiled Palmer by a shot in the Centenary Open.

Twelve years later, Jack Nicklaus also won the Masters and the US Open but went down by a stroke in the British Open. His defeat came at the hands of the mercurial Trevino who destroyed Tony Jacklin and denied Nicklaus by literally as well as metaphorically proving what it means to win when the chips are down. Thus was the PGA twice narrowly deprived the climax to the season that would have been its ultimate *raison d'être*.

The tournament had no pretensions to being the fourth anything when it began life in 1916 as a matchplay competition for the championship of the United States' fledgling Professional Golfers' Association. It was won by Jim Barnes, a Cornishman who had left England for America some time before. With hindsight, it was typical of the event's chequered existence that no sooner had it been started than it was stopped. The First World War called a halt to it in 1917 and 1918, then Barnes retained possession of the trophy by winning again in 1919.

Barnes was a fine golfer. He went on to win the 1921 US Open by nine strokes (a record margin during this century) and the 1925 Open at Prestwick, the last hurrah for the original Open venue. He was succeeded as PGA champion in 1920 by Jock Hutchison, another British expatriate and the losing finalist in the tournament's inaugural year.

The following decade was dominated by one man, Walter Hagen, although two others, Gene Sarazen and Leo Diegel, each found room to fit in a couple of wins. Hagen beat Barnes by 3 & 2 in the 1921 final, thus becoming the first native American champion. Sarazen took over in 1922 but it was something of a hollow victory as Hagen was not present to defend the title. It was thus apposite that in 1923 the two men met in the final at the Pelham Country Club, New York.

The event was, as ever until matchplay was abandoned in 1958, contested over 36 holes, and Hagen stood 2 down with only three to play. He won the next two holes to square matters and, after the 36th had been halved, the match went into sudden death. At the second extra hole,

Sarazen conjured up a miraculous recovery shot after a wayward drive, putting the ball within two feet of the pin. Hagen, for once flabbergasted rather than flamboyant, fluffed an easy pitch into a bunker and with that went his hopes of the championship.

He made amends with no half measures, winning the PGA from 1924 to 1927, a sequence beginning with a second triumph over Jim Barnes. Hagen is the only 20th-century golfer to have won the same major championship in four consecutive years, and it is a safe bet that the distinction will remain unique. He appears to have been less than enthusiastic about bidding for a fifth title in a row. Tournament officials only lured him to Baltimore at the eleventh hour, Hagen either having forgotten about his defence or being more concerned about raking in more dollars from yet another exhibition match.

He needn't have turned up. Diegel beat him in the semi-finals, thus avenging his defeat in the final of 1926, and then dispatched Al Espinosa by 6 & 5. When Hagen was asked for the trophy so that it could be presented to Diegel, he announced that he had lost it. He had apparently left it in a taxi. The cup materialized a few months later when it was discovered in the Chicago offices of Hagen's clubmakers.

Diegel retained the title – and this time had a trophy to show for it – in 1929, trouncing the reigning US Open champion Johnny Farrell by 6 & 4 in the final. Diegel employed a singular putting stance, with feet spread, elbows locked and the top of the putter shaft brushing against his

stomach. It looked terribly ungainly and uncomfortable but it certainly worked. He was a shade unlucky to win no more than two major championships, but that was the price of reaching one's peak during the age of Jones and Hagen. Jones won at least one major championship – if one includes the US Amateur – every year between 1923 and 1930, while Hagen, whose halcyon days predated the Masters, had a similar unbroken six-year span from 1924. This century only Jack Nicklaus, who won five majors in four years from 1970, has maintained such a run for longer than three seasons.

Neither Hagen nor Diegel were factors in the PGA after the 1920s. Gene Sarazen was, however. He lost an epic final to Tommy Armour in 1930 but he was back three years later to win for a third time, beating Willie Goggin with just seven clubs in his bag. Densmore Shute won twice and was runner-up once during this period; Paul Runyan also won twice, including an 8 & 7 hammering of Sam Snead in 1938, the most emphatic margin of victory in any final. Runyan produced marvellous golf that day, but nothing so astounding as the performance of Bobby Cruickshank against Al Watrous in one of the earlier rounds in 1932. He rallied to win from being 9 down with 12 holes to play – the biggest recovery known in an important matchplay competition – only to be eliminated later in the semi-finals.

While the war was raging in Europe, Byron Nelson was on the rampage in the PGA Championship. From 1939 to 1945, he was thrice the beaten finalist (losing once on the 36th green, once on the 37th and once at the 38th) and twice the winner. He beat Snead in 1940 and Sam Byrd in 1945, the latter being part of his unbelievable stretch of 11 consecutive tournament victories.

After the war, Ben Hogan won in 1946 and 1948. Snead, who had taken the title in 1942 in Nelson's rare absence from the final, picked it up again in 1949 and 1951 but Hogan was no longer in the field. His car accident in February 1949 meant his legs could not withstand the arduous chore of walking for a series of 36-hole matches. For this reason it is something of a fallacy – perpetuated by, among others, myself in the first paragraph of this chapter – to suggest that Hogan passed up the 1953 PGA in favour of the British Open. He never had any intention of playing in the PGA. He had not entered it for the previous four years and did not do so afterwards until it was switched to a strokeplay format, by which time he was well past his prime.

Below left The singular putting action of Leo Diegel. It was certainly effective. The great British golf writer Bernard Darwin was so impressed by Diegel's performance on the greens at Hoylake in his vain bid to stop Bobby Jones winning the British Open in 1930 that he coined a verb – 'to diegel' – which he conjugated, 'I diegel, thou diegelest, he diegels'.

Below right A double winner of the PGA in the 1930s, Densmore (Denny) Shute also won the British Open in a play-off and lost the US Open the same way.

Ben Hogan's last major championship before his horrific car crash. Hogan (putting) thrashed Mike Turnesa by 7 & 6 in the 1948 final at Norwood Hills, Missouri. By the following February, he was in hospital and fortunate to be alive.

But the legend of 1953 is not devoid of truth. That Hogan, unquestionably the best golfer in the world, was playing elsewhere (and in an overseas championship to boot) was not good for the morale of the PGA. Nor were champions like Walter Burkemo what was wanted: journeyman club professionals who happened to hit the jackpot that week. Not that Burkemo didn't deserve to win against Felice Torza in the 1953 final. Any man who can make up a 7-hole deficit in 18 holes is a worthy winner, and Burkemo went all the way to the last hurdle in 1954 as well before he was stopped by Chick Harbert, the last club pro – as opposed to tour player – to lift the trophy.

The PGA was losing its lustre. Doug Ford won in 1955 but nobody remembers him for that: instead, he's the man who holed out from a bunker at the 72nd green to clinch the Masters two years later. Jack Burke took the PGA in 1956 but his victory was already overshadowed by his sensational come-from-nowhere triumph at Augusta in the spring. Lionel Hebert followed them in 1957 and his 2 & 1 defeat of Dow Finsterwald was matchplay's last fling.

Television has a long history of antipathy towards matchplay, with its inherent risks of a final between two relative nonentities (Walter Burkemo and Chick Harbert, perhaps) and the chance that even a potentially mouth-watering tussle between Jack Nicklaus and Tom Watson could be ended well before the 18th green – that is, out of camera range and with no respect for the niceties of programme scheduling. It was the desire to pander to the small screen that led the PGA of America to make the move to strokeplay. It was pointed out to no avail both then and since that by doing this the PGA was digging its own grave; that one of the true attractions of the tournament was its valid claim to be the most important matchplay event in the world. It wasn't the format that was wrong but the cluttering up of the field with club pros to the exclusion of the regular tour players. The number of spots these no-hopers filled was not cut drastically for another 13 years – a costly prevarication.

Today, despite the recent revival in its fortunes, the PGA is paying the penalty for that step taken back in 1958. Look at it this way. The British and US Opens are without doubt the two most

THE USPGA CHAMPIONSHIP – WINNERS

Year	Venue	Winner	Year	Venue	Winner	Score
1916	Siwanoy	Jim Barnes	1952	Big Spring	Jim Turnesa	–
1917–8	No competition		1953	Birmingham	Walter Burkemo	–
1919	Engineers	Jim Barnes	1954	Keller	Chick Harbert	–
1920	Flossmoor	Jock Hutchison	1955	Meadowbrook	Doug Ford	–
1921	Inwood	Walter Hagen	1956	Blue Hill	Jack Burke	–
1922	Oakmont	Gene Sarazen	1957	Miami Valley	Lionel Hebert	–
1923	Pelham	†Gene Sarazen	*1958	Llanerch	Dow Finterswald	276
1924	French Lick	Walter Hagen	1959	Minneapolis	Bob Rosburg	277
1925	Olympia Fields	Walter Hagen	1960	Firestone	Jay Hebert	281
1926	Salisbury	Walter Hagen	1961	Olympia Fields	†Jerry Barber	277
1927	Cedar Crest	Walter Hagen	1962	Aronimink	Gary Player (SA)	278
1928	Baltimore	Leo Diegel	1963	Dallas	Jack Nicklaus	279
1929	Hillcrest	Leo Diegel	1964	Columbus	Bobby Nichols	271
1930	Fresh Meadow	Tommy Armour	1965	Laurel Valley	Dave Marr	280
1931	Wannamoisett	Tom Creavy	1966	Firestone	Al Geiberger	280
1932	Keller	Olin Dutra	1967	Columbine	†Don January	281
1933	Blue Mound	Gene Sarazen	1968	Pecan Valley	Julius Boros	281
1934	Park, NY	†Paul Runyan	1969	NCR, Dayton	Ray Floyd	276
1935	Twin Hills	Johnny Revolta	1970	Southern Hills	Dave Stockton	279
1936	Pinehurst	Densmore Shute	1971	PGA National	Jack Nicklaus	281
1937	Pittsburgh	†Densmore Shute	1972	Oakland Hills	Gary Player (SA)	281
1938	Shawnee	Paul Runyan	1973	Canterbury	Jack Nicklaus	277
1939	Pomonok	†Henry Picard	1974	Tanglewood	Lee Trevino	276
1940	Hershey	Byron Nelson	1975	Firestone	Jack Nicklaus	276
1941	Cherry Hills	†Vic Ghezzi	1976	Congressional	Dave Stockton	281
1942	Seaview	Sam Snead	1977	Pebble Beach	†Lanny Wadkins	282
1943	No competition		1978	Oakmont	†John Mahaffey	276
1944	Spokane	Bob Hamilton	1979	Oakland Hills	†David Graham (Aus)	272
1945	Morraine	Byron Nelson	1980	Oak Hill	Jack Nicklaus	274
1946	Portland	Ben Hogan	1981	Atlanta	Larry Nelson	273
1947	Plum Hollow	Jim Ferrier	1982	Southern Hills	Ray Floyd	272
1948	Norwood Hills	Ben Hogan	1983	Riviera	Hal Sutton	274
1949	Hermitage	Sam Snead	1984	Shoal Creek	Lee Trevino	273
1950	Scioto	Chandler Harper	1985	Cherry Hills	Hubert Green	278
1951	Oakmont	Sam Snead	1986	Inverness	Bob Tway	276

† won play-off   * prior to 1958 matchplay

prestigious championships in the world and they welcome, either through exemptions or via qualifying competitions, all professional golfers plus any amateurs who can fulfil the stipulated handicap requirements. The R & A, in particular, has made a huge effort to maximize the international appeal of the British version. The Masters is invitational, with specified categories of player gaining entry as of right but with absolutely no qualifying procedures. The PGA is, however, more parochial than the US Open or the Masters. Its qualifying competitions are regional affairs from which emerge a few club pros who provide cannon fodder for the big boys in the main event; at this rarefied level, they don't so much sort out the wheat from the chaff as the chaff from the dirt. The championship itself may be the fourth most coveted in the world but, as a strokeplay tournament, it can never rank higher than last of a small elite. At matchplay, it would be top of its class.

Nevertheless, for better or worse (and there's not much doubt which) the changes were rung in 1958, but the conversion to strokeplay did not reveal itself to be an instant panacea for the PGA's ills. Just as the British Open laboured in a slough of despond in the 1950s and only recovered in the next decade after receiving a life-saving injection of Palmer serum, the PGA suffered for 10 years and didn't receive the medicine appropriate to its malady until the 1970s.

It wasn't wholly deprived in the meantime, however. It had sentiment – Jay Hebert emulated his brother Lionel and won in 1960. It had drama – Bob Rosburg closed with a 66 to win by a stroke in 1959, and it would be hard to envisage anything more remarkable than Jerry Barber holing putts of 18, 35 and 60 feet on the last three greens in 1961 to tie the leader; hard, too, to imagine what poor Don January must have thought when he lost the play-off with a 68 to a 67. The PGA even had champions of calibre – like Gary Player in 1962 and Jack Nicklaus in 1963.

What it did lack was vision. The row between the tournament players and the officials of the PGA had turned so nasty by 1967 that a fortnight before play was to begin the players were openly talking of mutiny and threatening to pull out of the championship. In the end it was all so much hot air, but what Jack Nicklaus – who is invariably as articulate with his words as he is with his clubs – had to say on the eve of the competition was not.

'The PGA is killing its own tournament. The British Open is a major tournament and scheduling the PGA right behind it in July is not very smart.' It was also selfish. Palmer, the saviour of the Open, had opted to give it a miss in 1967 in order to acclimatize to the altitude and summer heat of Denver for what transpired to be another futile assault on the PGA.

Nicklaus continued: 'All the players would like to see the PGA be a better tournament than it is, but it won't be if it is going to be scheduled this way and if we continue to try to make golf courses famous by playing the PGA on them instead of playing the PGA on famous courses.'

Curing the two faults Nicklaus highlighted has enabled the PGA to re-establish itself, though the point that it would be stronger still if it reverted to matchplay remains in the suggestion box. The 1968 PGA, the last under the old regime, illustrated the championship's flaws perfectly. For a start, over 60 per cent of the field of 168 were club pros. Once again, the tournament was held immediately after the British Open, this time in the stifling, inhospitable heat of San Antonio, Texas, on a five-year-old condominium-lined course which had been awarded the honour because at the time of the nomination a former President of the PGA had a financial interest in the development of the Pecan Valley Country Club. It is only fair to mention that the course was better than the sceptics expected and so was the tournament. Julius Boros got up and down to save a difficult par at the final hole to edge out the luckless Palmer and Bob Charles by a shot and thus become, at 48 years and 140 days, the oldest winner of a major championship.

The shake-up affecting the organization of professional golf in America, to which I referred earlier, came soon afterwards. In 1969, the PGA Championship was moved to a new August slot which (except for 1971) it has kept. Ray Floyd won that one by a stroke from a plucky Gary Player, who had to endure several upsetting disturbances from anti-apartheid demonstrators which were timed and guaranteed to harm his golf. In 1970, the championship went to Southern Hills in Tulsa, another notable landmark because it indicated that the PGA of America was anxious to promote the status of its most prized possession. Southern Hills was only the fourth course to be used for the championship since the war which had previously been considered fit to host the US Open; in contrast, between 1970 and 1986 the authorities selected only four venues which had not already received the ultimate endorsement from the USGA. Having said that, there may be signs of confidence, though hopefully not of complacency, in the decision to take four consecutive PGAs from 1987 to non-US Open courses.

Dave Stockton won the first of his two titles in 1970 but he held it for just six months. The 1971 championship graced the PGA's own course at headquarters in Florida, the Sunshine State's debut as home to a major championship. The tournament was temporarily moved to February to avoid the unpleasant humidity of summer, although this precaution was evidently considered unnecessary when the PGA, having shifted offices, brought its championship back to Palm Beach Gardens in 1987. By 1971 the club professionals' representation had been substantially pruned – they now had a new event of their own, the Club Professionals' Championship – but they would not have been a threat to Jack Nicklaus even *en masse*. The Golden

Bear's victory made him the first man for 20 years to win a second PGA.

Over the past decade and more, most of the news has thankfully been made by the exploits of the golfers, like Gary Player who won for a second time in 1972. His magnificent 9-iron from a heavy lie in the rough at Oakland Hills' 16th hole in the last round, which cleared a cluster of weeping willows and a pond to finish a mere four feet from the stick, emphasized that the little South African has strength as well as guts. He sank the putt for the birdie that wrapped things up. Nicklaus resumed control in 1973 and 1975, but Trevino split his bid for a hat-trick by a single stroke at Tanglewood. Nicklaus had to wait until 1980 for a fifth PGA which equalled Hagen's tally. He won with ease, having seven shots in hand over the runner-up, Andy Bean.

If that PGA was a walkover, its four predecessors were all cliff-hangers. Stockton holed a par putt of 15 feet on the final green at Congressional to win in 1976, probably the longest putt ever made on the 72nd hole to win a major when its maker knew he needed it. Ecstasy for Stockton was followed by agony for Gene Littler. He had bravely overcome cancer of the lymph glands in the early 1970s and at Pebble Beach it looked as though the 1961 US Open champion was about to collect another big one. He led by five strokes with nine holes to play but bogeys on five of the first six holes on the back nine

Dave Stockton wins his second PGA title at Congressional, near Washington, by holing from five yards on the final green to deny the opportunity of a play-off to Ray Floyd, winner in 1969 and again in 1982, and Don January, champion in 1967 and victim of Jerry Barber's outrageous putting in 1961.

dumped him into a play-off with Lanny Wadkins. It was the first instance of sudden death resolving any major championship and Wadkins, having saved his skin with an almost impossible 20-foot putt at the first extra hole, sank one of six feet at the third to take it.

The unlikely victim of a collapse in the 1978 championship was Tom Watson. He held a four-stroke advantage as he turned for home on the Sunday afternoon but he was caught by Jerry Pate and John Mahaffey. The latter had lost a play-off for the 1975 US Open and it was his errors which paved the way for Pate to snatch his glorious victory at Atlanta the next summer, but at Oakmont there were no mistakes. Mahaffey birdied the second hole of overtime and, as he put it, 'went bananas'.

And the decade closed with a play-off. David Graham needed a par at the last hole at Oakland Hills to break Bobby Nichols's tournament record of 271 (established in 1964) and to match fellow-Australian Bruce Crampton's PGA single round record of 63 (set in 1975 and subsequently equalled by Ray Floyd in 1982 and Gary Player in

1984). Instead, he took a double-bogey six and opened the door to Ben Crenshaw. To Graham's eternal credit, he made a putt to stay alive at the first extra hole which was reminiscent of the one Wadkins had canned two years before. Like Wadkins, he prevailed two holes later. There was a savage sting in the tail for Crenshaw. His total of 272 was made up of four rounds below 70. Arnold Palmer had accomplished the same feat in the 1964 PGA and also discovered it wasn't good enough. At the time of writing, Lee Trevino (in the 1968 US Open and the 1984 PGA) is the only other man to shoot in the 60s on all four days of a major championship; the difference being that on both occasions he got his just deserts.

It was appropriate that in 1986 it should be at the Inverness Golf Club in Toledo, Ohio – the place where the tour pros were first welcomed into the clubhouse at the 1920 US Open – that the reputation of the PGA was boosted further, as was its right to be regarded as a major international championship. The PGA of America invited all 12 members of the European Ryder Cup team who in 1985 had caused the Americans to suffer their first defeat in the competition for 28 years. Not all of them accepted and only two made the halfway cut, but neither of those things detracted from a gesture which was widely applauded and seen in a favourable light when compared to the refusal of the officials at Augusta to do likewise in respect of the 1986 Masters.

The 1986 PGA also provided a classic championship. After the third day Greg Norman completed an unprecedented 'Saturday Slam' by leading all the year's four majors going into Sunday's final round. In fact, at Inverness a colossal and prolonged thunderstorm meant Sunday dragged into Monday, and for the third time that season Norman let slip his advantage. He was four shots clear of Bob Tway with eight holes to play but when they reached the 18th they were level. There Tway produced a shot destined to be remembered forever. He holed out from a bunker for a birdie three and a mortified Norman had to settle for second again. By the end of October he had beaten Tway by an infinitesimal margin in their race to top the US Money List. That will be of small satisfaction in the years ahead for Norman, but the PGA of America can proudly reflect that its 1986 championship served up a thrilling finale between two of the game's most successful current protagonists.

The contest between Tway and Norman was so exciting, so head-to-head, that one imagined it was matchplay. Maybe one day at the PGA it will be again.

'Over the hill,' said Hubert Green's critics, but at Cherry Hills in the 1985 USPGA Championship Green emphasized that his win at the 1978 US Open was no fluke.

Bob Tway bids to become the first golfer into orbit (with due deference to astronaut Alan Shepard) after holing from a bunker on the 72nd hole to clinch the 1986 championship at Inverness.

The US Tour: the American Dream

The 1986 United States PGA Tour was worth $25.5 million. Greg Norman won $653,296 of that. Both totals were records, albeit meaningless ones; the former being obliterated within 12 months and the latter inevitably destined to have a short life expectancy.

These vast, annually rising sums take no account of an additional $5 million in 'unofficial' money; the millions more available for the 50s-and-over brigade on the burgeoning Senior Tour; and the seven-figure cheques which sponsors queue up to hand over in order to associate their names with a variety of bonus schemes. One cannot ignore either the tens of millions annually raised for charity ('the leading money-winner on the PGA Tour' as the slogan has it) or the amounts ploughed into the player retirement plan. The tour is big business, involved in several diverse aspects of the sport and notably – and in some eyes controversially – in the construction of 'stadium golf courses'. The latter are purpose-built tournament sites, designed with such extraneous factors as spectator comfort in mind. As more new venues are opened (currently a dozen and counting), so the tour moves another event to one of its facilities.

Whether the US Tour should find it necessary to have an arm operating under the name Investments, Inc., is a moot point, not least within the membership. What is undeniable is that the tour has become an example of the 20th-century American dream *in excelsis*.

Its origins can be traced to the 1920s, when the United States echoed to the sounds of the motor car and popping champagne corks. Already there was a small nucleus of tournaments in existence which have maintained a place on the calendar: the US Open, of course, founded in 1895, the Western Open (1899), the Canadian Open (1904) and the Texas Open (1922). This quartet hardly constituted a quorum for the formation of what might properly be called a tour, but in the Roaring Twenties the circuit's development began in earnest.

Throughout the decade, tournaments sprang up on the West Coast and in Florida, the consequence of professionals moving to the warmer southern climes to escape the rigours of the north-east winter and wanting to keep sharp in competition. The Los Angeles Open was launched in 1926, the Pensacola Open in 1929, and both are still going strong. As the players moved eastwards from California in search of more money in Florida, more new tournaments were born in Texas and Louisiana to help them on their way towards the Atlantic. Their sojourn would customarily reach its conclusion at the Pinehurst resort in North Carolina in late March.

Then, as now, the tour theoretically followed the sun, and not just so the golfers could top up their tans. Many of the players would be back in the north during the summer at courses which had been closed while under frost and snow. They would mend clubs, teach the members and perhaps play occasionally in events organized by

Hagen doing what came naturally. His love of publicity, allied to his consummate ability, was a distinct boon in launching the professional golf circuit in the United States and in arousing public interest in the game throughout the world.

that time, the game was having to survive not only the tribulations of the American economy but also such factors as the retirement of Bobby Jones and a waning in the influence of Hagen and Sarazen.

As the dominance of these three declined into the past with the coincidental demise of hickory shafts, the circuit was revitalized by Snead, Byron Nelson, Ben Hogan, Ralph Guldahl, Jimmy Demaret and others in the new age of steel. These men took to the road. They liked to play golf and happened to be outstanding at it in an era when not many players were even good and it wasn't readily within reach of the ordinary man's pocket. As the American journalist Ross Goodner has put it: 'When Sam Snead won almost $20,000 in 1938 it seemed like all the money in the world to a nation that only recently had trouble finding someone who could spare a dime.'

Ben Hogan headed the Money List from 1940 to 1942, without beating Snead's mark, before golf in the United States was faced with another calamity as America joined the allied forces in the Second World War. There was no tour in 1943 but fund-raising exhibitions and clinics were encouraged and celebrities like Bing Crosby and Bob Hope raised thousands of dollars for the relief agencies. Both were confirmed golf nuts. In 1937, Crosby had inaugurated his own pro-am

Opposite **Ralph Guldahl had the 1937 Masters snatched from his grasp by Byron Nelson but he compensated in style by including two US Opens and the 1939 Masters among his tournament victories, which were all accumulated in a 10-year period up to the Second World War.**

their state golf association. Only the select few – like Walter Hagen and Gene Sarazen – could afford to spurn the regular income of a club job.

These two made money in exhibitions and it was from trips around the country on his personal lucrative circuit that Hagen realized the public would respond to the idea of a winter tour. Shortly afterwards, regional businesses and corporations started to appreciate that supporting the venture represented cheap advertising. Bob Harlow (Hagen's agent) and later Fred Corcoran (who would look after Sam Snead) became early directors of the PGA's Tournament Bureau, and from a schedule of just three events worth around $8500 in 1921 the little acorn grew into the giant oak we know now, spreading into all four seasons and occupying most weeks of the year. That explains why it has since been said that all pros today, as they check their healthy bank balances, should offer a silent prayer to Hagen and his endeavours on their behalf.

The expansion continued into the 1930s, despite the Great Depression. If the $7682 Horton Smith earned in topping the Money List in 1936 sounds rather paltry in comparision with Norman's haul precisely half a century later, it wasn't a bad reward for playing sport when a quarter of the population was unemployed and scores of golf clubs were filing for bankruptcy. At

Bob Hope (left) and Bing Crosby took the road to personal fortunes with their showbusiness careers but they will always be remembered in golfing circles for the tremendous help and enthusiasm they lavished on the game.

Byron Nelson. Several of the records he set in the 1940s, particularly in 1945, can safely be said to be unbeatable.

tournament at three courses on California's Monterey Peninsula, including Pebble Beach and Cypress Point. Bob Hope took the same road in 1960 with his Desert Classic, and since then other entertainers like Glen Campbell, Dean Martin and Andy Williams have amalgamated golf and showbiz on the tour.

Back in the 1940s, though, American golf came cautiously out of its year of enforced abstinence. Like the British government, the powers in Washington came to acknowledge that the pursuit of sport was not unpatriotic but provided desirable recreation in a period of stress. The trouble for the professional tour was that a large percentage of its best exponents were in the services and petrol rationing was not exactly conducive to long-distance travelling between venues. It was in this unpromising atmosphere of generally second-rate athletic achievement that Byron Nelson arrived not so much as a breath of fresh air but as a hurricane.

In 1944 Nelson practically doubled Snead's money record in winning six tournaments, and

yet that pales into insignificance compared with what he did in 1945. The bare bones of his accomplishments have been outlined in Chapter 3, to which one might add that he also won one other event (non-PGA approved because the purse did not meet the stipulated minimum), making 19 in all. That season he earned the equivalent of $63,335 in War Bonds, a staggering 14.5 per cent of the total available prize money. It would translate to nearly $3.7 million in 1986. Only Jack Nicklaus and Tom Watson have won more than that in their careers. Nelson's fabulous run throughout the 1940s created a record of 113 consecutive tournaments in the money (that is, without missing a cut), and another of 19 successive rounds below 70.

The US Tour annually updates its list of all-time records. Some, like Al Geiberger's 59 in the 1977 Memphis Classic which established a single-round best, will surely be eclipsed eventually, even if it takes until the next century. Other quirky ones, like the unknown Sam Trahan using only 18 putts for the final round of a tournament in Philadelphia in 1979, may not. But it is as safe as anything can be in golf when it comes to discussing the permanence of records to say that Nelson's 11 consecutive wins and several more of his marks will never be bettered. They are immortal. Those who cavil that for much of 1945 Hogan and Snead were not among the opposition have a scintilla of validity on their side, but there is no arguing with Nelson's stroke average of 68.33 on courses which were not short and had the disadvantage of being maintained in inferior condition to those the pros are accustomed to today; or with his cumulative total for the season of 320 under par. And even when Hogan and Snead were in attendance there was nothing they could do if 'Lord Byron' went about firing scores like 259, as he did in Seattle where the pack was left floundering 13 strokes adrift and Hogan needed a telescope to see Nelson a distant 20 shots away.

These record-shattering exploits shattered Nelson. He won five times in 1946 and was unlucky in the US Open (see page 71), but he had been so wearied by his relentless campaigning – in 1945 he had taken off just one week in 29 – that he effectively retired in 1947, though he still managed to be runner-up in the Masters that year and emerged to win the French Open as late as 1955.

With Hogan and Snead to the fore, the tour became more structured after the war and

professional golf consolidated its public appeal. The two great men clashed in the opening event of the 1950 schedule, the Los Angeles Open, Hogan's return to the fray after his awful accident. The crowd rooted for him during his brave bid to win first time out but, having tied with Snead, he lost the play-off 76 to 72.

The first of three crucial factors which were to inspire the golf boom of the 1960s and its subsequent sustained growth in America occurred in 1953. That was television. The medium which is now often maligned as having too powerful a hold on all sports introduced golf to a TV audience, and hence to millions of the unconverted, at the 1953 George S. May World Championship of Golf at the Tam O'Shanter Club in Chicago. Nelson had captured the then richest title in golf four times in the 1940s but never in the dramatic fashion Lew Worsham won it in 1953. Worsham holed a full wedge shot from over 100 yards out for an eagle two at the last to beat poor Chandler Harper by a stroke. Isao Aoki did the same thing to Jack Renner at the Hawaiian Open in 1983 to similar acclaim but with considerably less impact. The effect that Worsham's feat had on an uninitiated armchair gallery can be imagined. On its coast-to-coast

debut, at a stroke, golf had shown itself to be exciting.

Television coverage has since improved immeasurably, with longer hours, tricks like action replays and, above all, colour pictures. But before the advent of these refinements, golf had a second big boost in 1953. Dwight Eisenhower became President of the United States. As the ill-fated Prince of Wales had made golf a subject of conversation in Britain before the war, Eisenhower popularized golf in America. He was a member of Augusta and had a putting green laid out in the White House grounds. Other presidents, notably Gerald Ford, have since taken up the torch; and Ford's vice-president, Spiro T. Agnew, became the butt of countless jokes as he brought a new meaning to the notion of taking the game to the people. His errant shots regularly inflicted injuries on those who diced with death while watching him play in pro-ams.

The public became hooked on golf in the wake of Eisenhower's example. The tour prospered because of this increased interest and in 1958 the prize fund broke the $1 million barrier. In that year the leading money-winner and Masters champion was one Arnold Daniel Palmer; the third factor, the missing link.

Palmer won tournaments, lots of them, and did so with style. He simultaneously introduced the

Opposite **The US PGA Tour flourished in the 1950s because it had dozens of able players; some of them very able. Among the latter group was Cary Middlecoff, who won 37 times between 1947 and 1961, including the US Open in 1949 and 1956 and the Masters in 1955.**

When President Eisenhower entered the White House, golf received an enormous boost in the United States. Here the most powerful man in the western world is congratulated by his friend and partner, a Mr Palmer, after sinking a longish putt on the first hole at Merion during a charity exhibition match.

Palmer's patented hallmark. A casual hitch of the trousers as the object of adoring millions strides across another green in search of his ball in the hole.

he became the first man to take his earnings past $100,000 in a season (in 1963) and $1 million in a career (in 1968).

What the fans did not like was the large shadow of Jack Nicklaus, who was indeed pretty large in those days, which put Palmer in the shade all too frequently. They began to cheer Palmer and jeer Nicklaus, to scream with delight when he hit a rare loose shot. At the 1967 US Open they were even equipped with banners reading 'Right Here Jack' for display behind a hazard.

Palmer himself disdained this behaviour, though there was precious little he could do to dampen the ardour of his fervent supporters. He and Nicklaus remained good friends as well as keen rivals, constituting two-thirds of golf's Big Three.

The third man was Gary Player, who in 1961 became the first overseas golfer to head the Money List. On 7 November that year Nicklaus gave up chasing the ghost of Jones's record as an amateur and turned pro, with a reluctance surprising for a 21-year-old guaranteed at least $100,000 before he hit a ball in anger. He signed up with Mark McCormack, a Cleveland lawyer who was to make himself and his tremendous trio into exceedingly rich men.

From a famous handshake agreement with Palmer, his first client, McCormack has built up the world's foremost sports marketing and management company. He has had his fingers in more pies than the Queen of Hearts ever baked and in golf alone he has transformed the scene to the point where all the best players have managers, agents or representatives. Many of those players are under the umbrella of his flagship company, the International Management Group (IMG). He blazed the trail that led to players endorsing products which had nothing to do with their sport and stars being able to demand and receive tens of thousands of dollars in appearance fees from sponsors anxious to have them play in their tournaments. In short, he enabled his clients to capitalize on their skills. IMG also organizes tournaments and television rights and McCormack was responsible for the R & A, of which he is a member, becoming switched on to the commercial possibilities of the Open. In 1964 he was the brains behind the creation of the World Matchplay Championship, held at Wentworth, near London, each autumn, and as recently as 1986 he was the prime mover behind the setting up and acceptance of the Sony Ranking System of the world's top golfers.

words 'charge' and 'charisma' into the lexicon of golf. He not only played well but also looked good. He was to post-war golf what Hagen was between the wars, a hero for everyone. Watching him merely hitch up his trousers, the unconscious mannerism that became his trademark, was enough to drive grown men to frenzy. He enthralled women who didn't know the difference between a duck-hook and duck soup. He was followed religiously by a loyal band of boisterous supporters who acquired the name Arnie's Army. They celebrated raucously when Palmer won his 61 tour events and loved it when

THE UNITED STATES PGA TOUR

Year	Leading money winner	$	Tour purse	Year	Leading money winner	$	Tour purse
1934	Paul Runyan	6,767	–	1961	Gary Player (SA)	64,540	1,461,830
1935	Johnny Revolta	9,543	–	1962	Arnold Palmer	81,448	1,790,320
1936	Horton Smith	7,682	–	1963	Arnold Palmer	128,230	2,044,900
1937	Harry Cooper	14,138	–	1964	Jack Nicklaus	113,284	2,301,063
1938	Sam Snead	19,534	158,000	1965	Jack Nicklaus	140,752	2,848,515
1939	Henry Picard	10,303	121,000	1966	Billy Casper	121,944	3,704,445
1940	Ben Hogan	10,655	117,000	1967	Jack Nicklaus	188,998	3,979,162
1941	Ben Hogan	18,358	169,200	1968	Billy Casper	205,168	5,077,600
1942	Ben Hogan	13,143	116,650	1969	Frank Beard	164,707	5,465,875
1943	–	–	–	1970	Lee Trevino	157,037	6,751,523
1944	Byron Nelson	37,967	150,500	1971	Jack Nicklaus	244,490	7,116,000
1945	Byron Nelson	63,335	435,380	1972	Jack Nicklaus	320,542	7,596,749
1946	Ben Hogan	42,556	411,533	1973	Jack Nicklaus	308,362	8,657,225
1947	Jimmy Demaret	27,936	352,500	1974	Johnny Miller	353,021	8,165,941
1948	Ben Hogan	32,112	427,000	1975	Jack Nicklaus	298,149	7,895,450
1949	Sam Snead	31,593	338,200	1976	Jack Nicklaus	266,438	9,157,522
1950	Sam Snead	35,758	459,950	1977	Tom Watson	310,653	9,688,977
1951	Lloyd Mangrum	26,088	460,200	1978	Tom Watson	362,428	10,337,332
1952	Julius Boros	37,032	498,016	1979	Tom Watson	462,636	12,801,200
1953	Lew Worsham	34,002	562,704	1980	Tom Watson	530,808	13,371,786
1954	Bob Toski	65,819	600,819	1981	Tom Kite	375,698	14,175,393
1955	Julius Boros	63,121	782,010	1982	Craig Stadler	446,462	15,089,576
1956	Ted Kroll	72,835	847,070	1983	Hal Sutton	426,668	17,588,242
1957	Dick Mayer	65,835	820,360	1984	Tom Watson	476,260	21,251,382
1958	Arnold Palmer	42,607	1,005,800	1985	Curtis Strange	542,321	25,290,526
1959	Art Wall	53,167	1,225,205	1986	Greg Norman (Aus)	653,296	25,442,242
1960	Arnold Palmer	75,262	1,335,242				

Below left The former US Amateur champion Gene Littler enjoyed a successful career as a professional, winning the US Open and 28 other tour titles. In 1972 Littler underwent surgery for cancer of the lymph glands. The way he conquered his serious illness speaks volumes for the inner strength of the easy, sweet-swinging golfer his peers called 'Gene the Machine'.

Below right Two more tour titans. Tom Weiskopf (left) and Hale Irwin had respectively won 15 and 17 tour titles by the start of the 1987 season. Irwin's tally included two US Opens (1974 and 1979) while Weiskopf, who is widely regarded as a sad case of unfulfilled potential, added the British Open to his honours in 1973.

Duck pâté, screamed the headlines, mispronouncing the surname but cashing in on the pun when Jerry Pate made a rare scheduled visit to a water hazard to celebrate his win at the 1981 Memphis Classic. Apart from getting him soaked, his action refuted the allegation made by some sections of the media that the American tour players were a bunch of boring clones.

Deane Beman, Commissioner of the PGA Tour in the United States, seen here reliving his playing days with a respectable performance in the 1986 Open Championship at Turnberry.

McCormack is undoubtedly one of the most important men to have been involved in golf. His hunch about whom to sign in 1961 was as perceptive as the majority of his moves. The next year Palmer won the Masters and the Open, Nicklaus the US Open and Player the PGA. Palmer and Player remain in his stable but Nicklaus has long since bolted to set up his own conglomerate, Golden Bear Incorporated.

Though the 1960s belonged to the Big Three, they did not have it all their own way. Billy Casper, who won the US Open twice and the Masters once, topped the Money List in 1966 and 1968 with his consistent if not spectacular brand of quality golf, and Frank Beard surprisingly succeeded him in 1969. But a decade of expansion on every front was also more than tinged by controversy.

Golf is renowned as a colourful sport but skin-wise there was only one colour on tour going into the 1960s – white. The USPGA's regulations restricted membership to 'professional golfers of the Caucasian race, residing in North or South America'. In May 1961 this flagrantly racist policy led the state of California to refuse permission for the 1962 PGA Championship to be held in Los Angeles. The PGA removed the offending clause from its constitution later that year. At the Greater Hartford Open in August 1967, Charlie Sifford became the first black golfer to win on the US Tour.

By then the rumblings of discontent about the way the PGA was administering the circuit were getting ominously louder. The tour players had been growing increasingly restless about operating within an organization whose main base rested on the support of club pros. To cut a very long story short, they said to the PGA: 'We do things our way from now on.' The PGA replied: 'No chance', so the players formed a new body, the American Professional Golfers (APG).

The PGA felt it still held the whip hand in view of the courses, sponsors and television rights it had signed up. It was duly horrified to learn that these contracts weren't worth a nickel without the stars. Nobody was going to fork out good money to watch a tournament filled with anonymous sweater salesmen and grip repairers, otherwise known as club pros. On 1 December 1968 the APG announced a 28-event schedule for the new year, with in excess of $3.5 million prize money. The contest was over. In the time-honoured fashion the PGA's climbdown was hailed as a compromise. The tour players were welcomed back to the fold and their own organization, the Tournament Policy Board, was created. It was the first step towards full secession.

To the delight of the tour pros, in January 1969 Joe Dey agreed to leave his post as Executive Director of the USGA and became the first Commissioner of the Tournament Players' Division (TPD), the forerunner of today's USPGA Tour. Dey, then aged 61, was as respected as any figure in golf and his acceptance of the offer represented a major coup for the players, bestowing the TPD with immediate authority and status.

The split caused considerable bitterness among the club pros, who felt they had been kicked in the teeth and treated as second-class citizens by the boys on the glamour side of the game. Perhaps they had, but they had to resign themselves to a *fait accompli*. Dey served until March 1974 when Deane Beman (twice US Amateur and once British Amateur champion, but with only a moderate career as a tour pro behind him) assumed the reins.

On the golf course, Jack Nicklaus and Tom Watson dominated the tour in the 1970s. Only Lee Trevino (1970) and Johnny Miller (1974) were able to break their stranglehold on the title of leading money-winner. Indeed, their grip was not properly broken until Tom Kite took over from Watson in 1981 and ushered in a period of six different winners in as many years, concluding in 1986 with Greg Norman becoming only the second foreigner to top the Money List.

That takes us back to where we came in, Deane Beman being the man responsible for the developments mentioned at the start of this

Tom Kite won the Arnold Palmer Award for heading the US Money List in 1981, thus ending Tom Watson's four-year reign. As the picture makes evident, Kite also won the Bay Hill Classic in 1982. He chipped in on the first hole of a play-off against Jack Nicklaus and Denis Watson.

chapter. Several of his decisions have been disputed but there is no doubting the fact that he has made the US Tour a very wealthy place to make a living. Its headquarters are today located at one of its own 'stadium' sites in Ponte Vedra, Florida. From his office there, Beman has presided over the birth and rise of the Senior Tour, the rather less successful grooming of a secondary circuit, and the introduction of the all-exempt tour, which has eliminated the old system whereby the 'rabbits' had to pre-qualify for the main event. The idea, as with so many practices established in the United States, has been copied in Europe.

The US Tour runs from January to October, leaving the tail-end of the year free for American players to ply their trade elsewhere in the world without obligation to the mother circuit. Beman jealously guards his assets for the other 10 months, which is an understandable reaction designed to protect his tournament sponsors. It can have unfortunate consequences, however. The next chapter illustrates that an old financial adage – 'when America sneezes, the rest of the world catches a cold' – applies equally to golf.

Hal Sutton. He won the US Amateur in 1980, turned pro in 1981, won a tournament in 1982 and in 1983 won the USPGA Championship, the Tournament Players' Championship and topped the Money List. Sutton has been one of the more outstanding players to make the transition from amateur to professional in recent years and he generally averages a couple of wins a season.

Tour Talk is Universal

Golf has tournament circuits on every continent of the globe bar the Arctic and Antarctic. Before looking at how these have developed, following the example set in the United States, it is important to put the whole situation into context.

The United States has the most powerful golf tour in the world. It also has the richest. Those facts are inextricably connected. Part of the reason for this wealth is that American members of the US Tour cannot, except by fulfilling certain commitments, play abroad without a release from Commissioner Deane Beman's office. Often this will only be granted if the sponsor of the conflicting American event that week is agreeable, and in this way the interests of those who fund the tour are safeguarded. Of course, November and December tournaments in Japan, South Africa and Australia beckon itinerant

American pros who are then free from the constraints of their domestic obligations, but the significance of the Tour Commissioner's strength has never been more heavily emphasized than in September 1970 when the John Player tobacco company launched a £70,000 tournament at the Notts Golf Club in England.

To borrow an American expression, this was 'big bucks'. Christy O'Connor collected the first five-figure cheque ever presented in British golf – a staggering £24,375, nearly five times as much as Jack Nicklaus had earned for winning the Open at St Andrews. The Irishman's prize equalled the biggest on offer in the United States that year, converting to $60,000 in those heady days for sterling.

The tournament is now long defunct. Players were sunk almost as soon as they started. Their representative had blithely flown over to America with all that money behind him to complete the formalities of signing up the stars. He was told: 'No way.' It was an expensive lesson, even if O'Connor enjoyed it hugely.

Seve Ballesteros also learned there is a price to be paid for underestimating the authority and reaction of the Commissioner. In 1985 he refused to play in the required minimum of 15 American tournaments, something he was contracted to do under the terms which made him a tour member. Beman demonstrated that foreigners were to be treated no more leniently than natives by banning Ballesteros from all but four US Tour events in 1986 (the three majors, over which Beman has no control, plus the USF & G Classic in New Orleans at which Ballesteros was the defending champion). It may have been partly due to his enforced absence from top-class winter competition that the Spaniard faltered so dramatically and untypically when in sight of winning the 1986 Masters (see page 85). He is not normally associated with blow-ups.

Both these episodes make the point about the power of the US Tour, even though the incidents

Ireland's Christy O'Connor with the winner's trophy after the ill-fated John Player Classic in 1970.

were separated by 16 years. In fact, a great deal has changed since that day when John Players' unfortunate emissary received his rude shock. There has been a tremendous growth in the scale of professional golf everywhere, and nowhere more than in Europe, whose golfers have made their presence felt by winning tournaments in the United States. Tony Jacklin showed the way and subsequent major champions in the shape of Ballesteros, Bernhard Langer and Sandy Lyle have followed him.

The increasingly cosmopolitan nature of the US Tour has caused Beman to review his restrictive policies, especially for the sake of European and Japanese players whose countries operate major golf tours during the same months as the Americans. Although the regulations seem to fluctuate with the frequency of a St Andrews breeze, the present rule is that all overseas players who accept full membership of the US Tour are free to support their 'home circuits' as much as they want – provided they fulfil those 15 dates in the United States. The American influence is univerally pervasive, but that concession does indicate a measure of co-operation between Beman and his opposite numbers around the world. These include Ken Schofield, the Executive Director of the PGA European Tour.

Ballesteros, Langer and Lyle are currently the three most valuable jewels in Schofield's crown. The first two have been inspirations to the development of the game in their respective countries rather than the products of it, but all three are indisputably the results of the birth of the European Tour.

The British and Continental Tours used to be separate entities. The latter was basically a string of national Opens throughout mainland Europe. The former was operated by the British PGA which, as in the United States, exists primarily for the benefit of club professionals. The tour – such as it was – originally consisted of something like a tournament a month. The Vardon Trophy, named after Harry Vardon and awarded to the season's leading money-winner for topping the Order of Merit, was not instituted until 1937, when it was claimed by Charlie Whitcombe.

In the post-war years British golf was dominated by Commonwealth players like Bobby Locke and Peter Thomson, who almost shared the Open Championship between themselves. Another Australian, Norman von Nida, won a record seven tournaments, all in England, in 1947. That mark has never been

Norman von Nida won seven British tournaments in 1947, including this one, the Brand Lochryn event at Royal Mid-Surrey in April. It was one of the top tournaments of the season, with a prize fund of £1500. Watching von Nida's action is Dick Burton, the Englishman who won the last pre-war Open, at St Andrews in 1939.

bettered but in 1953 a Belgian, Flory van Donck, matched it with seven wins in six countries, including five continental Opens.

Mainland Europe fulfilled an important role in tournament golf before Ballesteros and Langer were born. Its function lay not so much in producing quality golfers – van Donck was an exception – as in providing tournaments, and the British marauders would often descend on these in force and with success. Peter Alliss won the Italian, Spanish and Portuguese Opens in consecutive weeks on one particularly fruitful excursion in 1958. Alliss, who is now famous throughout the world as a television commentator, was one of a group of touring British professionals of high, but not the highest, calibre. He, Eric Brown, Bernard Hunt, Dai Rees, Christy O'Connor, Neil Coles and others all made a good living from their travels but the gulf between the British players and the cream of American golf was distressingly emphasized every two years when the latter would customarily thrash their opponents in the Ryder Cup. The absence of the Open Championship trophy from a British mantelpiece from 1951 to 1969 was a further manifestation of the truth that the tournament circuit in Britain and Europe was

Above left Left to right: Tony Jacklin, John Jacobs and Peter Alliss. The first two were instrumental in causing the European golf boom at the beginning of the 1970s, while Alliss has successfully converted his career from respected golfer to respected golf commentator.

Above right Although it was Jacklin who took the limelight and two major championships around the turn of the last decade, it was Peter Oosterhuis who lifted the Vardon Trophy for being the leading official money winner in Europe from 1971 to 1974.

merely a pale shadow of the one across the Atlantic.

Then, much as in America, three things happened. In America these were television, Eisenhower and Palmer. In Europe they were the big ball, Tony Jacklin and John Jacobs.

In 1968 the British PGA, heeding those who considered the 1.68-inch ball to be a factor behind America's supremacy in professional golf, announced it would be compulsory in all its tournaments for a three-year experimental period. This controversial decision heralded the beginning of the end of the 1.62-inch ball for professionals (though it was permitted in the Open until 1974) and initiated the process by which nearly all club golfers in Britain today play the big ball.

The chances of the ruling being revoked were reduced within 18 months when Tony Jacklin won the 1969 Open at Lytham (ironically, with the small ball) and within another 12 months they had vanished altogether in the wake of Jacklin's massacre of the Americans in their own national championship (this time with the big one). British golf had its king, and the time was ripe to capitalize on his success.

In 1971 John Jacobs was appointed Tournament Director-General of the PGA, relieving the then secretary, Major John Bywaters, of a massive chunk of his colossal workload. Jacobs was brought in to make the tour side more 'business-like' and that he did, proving himself to be as astute an administrator as he was capable professional and is esteemed teacher.

He did not have an easy baptism. Three major sponsors had pulled out after 1970, including Players following the Nottingham fiasco. The

continental tournaments suddenly looked extremely attractive and six of them – the Algarve, Spanish, Italian, French, German and Swiss Opens – counted for the Ryder Cup points table and the Order of Merit in 1971 by guaranteeing a minimum purse of £10,000, more money than any other event under the auspices of the PGA.

Into this cold climate stepped Jacobs. He shuffled the schedule so that the richest tournaments were allocated the best dates, and during those weeks he prohibited his star players from competing outside Europe. He co-ordinated the continental Opens as part of his package and stipulated minimum prize funds for Order of Merit events, which lost him some sponsors but gained others (even John Player again briefly, until the company learned that Turnberry in the autumn can be about as suitable as the Arctic for the staging of a golf tournament).

Jacobs set himself a target of £200,000 in total prize money for 1972. He doubled that, a spectacular vindication of his insistence on not having to answer to a committee and financial evidence of the drawing power of Jacklin and Peter Oosterhuis, who was to collect the Vardon Trophy in four successive seasons from 1971. Oosterhuis left Britain for America in 1975 but he won only once in 12 years of arduous campaigning on the US Tour, proof positive of how relatively easy it was then to excel in Europe and how hard it is still to stand out in the United States.

The year Oosterhuis departed from British shores also saw the creation of a separate Tournament Players' Division within the PGA (a copy from the United States) and the departure of Jacobs from the hot seat. Ken Schofield replaced him and the subsequent increase in the prosperity of the tour has been inexorable.

That verdict is not delivered with just money in mind. Schofield deserves congratulations for lifting purses from around £600,000 to over £7 million and rising, but he has been enormously assisted in his endeavours by the exploits of Severiano Ballesteros. These two men were the second wave of the revolution.

Ballesteros was a virtual unknown when he audaciously led the field by two strokes with a round to play in the 1976 Open Championship at Royal Birkdale. His own recklessness and the brilliance of Johnny Miller cost him the title but he finished tied for second with Jack Nicklaus thanks to a characteristically ingenious chip shot to the

THE PGA EUROPEAN TOUR

Year	Vardon Trophy	Year	Vardon Trophy	Year	Vardon Trophy	Leading money winner*	£	Tour purse
1937	Charlie Whitcombe	1957	Eric Brown	1972	Peter Oosterhuis	Bob Charles (NZ)	18,538	430,185
1938	Henry Cotton	1958	Bernard Hunt	1973	Peter Oosterhuis	Tony Jacklin	24,839	509,500
1939	Reg Whitcombe	1959	Dai Rees	1974	Peter Oosterhuis	Peter Oosterhuis	32,127	604,800
1940–5	–	1960	Bernard Hunt	1975	Dale Hayes (SA)	Dale Hayes (SA)	20,507	607,327
1946	Bobby Locke (SA)	1961	Christy O'Connor (Ire)	1976	Seve Ballesteros (Sp)	Seve Ballesteros (Sp)	39,504	894,668
1947	Norman von Nida (Aus)	1962	Christy O'Connor (Ire)	1977	Seve Ballesteros (Sp)	Seve Ballesteros (Sp)	46,436	1,024,416
1948	Charlie Ward	1963	Neil Coles	1978	Seve Ballesteros (Sp)	Seve Ballesteros (Sp)	54,348	1,195,187
1949	Charlie Ward	1964	Peter Alliss	1979	Sandy Lyle	Sandy Lyle	49,233	1,442,220
1950	Bobby Locke (SA)	1965	Bernard Hunt	1980	Sandy Lyle	Greg Norman (Aus)	74,829	1,711,930
1951	John Panton	1966	Peter Alliss	1981	Bernhard Langer (Ger)	Bernhard Langer (Ger)	95,991	1,806,480
1952	Harry Weetman	1967	Malcolm Gregson	1982	Greg Norman (Aus)	Sandy Lyle	86,141	2,298,035
1953	Flory van Donck (Bel)	1968	Brian Huggett	1983	Nick Faldo	Nick Faldo	140,761	2,819,618
1954	Bobby Locke (SA)	1969	Bernard Gallacher	1984	Bernhard Langer (Ger)	Bernhard Langer (Ger)	160,883	3,405,137
1955	Dai Rees	1970	Neil Coles	1985	Sandy Lyle	Sandy Lyle	199,020	4,758,533
1956	Harry Weetman	1971	Peter Oosterhuis	1986	Seve Ballesteros (Sp)	Seve Ballesteros (Sp)	259,275	5,660,478

* Includes non-official earnings

final green. Three weeks later Ballesteros won the Dutch Open and from that day his own career has flourished almost in tandem with the fortunes of the whole tour. Exactly 10 years on, Ballesteros became the first man to earn in excess of £1 million prize money in Europe when he won the Dutch Open again. On both occasions his victory margin was eight shots.

Ballesteros was not the only successful continental golfer in the mid-1970s. His fellow-Spaniards Manuel Pinero, Francisco Abreu and Salvador Balbuena were also tournament victors in 1976, as was Italy's Baldovino Dassu, but the potential of this 19-year-old prodigy from Pedrena, on Spain's northern coast, exicted everybody. He headed the Order of Merit in 1976 and that winter he and Pinero had the nerve to beat the crack American duo of Jerry Pate and Dave Stockton (respectively the reigning US Open and PGA champions) at the World Cup in California.

It is no exaggeration to equate Ballesteros with Arnold Palmer. They both gave the impression of trying to beat the golf course into submission (I use the past tense now that Palmer is beyond his prime and Ballesteros is proud of having switched to more clinical and less cavalier methods of attack). Both men could putt like demons – indeed Ballesteros still does, employing his putter with the deadly precision of a matador's sword. They pulled in the crowds with their exciting brand of golf, which in turn attracted sponsors and television. Finally, both breathed life into their respective circuits at critical moments. In Europe the timing could not have been more propitious. At the conclusion of the 1976 season,

Below left Addressing the issues – Mark McCormack, founder of the International Management Group (IMG) and one of the most powerful and influential men in sport. Looking on – Ken Schofield, now the Executive Director of the PGA European Tour.

Left The World Matchplay Championship is one of McCormack's innovations and Sandy Lyle (right) is one of IMG's clients. Here Lyle receives the damp commiserations of Severiano Ballesteros after losing at the first extra hole of the 1982 Matchplay final. Lyle, who won the Open in 1985, is one of the European golfers to have benefited from the Spaniard's example at the highest levels of the game. The Matchplay, although not an official tour event, has gained in stature throughout the years and is one of the most eagerly awaited weeks on the European golf calendar.

Two more men who have prevented Ballesteros having the European scene to himself. In 1983 Nick Faldo collected these five trophies and became the first player to win over £100,000 in a season in Europe. Two years later Bernhard Langer defied Ballesteros in the last round at Augusta to become the second European winner of the Masters, for all his anguish at this putt on the 15th lipping out.

Ken Schofield announced the formal merger of the British and Continental Tours under the united banner of the European Tournament Players' Division, outside the PGA. This has evolved into the modern European Tour.

Ballesteros was the unofficial flagship of the new body. He was the principal reason for continentals being called in as reinforcements to help the ailing British cause in the Ryder Cup from 1979. That year he won the Open Championship; the next April he bearded the Americans in their own den by winning the Masters. Such stirring deeds encouraged other Europeans to believe: 'If he can do it, so can I.' Langer and Lyle have, both capturing major championships in 1985, and in March 1987 Lyle added the United States' Tournament Players' Championship, golf's putative 'fifth major'.

Apart from these three, the only two other recipients of the Vardon Trophy since 1975 have been Greg Norman (1982) and Nick Faldo (1983). Norman confessed to treating his European experience as a stepping stone to the US Tour and his attitude was totally justified by his sensational performances in 1986. Faldo's *annus mirabilis* included five tournament victories, the sort of thing that is routine for Ballesteros but exceptional for anyone else. Faldo has not, at the time of writing, attained the heady heights of the other four, but he may yet.

It would be a mistake to assume all has been sweetness and light in the last decade. There have been ructions between the authorities and Ballesteros over his demands to be paid appearance money, which, although he by no means invented the concept, has been a crusade long associated with him. The row reached its unhappy peak in 1981 when Ballesteros shunned Europe for much of the year. The matter has

never been resolved to the satisfaction of the tour, whose officials would like to see appearance money outlawed as it is in America and the cash used to build up the prize funds; and it is never likely to be so long as sponsors insist on their right to pay whomever they want to play in their tournaments. The irony is that if the John Player Classic was to be launched today the organizers would probably not even try to sign up any Americans, with the possible exceptions of Nicklaus and Watson. They would be delighted to make do with Messrs Ballesteros, Langer, Lyle, Norman and Faldo – for a fee, of course.

Television coverage has been responsible for bringing in more sponsors and therefore more money, a development facilitated when Schofield arranged for a Sunday finish to become the norm. Most British tournaments are televised and, as the composition of the Ryder Cup teams since 1979 illustrates, it is still Britain which breeds the majority of Europe's leading players. In addition to Faldo and Lyle, these include Howard Clark, Sam Torrance and Ian Woosnam, with plenty of promising prospects like David Feherty, Robert Lee, Philip Parkin and Ronan Rafferty appearing to be candidates for high honours.

But the growth area for golf in Europe undoubtedly lies on the continent. A few blinkered British professionals complain about their cross-Channel colleagues annually gaining a larger slice of the tournament cake, which means extra hassle and cost for them to compete abroad. However, to object to over half the 30-odd events on the schedule being held on the continent is simply unrealistic. It ignores such essential ingredients as money – for example, the Swiss Open is at present the richest event under Ken Schofield's control – and climate. It is obviously not feasible to operate a tour from March to November without spending a considerable amount of time in the warmer weather of the south. Indeed, Schofield has rewritten the geography text books by taking the European Tour to North Africa.

The moaners fail to recognize that the tour is no longer the preserve of the British. Spain in particular has regularly produced quality players, in numbers out of all proportion to the popularity of the game among Spaniards. Ballesteros is the outstanding example and Jose-Maria Olazabal the most recent. As a first-year (rookie) professional in 1986, Olazabal was second to Ballesteros on the Order of Merit, though admittedly over £100,000 adrift as Seve smashed Sandy Lyle's official money record by amassing £242,209 to collect his fourth Vardon Trophy. The Swedes too have been steadily mounting an impressive array of talent. It is disconcerting for some Britons to reflect that golfers from the four home countries filled only five of the top 10 places on the 1986 Order of Merit.

The European Tour is now truly European and in a healthy state. It has adopted several American innovations, such as qualifying schools, an all-exempt tour and the establishment of a separate body (PGA European Tour Enterprises Ltd) to exploit the earnings potential of the tour's activities and to generate additional income therefrom. But its greatest contribution to professional golf has also been its good fortune: to be the spawning ground for the likes of Ballesteros, Langer and Lyle. It is the impact its progeny have had on the game worldwide that merits the tour's extended treatment here.

If cash were the sole criteria of importance, the European Tour would be a distant third to those of the United States and Japan. The Japanese PGA circuit carries around 50 per cent more prize money than its European counterpart. In fact, tournament golf in Japan has been perhaps the most remarkable growth story in sport during the latter half of this century. Japan surprisingly won the 1957 World

Tsuneyuki (Tommy) Nakajima of Japan dominates his domestic tour but up until now he has found it rather hard going when confronted by the big names from elsewhere around the world, a point emphasized here at the 1986 Open Championship at Turnberry.

The Australian golf circuit has endured more than its share of trials and tribulations but it never ceases to spawn fine golfers. Australia won the first two Dunhill Cup competitions at St Andrews, the winning team in 1986 being (from left to right) David Graham, Rodger Davis and Greg Norman.

Cup (then called the Canada Cup) at Kasumigaseki just outside Tokyo. Ever since, the country has taken to golf with almost absurd enthusiasm.

As far as the professional tour goes, this has led to a calendar of over 40 tournaments from March to December. The stars of that shock World Cup victory – Torakichi (Pete) Nakamura and Koichi Ono – have been superseded by Isao Aoki and Tsuneyuki (Tommy) Nakajima as the heroes of Japanese golf. Aoki, as outlined on page 51, has enjoyed success outside his homeland but Nakajima, belying the Anglicizing of his first name, has not been able to translate his phenomenal prowess in Japan into titles abroad in the fashion one would expect. It is nothing unusual for him to win half-a-dozen domestic tournaments a season and pick up a bucketful of yen, but this golfing giant from the east has found that his astounding achievements at home have been dwarfed overseas by his failure to grab some excellent opportunities to win, notably in the 1986 Open at Turnberry where his fallibility on the greens in the last round rendered him incapable of threatening Greg Norman.

This is symptomatic of the malady which afflicts Japanese golf. Nakajima and the likes of Masahiro Kuramoto and the three Ozaki brothers – known colloquially as Jet, Joe and Jumbo – are unwilling to forego the commercial endorsements available at home and as a result they lock themselves into their own circuit. This means that at the highest level the Japanese suffer from a lack of international competition, and sometimes it shows. They are terribly vulnerable to the predators from America and Europe who swoop down on their lucrative series of tournaments each November, a point emphasized by the fact that when Nakajima won the Dunlop Phoenix in 1985 he was the first native player to bank his country's largest golf prize in the 13 years since the tournament's inception. Thus it is reasonable to say that the Japanese Tour may be second in terms of money but is a poor third in class.

The United States, European and Japanese tours are leagues ahead of the rest. The Australia/ New Zealand circuit is a rambling trek of some 15 tournaments worth less than a £1 million, with a southern hemisphere midwinter break from May to October. The only events with any real international status are the Australian Open in November and the Australian Masters in February. The purses are otherwise poor and the circuit's organization is undermined by the incessant bickering between a plethora of parties with different vested interests. Despite this, there have been many fine Antipodean golfers, including Peter Thomson, Kel Nagle, David Graham and Greg Norman from Australia and Bob Charles from New Zealand. Norman put his humbler compatriots firmly in their place when huge appearance fees lured him home in October and November 1986. He rounded off an outstanding year's golf by winning four times in six outings.

On the other side of the Indian Ocean, South Africa offers the peripatetic golfer sun and the risk of political repercussions, but little money, between November and March. This beleaguered and economically ravaged country can only raise around £300,000 for its Sunshine Tour, but the land of Gary Player and Bobby Locke also stages the Million Dollar Challenge, a select international and invitational event held at the luxurious Sun City resort in the controversial 'tribal homeland' of Bophuthatswana, which is regarded by the rest of the world as a fiction of apartheid rather than an autonomous state. This accounts for the US Tour abandoning its usual winter policy of *laissez faire* in 1986 and instead strongly urging its players not to go to Sun City: a piece of interventionism which was largely successful. But as the eponymous title suggests, the money at Sun City is fantastic, and the US$500,000 Johnny Miller collected for winning the inaugural five-man event in 1982 is comfortably the biggest cheque ever presented to the winner of a golf tournament.

If Miller got a lot then, the luckless Englishman, Gordon Brand, was a victim of the 'you play now, we pay maybe' philosophy of the Nigerians after he had apparently earned the £16,500 first prize at their Open Championship in February 1986. The Nigerian Open was the richest of the five legs on the Safari Tour, which serves European golfers as an alternative winter tune-up destination to South Africa, but the Nigerian government's refusal to pay up in full meant the future of the western segment of the circuit was thrown into jeopardy and it was cancelled for early 1987, though the Safari Tour still lumbers on in truncated form in the south-east of Africa.

That leaves the Asia Tour, started in 1959. Today it boasts over £1 million available in a unique amalgam of the national Opens of exotic eastern countries like Hong Kong, India and Thailand. The circuit's protagonists tend to be

natives of the host countries, flying visitors or novice players from the United States and Europe, and a few luminaries from the Antipodes and Japan. The only local golfers to emerge who could honestly be described as better than competent are 'Mr Lu' (Lu Liang Huan), who chased home Lee Trevino in the Open at Birkdale in 1971, and T. C. (Tze-Chung) Chen, who flopped disastrously when he seemed to have the 1985 US Open within his grasp. Both are Taiwanese.

There are sundry other golf tournaments around the world, including several in Canada and South America, although a futile attempt to promote the latter as a full-scale tour has to be regarded as one of the few failures of IMG and Mark McCormack, who has been the *eminence grise* behind many of the developments discussed in this chapter. McCormack recalls: 'We felt it was good for golf and thought it would be good for ourselves, but the currencies were devaluing so fast it was unbelievable and we got absolutely murdered.'

There is no reason why McCormack should have purely altruistic motives, but 'good for golf' is an apt motto with which to conclude these last two chapters. It is doubtful that Walter Hagen and the American pioneers of the 1920s could ever have foreseen what their fledgling golf tour would lead to, but good for golf it has certainly been.

Above left Agony and ecstasy for Nick Price. The South African has just failed to hole a 25-footer on the 18th green in the third round of the 1986 Masters, but nevertheless he has broken the 36-year-old course record with his nine-under-par 63. Price is one of several South Africans to have thrived on the international stage in the wake of Gary Player and Bobby Locke.

Above right T. C. Chen looked a certain winner of the 1985 US Open until he had a double-hit on the 5th hole of the final round at Oakland Hills. He took a four-over-par eight on the hole and eventually lost by a shot to Andy North. Despite that appalling blow, Chen has matured into a genuinely top-class golfer and when he won the Los Angeles Open in February 1987 he became the first Taiwanese to win in the United States.

Sam Ryder's Legacy: the King of Cups

An American friend of mine remarked recently: 'You know, golf is in its cups.' I know what he means. He wasn't exactly casting aspersions on the state of the sport, which is generally healthy and prosperous, but reflecting the modern passion for team events: a mania which has led to a multitude of Cup competitions.

The time was when the Ryder Cup, inaugurated in 1927, was the only professional team competition on the calendar, and that only concerned golfers from Great Britain and the United States. Today golf has more cups than the china department at Harrods. The most venerable of these others is the World Cup, the dream-come-true of an American philanthropist, John Jay Hopkins. It was started in Montreal in 1953 (hence its original name of the Canada Cup) and after years of offering relative peanuts for prize money – and being surprised when all too often it got monkeys – the World Cup was spectacularly revamped in 1985 with a purse worthy of its name: $644,000 in fact. As if exhausted by the efforts involved in raising this bonanza, the new chief, Burch Riber, cancelled the 1986 event, but with the firm assurance that the World Cup would return permanently after a 12-month hiatus and be the stronger for the rest.

Perhaps the main reason for the temporary demise of the World Cup was the launch of the $1 million-plus Dunhill Cup at St Andrews in 1985. This Mark McCormack-inspired international extravaganza boils down to three-man teams from 16 different countries competing for a top cheque of $100,000 per head in a match-medal knockout format. McCormack has always had a keen and eager eye for the half-chance and the previous stinginess of the World Cup's prize funds enabled him to introduce another lucrative tournament into the already congested autumn fixture list. It helps, of course, that several of the stars competing in it are clients of his.

The Dunhill Cup, as the name makes plain, is an unashamedly commercial enterprise, as are the Chrysler Cup (between the Senior golfers of the United States and the Rest of the World) and the Nissan Cup (involving six-man teams from the American, European, Japanese and Australian PGA Tours). The latter was, like the Dunhill, only instituted in 1985, and the staging of two such mega-productions at the tail-end of the season is conclusive evidence of the way sponsors are practically queueing up to pour more cash into golf's brimming coffers.

But welcome though these affairs are as alternatives to the staple weekly diet of 72-hole individual strokeplay tournaments, they have not forsaken strokeplay for matchplay, largely because television wants matches guaranteed to go to the 18th green – and television talks big money. Money is basically the *raison d'être* of all these competitions, if only because that is their only means of inducing the world's best players to participate. Not so the Ryder Cup. That is something different and something special.

The Ryder Cup is played for patriotism: on the one side for Uncle Sam and the American way, on the other for Queen and Country, the Irish Tricolour and assorted continental causes. What used to be the Great Britain & Ireland team was expanded from 1979 to take in the whole of Europe. The reason was simple. The Ryder Cup had become not so much a series of matches as a series of massacres: the British had won only once since the war. (Incidentally, 'British' is acceptable shorthand. The team was not formally called Great Britain & Ireland until 1973, but Irishmen had long been included in it because golf in Ireland is organized without regard for the North/South partition, and Irish professionals were registered with the British PGA. I trust that to refer to the GB & I players as 'British', if only for convenience, will not offend Republican sensitivities.) Accordingly, in 1979 the rest of Europe was drafted in to make the contest a contest again. Any purists who regretted such a fundamental tampering with tradition had their

uneasy consciences assuaged and their hearts lifted when Europe comprehensively defeated the United States at The Belfry, near Birmingham, in the 1985 encounter. It was the Americans' first reverse in 28 years, a statistic which bears adequate testimony to their post-war dominance, and which the generous Sam Ryder probably never imagined could have occurred.

The Ryder Cup began in 1927. It takes its name from Samuel Ryder, a St Albans businessman who made a fortune from selling penny packets of seed. He was prompted to donate the small solid gold trophy after attending the second unofficial match between teams of British and American professionals held at Wentworth in June 1926. Like its forerunner at Gleneagles in 1921, it resulted in a resounding victory for the home team, this time by the almost unbelievable margin of 13½ points to 1½. Abe Mitchell, Ryder's personal professional, thrashed the defending Open champion, Jim Barnes, by 8 & 7, and in the foursomes he and George Duncan routed Barnes and the great Walter Hagen by 9 & 8. Ryder was so impressed by what he saw and by the camaraderie among the players that he declared words to the effect, 'We must do this more often.' And he did something about it. He had the

famous cup made up and engraved, using Mitchell as the model for the little golfer who stands proudly atop the trophy today.

The first Ryder Cup match took place at Worcester, Massachusetts, the following June. Since Ryder had not endowed the trophy, an appeal for funds was launched by George Philpot, the Editor of *Golf Illustrated*, who also doubled as team manager, and the squad duly embarked from Southampton on a mission with a dual purpose – to return with the Ryder Cup and the US Open. Seldom has optimism been so misplaced. Indeed, at the time of writing the sombre truth is that the Americans have never failed to win the Ryder Cup on home soil, and Tony Jacklin (in 1970) is the only European golfer to become US Open champion since Ryder's crusade was waved off in style 60 years ago. And style it unquestionably was.

It is amusing to recall that when Jacklin himself was appointed Ryder Cup captain for the first time in 1983, he insisted his men must make the journey to the United States 'first-class all the way'. He meant flying on Concorde. Compared to the *Aquitania*, the veritable hotel with a hull which transported the 1927 British team to New York on a leisurely and luxurious five-day

Aboard the *Aquitania* prior to departing for the United States and the first Ryder Cup match. Left to right: George Philpot (team manager), Samuel Ryder (who did not travel), George Gadd, Arthur Havers, George Duncan, Ted Ray, Fred Robson, Archie Compston, Charlie Whitcombe and Abe Mitchell (who must have fallen ill shortly after this was taken). Team members not shown are Aubrey Boomer and Herbert Jolly.

voyage, the winged wonder is like a speedboat with hostesses. 'The floating palace' was how the liner was described by an anonymous author in the contemporary issue of *PGA Journal*. 'Lifts to all decks, lounges, smoke rooms, ballroom, swimming bath and gymnasium were among the outstanding features.'

But old J. H. Taylor, one of the selectors, was at pains to stress 'it is no casual picnic'. The American domination of the sport was a new, disturbing and totally unacceptable phenomenon to British golfers in the 1920s. Hagen and Bobby Jones were usurpers of the British birthright to rule the world of golf and Taylor and his colleagues were determined that the proper order of things should be reasserted.

Their aspirations suffered an immediate blow when Abe Mitchell went down with appendicitis just after boarding the *Aquitania* and he had to disembark for hospital. Ryder wrote to his friend and mentor: 'Let us hope our team will win, but it is the play without the Prince of Denmark.'

Ted Ray was nominated captain in Mitchell's absence. His opposite number was Hagen, who was to lead his side in every one of the six pre-war contests, albeit in a non-playing capacity in 1937. Hagen would have approved of the creature comforts enjoyed by his rivals on their Atlantic crossing, but the British were not accustomed to being treated like celebrities and they were further disorientated when their ship berthed. On landing

in America, they were introduced to 'a world of luxury and plenty', as Arthur Havers put it. Hagen might have choreographed the whole show – a waiving of customs formalities, a motorcycle escort through Manhattan, limousines permanently at the players' disposal, typically transatlantic hospitality and kindness, and clubhouses equipped with every amenity and furnished to the highest standards. And so it went on.

Totally overawed off the course, the British were overwhelmed on it. They lost 2½–9½. (From 1927 to 1959, the competition consisted of one day of four 36-hole foursomes and another of eight 36-hole singles.) It was generally agreed that the major difference between the teams lay in the short game, especially putting. That has been a familiar refrain down the years.

Although after the war the Ryder Cup often seemed to have degenerated into a grandiose Anglo-American public relations exercise, it was never thus in the 1920s and '30s. The 1929 match at Moortown, Leeds, brought the British the revenge they had anticipated with what in hindsight can only be regarded as complacency bordering on stupidity. The heroes for the home team were Duncan, who delighted in tearing Hagen apart by the astonishing margin of 10 & 8 – a Ryder Cup singles record – and 22-year-old Henry Cotton, who supplied the vital last point by defeating Al Watrous 4 & 3. A month later Hagen cut short any gloating by winning his fourth Open title at Muirfield.

At the end of that year, on 9 December, Sam Ryder signed over his trophy to the PGA under a Deed of Trust, confirming it to be the reward for the winners of a biennial matchplay international 'between two teams of professional golfers, one team representing Great Britain and the other team representing the United States of America'. From that date, the administration of the Ryder Cup in their respective countries has been undertaken by the British PGA and the PGA of America, *not* the PGA European Tour and the American PGA Tour.

From the cold of a Yorkshire spring in 1929, the scene switched to the enervating heat of an Ohio summer in 1931. The temperature permanently hovered around 100°F and people all over the Columbus area were dying from heat exhaustion and dehydration. Fred Pignon, the British manager, commented: 'In this weather, golf is not a game – it is a form of torture.' He also echoed Havers's remarks about the 'almost embarrassing hospitality'. Pignon said: 'Until you have been the guest of an American golfer you may think you know something about lavish hospitality, but they begin at the place which we consider the high limit.'

The British started badly and fizzled out altogether in the withering heat. Their hopes were faint anyway, but made even more frail by the absence of Cotton, who opted out because he could not resolve his squabbles with the PGA about travelling arrangements and money.

Cotton, despite his late flourish at Moortown, was only ever a sporadic supporter of his country in the Ryder Cup. He didn't play in 1933 or 1935 either, being precluded by the strict residence clause in the Deed of Trust because he was based in Belgium, and in 1949 he refused to play under the captaincy of Charlie Whitcombe. Nevertheless, he did agree to serve as non-playing captain in 1953.

Cotton was the best British golfer since the Great Triumvirate – and many experts would argue that is still the case – but episodes like those above did nothing to boost his popularity, which in some quarters was already jeopardized by his confident manner and habit of saying what he thought. Cotton could only get away with it because he was good, very good, and he worked extraordinarily hard to stay that way. Although his efforts to further his own career and simultaneously raise the status of the professional golfer were not always appreciated at the time (envy of his sophisticated lifestyle, jealousy of his talent and a conservative respect for near-feudal conventions saw to that), that did not worry Cotton, and in later life he was accorded much of the praise which was withheld 50 years before.

His maverick counterpart in America was, of course, the flamboyant Hagen, who adored matchplay and the Ryder Cup. He repaid his 1929 mauling at the hands of George Duncan by pairing up with Densmore Shute to crush Duncan and Arthur Havers by 10 & 9 in the foursomes at Scioto in 1931, the most emphatic margin of victory in any Ryder Cup match. The next day Hagen faced Charlie Whitcombe in the singles, an occasion prefaced by a classic cameo of vintage Hagen. As the two men stood on the first tee, a waiter sauntered over and handed a Martini to the American skipper. Hagen, never one to let golf get in the way of a good time and not averse to drinking and driving, downed the cocktail before cracking a marvellous tee shot down the middle of the fairway. Naturally, like his team, he won.

Sam Ryder (left) presents his trophy to the victorious British captain, George Duncan, at Moortown in 1929.

The 1933 match at Southport & Ainsdale provided a fantastic finish, one which for sheer theatre has only been equalled by the tied match of 1969, held at nearby Royal Birkdale.

J. H. Taylor was the non-playing British captain, and he ordered his troops out on to the beach at 6.30 each morning to undergo a rigorous training regime. As Red Rum was later to prove in three Grand Nationals, a few gallops on Southport sands is a sound recipe for success, and Taylor's men came out of the stalls like racehorses. They took a foursomes lead for the first time in the four meetings, and therefore needed to share the eight singles to regain the Ryder Cup.

There were at least 15,000 people, reckoned then to be the largest attendance on a British golf course, swarming over the sandhills on that second afternoon. Some had come to see the golf, others to see the Prince of Wales who was among their number. For sure the Prince was there to see the golf; and, to stretch creative licence to breaking point, it may be that he was instrumental in Britain's famous victory.

The whole issue rested on the final singles. With the contest dead level, Syd Easterbrook and Denny Shute came to the last hole, a par-4, all square. In American eyes, what followed was a tragedy of errors. After three hacks each, both men lay about 15 feet from the cup, with Easterbrook furthest away. He knocked his putt a

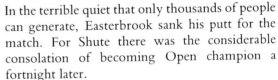

An enormous audience surrounds the 16th green at Southport & Ainsdale for the singles match between Walter Hagen and Arthur Lacey in 1933. Hagen won their duel but the American team lost a marvellous and tense encounter.

The defeated American captain, Hagen (to the right of the stand), leads the cheers for the Prince of Wales (saluting) after Britain's triumph in 1933, their last taste of success for 24 years.

yard past the hole. At that moment, Hagen, as one might expect, was chatting amiably to the Prince. He contemplated yelling out to Shute not to charge his putt – the Americans only required a half to retain the trophy. Instead, perhaps swayed by respect for the finer points of decorum, he remained silent. Shute did charge the putt, and then missed the four-footer he had coming back.

In the terrible quiet that only thousands of people can generate, Easterbrook sank his putt for the match. For Shute there was the considerable consolation of becoming Open champion a fortnight later.

'In giving this Cup I am naturally impartial but, of course, we over here are very pleased to have won,' the Prince wittily observed at the prize-giving ceremony. Sam Ryder never saw Britain do anything else. He never travelled to the United States and by the time the Americans recorded their first of eight away victories in 1937, again at S & A, he was dead.

That shocking defeat followed the expected drubbing in New Jersey in 1935. The British had been pathetic there and several commentators regarded their performance in 1937 as, with one or two notable exceptions, even more spineless. *Golf Illustrated* queried acidly: 'Is it any use pretending that the Americans are unbeatable when, in point of fact, they threw the foursomes at us, a gift which we, with equal courtesy, refused to accept?'

At least Cotton went on from Southport to take the Open Championship at Carnoustie, but otherwise the writing was indelibly on the wall. The Americans had invariably won with ease at home. In Britain they had twice been thwarted narrowly before comfortably confirming their

of the game and that Americans could pop over and win the Open Championship almost at will.

In fact, it was at the behest of the Americans that the Ryder Cup was resumed as promptly as 1947, and thanks to the munificence of Bob Hudson, an Oregon fruit packer, that the British could afford to make the long trip to the American north-west. Hudson financed the whole expedition, blazing a trail of sponsorship that has been followed by several wealthy individuals and companies, without which the Ryder Cup may well have died long before it was revived in 1979.

It rained so hard in 1947 at Portland that the match was almost a washout. It was nearly a whitewash too. The British lost 1–11. The meeting at Ganton two years later was preceded by Hogan's complaint about the British clubs (see page 32), but this was compensated for by some brilliant golf. The home players snatched a 3–1 foursomes lead and acquitted themselves superbly in the singles, but it wasn't sufficient. They couldn't find another gear in the face of a scintillating barrage of birdies from their opponents which caused the scoreboard operators to run out of 3s. The match was lost 5–7.

The Americans held a 3–1 advantage after the first day in 1953 and 1957. They lost one match and should have lost both. In 1953 at Wentworth, Peter Alliss took four to get down from beside the last green; shortly afterwards, Bernard Hunt missed from a yard on the same hole. Had Alliss done the job in three and Hunt made his putt, Britain would have won. Instead the two babes

'Toots' Cotton, wife of the 1953 British captain Henry, was renowned for her fiery temper. She is seen below ripping up a newspaper placard which read: 'Henry Cotton "kicks" Ryder Cup members', a story which broke after Britain lost the first day's foursomes 1–3 at Wentworth. 'Henry didn't do that,' Toots proclaimed. 'Why don't you print the truth?'
Despite their overnight deficit, the British should have won at Wentworth. They still looked likely to earn a tie until Bernard Hunt, above, missed this putt from a yard on the final green against Dave Douglas.

authority in 1937. But the British did have the immense satisfaction of actually having won a couple of times. Nobody knew then, even if many suspected, what a rare occurrence that would become. In those days of pre-war innocence the Ryder Cup was a meaningful sporting battle, hence the attention given to the period here.

In between Britain rescuing Europe in the Second World War and Europe rescuing Britain from golfing annihilation, there were 16 Ryder Cup matches. Only four of them – 1949, 1953, 1957 and 1969 – were close enough to merit mention, though a few words are necessary to to explain how on the whole there came to be such a disparity in the strengths of the teams.

The war exacerbated the differences between the countries. In the United States there was still plenty of cash around to maintain the standards of living experienced briefly by the three visiting pre-war British Ryder Cup teams; quality was attainable. In Britain, rationing was the order of the day; austerity was the watchword. In these diverse economic climates the professional tour boomed in America, providing a marvellous means for a man to make a living from tournament golf, whereas in Britain the poor pro spent most of the time in his shop. No wonder he was so regularly outclassed in every department

THE RYDER CUP

Year	Venue	USA captain	GB/Eur capt	Winners	Score	
1927	Worcester, USA	Walter Hagen	Ted Ray	USA	9½	2½
1929	Moortown, England	Walter Hagen	George Duncan	Britain	7	5
1931	Scioto, USA	Walter Hagen	Charlie Whitcombe	USA	9	3
1933	Southport & Ainsdale, Eng	Walter Hagen	*J. H. Taylor	Britain	6½	5½
1935	Ridgewood, USA	Walter Hagen	Charlie Whitcombe	USA	9	3
1937	Southport & Ainsdale, Eng	*Walter Hagen	Charlie Whitcombe	USA	8	4
1947	Portland, USA	Ben Hogan	Henry Cotton	USA	11	1
1949	Ganton, England	*Ben Hogan	*Charlie Whitcombe	USA	7	5
1951	Pinehurst, USA	Sam Snead	*Arthur Lacey	USA	9½	2½
1953	Wentworth, England	Lloyd Mangrum	*Henry Cotton	USA	6½	5½
1955	Palm Springs, USA	Chick Harbert	Dai Rees	USA	8	4
1957	Lindrick, England	Jack Burke	Dai Rees	Britain	7½	4½
1959	Palm Desert, USA	Sam Snead	Dai Rees	USA	8½	3½
1961	Lytham, England	Jerry Barber	Dai Rees	USA	14½	9½
1963	Atlanta, USA	Arnold Palmer	*Johnny Fallon	USA	23	9
1965	Birkdale, England	*Byron Nelson	*Harry Weetman	USA	19½	12½
1967	Houston, USA	*Ben Hogan	*Dai Rees	USA	23½	8½
1969	Birkdale, England	*Sam Snead	*Eric Brown	tied	16	16
1971	St Louis, USA	*Jay Hebert	*Eric Brown	USA	18½	13½
1973	Muirfield, Scotland	*Jack Burke	*Bernard Hunt	USA	19	13
1975	Laurel Valley, USA	*Arnold Palmer	*Bernard Hunt	USA	21	11
1977	Lytham, England	*Dow Finsterwald	*Brian Huggett	USA	12½	7½
1979	Greenbrier, USA	*Billy Casper	*John Jacobs	USA	17	11
1981	Walton Heath, England	*Dave Marr	*John Jacobs	USA	18½	9½
1983	PGA National, USA	*Jack Nicklaus	*Tony Jacklin	USA	14½	13½
1985	The Belfry, England	*Lee Trevino	*Tony Jacklin	Europe	16½	11½

* non-playing captain

Peter Alliss (left) congratulates his captain, Dai Rees, after Britain's memorable win at Lindrick in 1957. Behind them is Max Faulkner, the 1951 Open champion, who was omitted from the singles at his own suggestion.

were left to carry the can for a heartbreaking defeat. But they were back in 1957 when, inspired by a vast and enthusiastic Yorkshire crowd at Lindrick and the leadership of Dai Rees, the team stormed home by 6½–1½ in the singles to earn Britain's third and last victory.

By 1961, though, it was recognized that British triumphs were not likely to be commonplace, so an era of fiddling with the format was ushered in. With spurious logic, the matches were reduced from 36 to 18 holes apiece to create more games, thereby increasing the number of points to fight for. The only impact of this was to increase the number of points won by the Americans. The one glorious exception was in 1969 when the teams finished level at 16–16.

Tony Jacklin was the local hero, as he had been in the Open at Lytham two months previously. Having beaten Jack Nicklaus 4 & 3 in the morning singles, he took him on again in the afternoon. Jacklin holed a monstrous putt to win the 17th, and the resulting roar led Brian Huggett up ahead to believe he had a five-footer on the 18th to clinch the Ryder Cup. He bravely sank it, only to learn that Jacklin had not won but was level playing the last. So were the teams. The situation was a repeat of 1933 and the finale nearly was too. Nicklaus eventually lay four feet from the cup, Jacklin was a yard away, both in three. Nicklaus

Opposite Brian Huggett holes from five feet to halve his crucial singles with Billy Casper at Royal Birkdale in 1969. He mistakenly believed that he had just won the Ryder Cup. . . .

knocked in his knee-trembler and, in an unforgettable sporting gesture, conceded Jacklin's putt for the half with the words: 'I don't think that you'd have missed that, Tony, but I'm not going to give you the chance.' The Americans then graciously agreed that each side would hold the cup for a year.

But by and large, the history of the Ryder Cup from 1947 to 1977 is rather like a mirror image of the Lions v the Christians in Roman times. The lions' supporters (ie. the American spectators) soon got bored with an almost permanent state of no-contest which, apart from inconsequential sideshows like Brian Barnes twice beating Nicklaus in the singles in 1975, is what they got in their home ring. Perversely, the Christians were begging to be thrown in again. Headlines like 'We Can Do It This Time' and 'Everything Points To Another Lindrick' were followed by dispiriting tales of another British defeat, usually accompanied by a few caustic barbs aimed at the selectors. Finding the silver lining was a popular pastime of the day but the truth is that, for all the optimistic predictions, it was not until the

continent reinforced the British challenge in 1979 that post-war victory became a serious possibility, and not until 1985 did it actually become a probability. Lindrick and Birkdale represented remarkable British performances but in many ways they were really flashes in the pan. Occasions like those kept non-Britons out in the cold longer than might otherwise have been the case. They meant that when reform was introduced it was continental rather than the oft-mooted Commonwealth players who came in.

Following Britain's defeat at Lytham in 1977, Jack Nicklaus wrote to Lord Derby, the President of the British PGA, saying he was afraid the Ryder Cup would die unless something was done. He suggested that the British team be expanded to a European one. At a special committee meeting, the PGA decided to vary the Deed of Trust under the powers vested in them and give effect to Nicklaus's wishes.

It was a logical step, given the recent formation of the European TPD. Seve Ballesteros and Antonio Garrido of Spain joined 10 Britons at The Greenbrier in 1979 but the new recruits only got

. . . The end of a fantastic match. Jack Nicklaus (left) and Tony Jacklin shake hands after Nicklaus had sportingly conceded a short putt to Jacklin which ensured that their game and the entire contest finished all square.

One of golf's great shots from one of its greatest shot-makers. Seve Ballesteros carves a 3-wood 245 yards from an awkward lie in a bunker to the front edge of the 18th hole at PGA National, Florida, in 1983. This stroke of genius enabled him to get a half with Fuzzy Zoeller in the top singles but that in itself was a disappointment after Ballesteros had been 3 up at one time.

one point between them. Larry Nelson was pitched against Ballesteros four times that week and won the lot. At Walton Heath two years later Nelson extended his personal record in the matches to a unique nine wins from nine starts, but Ballesteros was not among the three Europeans in the home team. He was peevishly omitted because of his recurring rows with the European Tour, and to nobody's surprise the Americans won easily.

But Ballesteros was back for Florida in 1983. He replaced his compatriot, Manuel Pinero, while Bernhard Langer and Jose-Maria Canizares remained in the squad. The three provided a forceful demonstration of the difference the continentals had made by helping Europe to hound its opponents down to the line. The United States won by 14½–13½, the closest-ever finish in America, though for much of a thrilling afternoon it seemed Europe would win. In the end, both Ballesteros and Canizares had to rue letting slip three-hole leads.

In 1985, with Tony Jacklin retained as captain, it all came right for Europe. Four Spaniards – Ballesteros, Pinero, Canizares and Jose Rivero – were in a team which included the Masters winner Langer and Open champion Lyle. Victory was likely from the moment Craig Stadler missed a tiny putt on the last green of the second morning's fourballs. That allowed the Europeans to go into lunch tied at 6–6 and they rammed home this immense psychological boost by running away

with the second series of foursomes and the next day's singles. The 16½–11½ defeat was the heaviest ever inflicted on the Americans in the Ryder Cup. For Jacklin, vengeance was sweet. The Americans were led by Lee Trevino, his old adversary.

There were many complaints at The Belfry from visiting players disgruntled at the overt partisanship of the huge crowds. The fans certainly left no doubt as to where their sympathies lay, but that is nothing new in matchplay competition.

Back in 1905, Harry Vardon and J. H. Taylor of England were so upset by the behaviour of the spectators at St Andrews during a £400 challenge match against James Braid and Sandy Herd of Scotland that they contemplated quitting. They didn't, and they went on to win. After the 1949 Ryder Cup at Ganton, Henry Longhurst rebuked the crowds: 'It is all right to cheer when your own man puts his ball on the green. It is quite inexcusable to let out a roar when the opposition drives into the woods.' Dow Finsterwald, the American skipper in 1977, said: 'You've got real trouble if those people out there were representative of your normal crowds. There were an awful lot who seemed to think this was a war, not a golf match.'

Similar sentiments were expressed at The Belfry by Americans who felt the audiences in the United States, rendered blasé by victory upon victory, would never have behaved like that. Peter Alliss, who has known rough and smooth in the Ryder Cup, reckons it's simply sour grapes.

'The Americans have always been great winners, full of "If only you guys could win once in a while to stimulate interest" and that sort of stuff – which, of course, is utter humbug; none of them want to be on a losing Ryder Cup team, as the reactions of Tommy Bolt at Lindrick and Hal Sutton at The Belfry testified. Alliss goes on: 'If you play abroad, at whatever sport, the locals will support their team. As for galleries in the States being polite and sporting, when I beat Arnold Palmer at Atlanta in 1963 I thought I was going to get lynched. But that side is all forgotten now and it's not even worth bothering about really. It's just something that's bound to happen.'

Matchplay, unlike strokeplay, is about winners and losers, not firsts and seconds. It is blood and guts golf. The Ryder Cup stirs these emotions, nowadays mixing them with the kind of commercial trappings found at the Open and adding a large dash of genuinely patriotic fervour which has no other proper outlet in what is mostly an individual, non-nationalistic sport. The combination produces a powerful cocktail which in 1985 caused Sam Torrance, on sinking the winning putt, to exclaim tearfully: 'If I ever win the Open it couldn't feel any better than this.' Both Ballesteros and Lyle, who have won it, agreed he was right.

Even the Americans are not immune. Jack Nicklaus declared his captaincy of the 1983 team had forced him to endure the most nerve-jangling moments of *his* career, and Jack has known a few tense ones. Billy Casper perhaps put it best with his comment: 'When the starter on the first tee says: "And now, playing for the United States . . ." it's an experience you can never forget.'

Americans are guaranteed a share of a healthy purse when they play against the Japanese Tour in the alternate even-numbered years, and still some of them find an excuse not to turn up. The Ryder Cup offers no prize money, but the best players on either side of the Atlantic are desperate to make their teams. Money is not quite everything in sport. In the most important golf international in the world, representative honours count for a bit as well.

At last! Sam Torrance's putt on the 18th green at The Belfry in 1985 gave him victory over US Open champion Andy North and put the seal on a tremendous day for European golf, one which saw the Americans vanquished for the first time in 28 years. His joy contrasted sharply with the misery of Craig Stadler, who missed his putt (below) in this fourball match with Curtis Strange against Langer and Lyle. Stadler stands in disconsolate isolation to the right of the 18th green, which in happier circumstances he would doubtless acknowledge to be a marvellous arena for tournament golf.

CHAPTER ELEVEN

The Amateurs:
Not Just for Fun

Professionals have constituted the vast majority of the golfers discussed in this book so far. They represent, of course, the tiniest tip of the iceberg, numerically an insignificant minority compared with the millions of amateurs who play the game.

It would be wrong to say that a massive proportion of those amateurs play golf for fun. Most of them do at least some of the time, but on other occasions there is nothing the humblest exponent of the game takes more seriously than a three-foot putt. This chapter is not concerned with him, the archetypal club hacker, but with the top echelon of amateur golfers: men whose abilities justified some on-course solemnity; many of whom could have made handsome livings as professionals had they wished to, and some who later did; and a few who were as good as anyone produced from the paid ranks of their contemporaries. And, despite the past tense

employed in that last sentence, there are still some amateurs around today who fulfil the first two of those three categories.

Just as Prestwick founded the Open in 1860, it also hosted the tournament which was the precursor of the Amateur Championship (or British Amateur as it is often known as to save confusion). The club inaugurated a foursomes competition in 1857, but in the two subsequent years, prior to the birth of the Open, the event was held as an individual knockout. The Amateur itself did not begin until 1885, and that was seven years after the grand old universities of Oxford and Cambridge had fought out their first fixture at the London Scottish Golf Club in Wimbledon.

The 1885 Amateur was staged at Royal Liverpool, Hoylake, and won by a local member, Allan MacFie. For a long time it was not regarded as the first official British Amateur – that distinction belonged to the 1886 event at St

Harold Hilton on the way to completing the first leg of his historic double act by winning the Amateur Championship at Prestwick in June 1911. Three months later he added the American title at Apawamis, New York.

Andrews – but it was belatedly accorded the honour in 1922 after the R & A had assumed sole responsibility for the organization of the championship.

The early years were dominated by John Ball and Harold Hilton (see page 38), though Horace Hutchinson, Johnny Laidlay, Freddie Tait and Robert Maxwell were each victorious twice before the Frist World War. Ball's record of eight titles is as safe as Byron Nelson's mark of 11 consecutive professional tournament wins. When Michael Bonallack retired in the 1970s with his name engraved five times on the trophy (which, incidentally, dwarfs the claret jug presented to the Open champion), the already remote possibility of Ball being overhauled vanished completely. It is surely inconceivable today that anyone good enough to threaten Ball's mark would remain an amateur sufficiently long to rewrite the history books. By way of a footnote, perhaps the strangest statistic about Ball's remarkable tally is that he never won the Amateur in consecutive years.

The United States Amateur Championship survived a false start before eventually getting the winner the winner thought it deserved. As described on page 23, the egotistical Charles Blair Macdonald became the first official US Amateur champion in 1895. In strictly tournament terms though, a more significant occurrence was Walter Travis's triumph in 1900.

Travis was born in Australia but emigrated to the United States in his early teens and became an American citizen. He didn't take up golf until he was 35, yet at the age of 39 he won the Amateur Championship of his adopted country. By 1903 he had won it three times, and the following year he astounded and appalled his ill-tempered hosts at Sandwich by becoming the first overseas winner of the British Amateur. Travis was startled and upset by the lukewarm, not to say intermittently hostile, reception that greeted him at Royal St George's, which was in stark contrast to the friendly treatment he had sampled when in Britain previously. The difference then was that he had not been a competitor.

In Travis's own words: 'I have always enjoyed the reputation of being a short driver.' He also had another reputation as a deadly putter, but just before the championship he had lost his customarily uncanny feel and touch. In desperation he borrowed a centre-shafted Schenectady putter from an American spectator. He then proceeded to putt players of the calibre of

Hilton and Hutchinson into defeat before wearing down the long-hitting Ted Blackwell by 4 & 3 in the 36-hole final. Deafening silence acknowledged the *dénouement* and the R & A soon banned the centre-shafted putter. Not surprisingly, Travis didn't play in the British Amateur again. Ironically, nor could he ever recapture that magic with the Schenectady.

Travis was in the very vanguard of the American challenge to the British dominance of the game; a challenge which was to prove utterly successful after the First World War. The 'Old Man', as he was nicknamed back home, was an inspiration to his countrymen, an outstanding example of how doggedness and diligence could reap substantial rewards. It was amateur golf that appealed to the American public at the turn of the century, partly because they realized their home-bred professionals were no match for the Great

Walter Travis, born in Australia, a citizen of the United States and Amateur champion of the British Isles in 1904. Here he shows the style of one of golf's great late developers.

Jerry Travers putting on the 18th green at Baltusrol during the third round of the 1915 US Open, which he eventually won. Travers was one of five American amateurs to win their national Open in the 20 years from 1913. Another was Chick Evans (below), who won both the US Open and US Amateur in 1916.

Triumvirate and a few other leading Britons and Travis had demonstrated that American amateurs could lick the British in their own backyard.

Travis's mantle was taken up by Jerome Travers, the son of a wealthy New York family, who combined on-course excellence with a socialite existence. Travers won four US Amateurs and a US Open between 1907 and 1915, but during that period he indulged his sybaritic tendencies to such an extent that twice he didn't even bother to enter the US Amateur. Francis Ouimet, who preceded Travers as US Open champion by two years, immediately succeeded him as US Amateur champion in 1914. Bob Gardner then emulated H. J. Whigham, Macdonald's son-in-law, and Chandler Egan by winning for a second time, and in 1916 Chick Evans did what only John Ball (1890) had done and Bobby Jones (1930) was to do by winning a country's Open and Amateur Championships in the same year. Evans won the US Open at Minikahda and the Amateur at Merion in Philadelphia.

Evans was to win the US Amateur once more, in 1920. So was Ouimet, in the far future of 1931. In between times was Bobby Jones. After 1923 – when he won his first major championship, the US Open – Jones won the US Amateur in five of the next seven seasons. On the two occasions he missed out (1926 and 1929) he compensated in style by taking his second and third US Opens.

Jones didn't just win in his finals: he slaughtered his adversaries. Remembering that all matches were then played over 36 holes (though none went anywhere near the distance), consider these

facts. In 1924, Jones thrashed George von Elm by 9 & 8 having disposed of Ouimet by 11 & 10 in the semi-finals. The following September he beat Watts Gunn, his colleague and protégé from the East Lake club in his hometown of Atlanta, Georgia, by 8 & 7. Chick Evans succumbed by the same margin in 1927, this after poor Ouimet had again gone down by 11 & 10 in the semi-finals. No wonder Ouimet would later claim: 'I played some pretty darn creditable golf in the Amateur in the twenties. Then I'd run into Bobby, and he would absolutely annihilate me. You have no idea how good Bobby was!'

In 1928 Jones provided further incontrovertible evidence of his superiority. He faced Phil Perkins, the British Amateur champion, in the final of the US Amateur and crushed him 10 & 9. It was probably no consolation to Perkins that Jones had prevailed in the two previous rounds by 14 & 13 and 13 & 12, because the Englishman's humiliation occurred a mere fortnight after Jones had inflicted a 13 & 12 defeat on him in the top singles at the fifth Walker Cup international, of which more in a moment.

By the end of 1929 Jones had done more than enough to be regarded by posterity as a giant among golfers. Within another 12 months he had established himself as one of the most accomplished sportsmen in history. His Impregnable Quadrilateral in 1930 is the epitome of athletic perfection. It is also truly impregnable. Jones won the British Amateur at St Andrews on 31 May by beating Roger Wethered 7 & 6; lifted the British Open at Hoylake on 20 June, having two shots to spare over his professional compatriots, Leo Diegel and Macdonald Smith; retained his US Open title on 12 July at Interlachen, Minneapolis, with Smith again two strokes in arrears; and finally won his fifth US Amateur on 27 September at Merion, where he had also won his first, by overwhelming Gene Homans 8 & 7 in his last seriously competitive round.

The *New York Times* declared on the morning after Merion that 'Bobby Jones not only became the national Amateur champion for 1930 but the holder of a record that probably will survive through the ages'. That's as safe a wager as betting on the religion of the next Pope. The feat will never be matched; nor, surely, will his performance of beating the field for eight years, and at the highest level, more regularly than it beat him. Byron Nelson did it memorably for one long year in 1945. Ben Hogan did so spasmodically, if gloriously, in the early 1950s. Nobody else, not even Jack Nicklaus, has really come close.

Maintaining this peak drained Jones. On telling his biographer, O. B. Keeler, of his intention to retire, he added: 'I'll never give up golf. I love it too well, and it has meant too much in my life. But it will be an easier and more gracious trail from now on.' The *New York Times* announced the news in November 1930 with the rhyming tribute: 'With dignity he quit the memorable scene on which he nothing common did, or mean.' How true that is. Jones was so brutal with his brilliance that his hapless rivals may have been excused for loathing him. But Jones was deified, not despised. Gene Sarazen once said of partnering Jones in a tournament: 'He made you feel that you were playing with a friend, and you were.'

Jones's win in the British Amateur made him the only man to have a complete collection of all four legs of the Impregnable Quadrilateral. A select few – Harold Hilton, Lawson Little, Arnold Palmer and Jack Nicklaus – have won three. Anyone who suggests that Jones's victories in the two Amateurs cannot be considerd to have the status of those in the Opens need only reflect that in 1926 Jones won both Opens but went down in

The completion of the Impregnable Quadrilateral. The crowd rushes on to the 11th green at Merion after Jones had beaten Gene Homans in the final of the 1930 US Amateur.

The fruits of the Grand Slam. Jones and O. B. Keeler with, from left to right, the trophies of the British Amateur, the Open Championship, the Walker Cup (Jones had captained the United States to victory at Sandwich), the US Open and the US Amateur.

Performers of distinction. Bernard Darwin is on the right of this picture, standing with Paul Hunter of the United States whom he beat by 2 & 1 at Hoylake in the unofficial international of 1921. Darwin is revered as probably the greatest ever golf writer but, as that result showed, he was a fine golfer too. He proved the point again when he defeated William Fownes, the son of the founder of Oakmont, in the first Walker Cup match of 1922. Henry Longhurst (below) was a capable golfer as well, good enough to win the German Amateur in 1936, the same year that he covered Britain's ignominious display in the Walker Cup at Pine Valley. Longhurst, seen here at the 1975 Open, was not only another marvellous writer but also justly renowned for his skilful television commentaries.

both of the major Amateurs. Amateur golf was extraordinarily strong in the 1920s. In the two Amateurs Jones lost in America, his conquerors were an avenging George von Elm in the final of 1926 (you may recall him from the marathon US Open of 1931) and Johnny Goodman in the first round in 1929. Goodman was a rising star who fulfilled his immense potential by winning the US Open in 1933 and the US Amateur in 1937.

It is obvious that, quite apart from Jones, the Americans were then producing amateurs of the highest quality: men who could beat their professional counterparts in the US Open. They could also beat the British, as they have proved repeatedly since the inception of the Walker Cup between the United States and Great Britain in 1922, which is where we left the British scene in those pre-Jones days.

The Walker Cup takes its name from George Herbert Walker, the president of the USGA in 1920. He offered to donate an International Challenge Trophy for a competition involving all countries who wished to send amateur teams to the United States in 1921. Nobody pitched up. Disconcerted but not discouraged, the Americans quickly dispatched an elite eight-man party (it included Jones, Ouimet and Evans) to tackle the British in an international at Hoylake. The visitors won 9–3. Tommy Armour represented the hosts, which is a historical curiosity because, having changed nationalities, he played for the United States at Wentworth in the professionals' match of 1926 which led Sam Ryder to inaugurate his Cup. Armour, on the losing side in both unofficial matches, never actually took part in either the Walker or Ryder Cups.

In the spring of 1922, the R & A announced it would send a team to the United States to contest the Walker Cup. The modest Mr Walker was mortified that his name had been appended to the trophy but at least the event had got off the ground. The rest of the world had blown its chance – the Walker Cup was to be exclusively between the old power and the new.

It has to be said that the old has not done very well. The Americans have won 28 of the 31 meetings. The British and Irish won in 1938 and 1971 – both times at St Andrews – and tied a memorable match at Baltimore in 1965.

As befits an amateur gathering, the Walker Cup is proud of its Olympian ideals. The taking part is what matters. Winning is important too, but the making or missing of a three-foot putt is not relevant to the meaning of life or the whereabouts of the next gin and tonic. Try telling that to the players, of course – they're the ones who sweat over those short putts. But the Walker Cup has admirably maintained its Corinthian flavour, and at times that has been all that has kept it going. Unlike the Ryder Cup, there was no semblance of equality in the results in the early days, and in the modern era there is no natural association with mainland Europe or elsewhere which could justify a strengthening of the British challenge without fundamentally altering the special nature of the event.

THE WALKER CUP

Year	Venue	Winners	Score	
1922	National Golf Links, USA	USA	8	4
1923	St Andrews, Scotland	USA	6½	5½
1924	Garden City, USA	USA	9	3
1926	St Andrews, Scotland	USA	6½	5½
1928	Chicago, USA	USA	11	1
1930	Sandwich, England	USA	10	2
1932	Brookline, USA	USA	9½	2½
1934	St Andrews, Scotland	USA	9½	2½
1936	Pine Valley, USA	USA	10½	1½
1938	St Andrews, Scotland	Britain	7½	4½
1947	St Andrews, Scotland	USA	8	4
1949	Winged Foot, USA	USA	10	2
1951	Birkdale, England	USA	7½	4½
1953	Kittansett Club, USA	USA	9	3
1955	St Andrews, Scotland	USA	10	2
1957	Minikahda, USA	USA	8½	3½
1959	Muirfield, Scotland	USA	9	3
1961	Seattle, USA	USA	11	1
1963	Turnberry, Scotland	USA	14	10
1965	Baltimore, USA	tied	12	12
1967	Sandwich, England	USA	15	9
1969	Milwaukee, USA	USA	13	11
1971	St Andrews, Scotland	Britain	13	11
1973	Brookline, USA	USA	14	10
1975	St Andrews, Scotland	USA	15½	8½
1977	Shinnecock Hills, USA	USA	16	8
1979	Muirfield, Scotland	USA	15½	8½
1981	Cypress Point, USA	USA	15	9
1983	Hoylake, England	USA	13½	10½
1985	Pine Valley, USA	USA	13	11

A familiar sight. The American captain, in this case Bob Gardner (right) in 1923, takes possession of the Walker Cup.

In a burst of enthusiasm, the Walker Cup was initially an annual reunion. It began in 1922 at Charlie Macdonald's National Golf Links, when it featured an unscheduled performance by Bernard Darwin, who had been sent to cover the occasion for *The Times* and found himself playing in place of the indisposed British captain, Robert Harris. Darwin recovered from 3 down after three holes to beat William Fownes in the singles, thus furthering his reputation as the best of all golf writers to one as the best golfer of all golf writers.

The 1923 match at St Andrews provided a reliable indicator of how the British could snatch defeat from the jaws of victory. Willis Mackenzie lost having been 6 up after 14 holes (all matches were over 36 holes) while Roger Wethered and Ernest Holderness halved with Francis Ouimet and lost to Frederick Wright, respectively, despite both having been 2 up with three to play. The upshot of these disasters was that the home team lost 6½–5½, a margin that swelled to 9–3 the following September at Garden City, New York.

The match became a biennial fixture after that, which saved a few Britons from the torture of playing Bobby Jones. Either side of pulverizing Phil Perkins, he beat Cyril Tolley 12 & 11 in 1926 and Wethered 9 & 8 in 1930. Those three, together with Holderness, were the best amateurs in Britain in the 1920s, and yet putting them in with Jones was like sending lambs to the slaughter.

The lambs were well and truly slaughtered at Pine Valley in 1936. They halved three matches and lost the other nine. Without a point to show for his country's endeavours, Henry Longhurst, the famous television commentator and golf correspondent of *The Sunday Times*, observed: 'The British side of the scoreboard looked like a daisy chain, with twelve noughts one beneath the other.' Things could have been still more

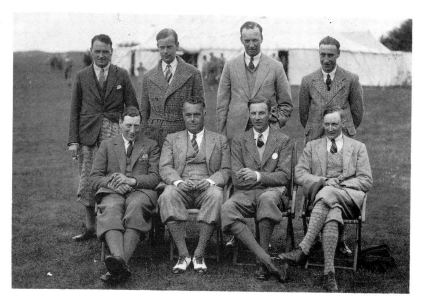

Britain's team for the 1930 Walker Cup at Sandwich. Left to right: (standing) Willie Campbell, Rex Hartley, Jack Stout and John Smith; (seated) Tony Torrance, Cyril Tolley, Roger Wethered and Sir Ernest Holderness. Strong though the British team was, it was no match for the likes of Bobby Jones, George von Elm, Jimmy Johnston and Francis Ouimet. The United States won by 10 points to 2.

THE BRITISH AND UNITED STATES AMATEUR CHAMPIONSHIPS – WINNERS

Year	British	United States	Year	British	United States	Year	British	United States
1885	Allan MacFie	–	1919	No competition	Davey Herron	1955	Joe Conrad (USA)	Harvie Ward
1886	Horace Hutchinson	–	1920	Cyril Tolley	Chick Evans	1956	John Beharrell	Harvie Ward
1887	Horace Hutchinson	–	1921	Willie Hunter	Jesse Guilford	1957	Reid Jack	Hillman Robbins
1888	John Ball	–	1922	Ernest Holderness	Jess Sweetser	1958	Joe Carr (Ire)	Charlie Coe
1889	Johnny Laidlay	–	1923	Roger Wethered	Max Marston	1959	Deane Beman (USA)	Jack Nicklaus
1890	John Ball	–	1924	Ernest Holderness	Bobby Jones	1960	Joe Carr (Ire)	Deane Beman
1891	Johnny Laidlay	–	1925	Robert Harris	Bobby Jones	1961	Michael Bonallack	Jack Nicklaus
1892	John Ball	–	1926	Jess Sweetser (USA)	George von Elm	1962	Richard Davies (USA)	Labron Harris
1893	Peter Anderson	–	1927	Dr William Tweddell	Bobby Jones	1963	Michael Lunt	Deane Beman
1894	John Ball	–	1928	Phil Perkins	Bobby Jones	1964	Gordon Clark	William Campbell
1895	L. Balfour-Melville	Charles Macdonald	1929	Cyril Tolley	Jimmy Johnston	1965	Michael Bonallack	Bob Murphy
1896	Freddie Tait	H. J. Whigham	1930	Bobby Jones (USA)	Bobby Jones	1966	Bobby Cole (SA)	Gary Cowan (Can)
1897	Jack Allan	H. J. Whigham	1931	Eric Martin Smith	Francis Ouimet	1967	Bob Dickson (USA)	Bob Dickson
1898	Freddie Tait	Findlay Douglas	1932	John de Forest	Ross Somerville (Can)	1968	Michael Bonallack	Bruce Fleisher
1899	John Ball	H. M. Harriman	1933	Hon Michael Scott	George Dunlap	1969	Michael Bonallack	Steve Melnyk
1900	Harold Hilton	Walter Travis	1934	Lawson Little (USA)	Lawson Little	1970	Michael Bonallack	Lanny Wadkins
1901	Harold Hilton	Walter Travis	1935	Lawson Little (USA)	Lawson Little	1971	Steve Melnyk (USA)	Gary Cowan (Can)
1902	Charles Hutchings	Louis James	1936	Hector Thomson	Johnny Fischer	1972	Trevor Homer	Vinny Giles
1903	Robert Maxwell	Walter Travis	1937	Robert Sweeny (USA)	Johnny Goodman	1973	Dick Siderowf (USA)	Craig Stadler
1904	Walter Travis (USA)	Chandler Egan	1938	Charlie Yates (USA)	Willie Turnesa	1974	Trevor Homer	Jerry Pate
1905	Gordon Barry	Chandler Egan	1939	Alec Kyle	Bud Ward	1975	Vinny Giles (USA)	Fred Ridley
1906	James Robb	Eben Byers	1940	No competition	Dick Chapman	1976	Dick Siderowf (USA)	Bill Sander
1907	John Ball	Jerome Travers	1941	No competition	Bud Ward	1977	Peter McEvoy	John Fought
1908	E. A. Lassen	Jerome Travers	1942–5	No competition	No competition	1978	Peter McEvoy	John Cook
1909	Robert Maxwell	Bob Gardner	1946	James Bruen (Ire)	Ted Bishop	1979	Jay Sigel (USA)	Mark O'Meara
1910	John Ball	William Fownes	1947	Willie Turnesa (USA)	Skee Riegel	1980	Duncan Evans	Hal Sutton
1911	Harold Hilton	Harold Hilton (GB)	1948	Frank Stranahan (USA)	Willie Turnesa	1981	Philippe Ploujoux (Fr)	Nathaniel Crosby
1912	John Ball	Jerome Travers	1949	Sam McCready	Charlie Coe	1982	Martin Thompson	Jay Sigel
1913	Harold Hilton	Jerome Travers	1950	Frank Stranahan (USA)	Sam Urzetta	1983	Philip Parkin	Jay Sigel
1914	J. L. C. Jenkins	Francis Ouimet	1951	Dick Chapman (USA)	Billy Maxwell	1984	Jose-Maria Olazabal (Sp)	Scott Verplank
1915	No competition	Bob Gardner	1952	Harvie Ward (USA)	Jack Westland	1985	Garth McGimpsey	Sam Randolph
1916	No competition	Chick Evans	1953	Joe Carr (Ire)	Gene Littler	1986	David Curry	Buddy Alexander
1917–8	No competition	No competition	1954	Doug Bachli (Aus)	Arnold Palmer			

Lawson Little, a superb amateur whose subsequent professional career was highlighted by his victory in the 1940 US Open.

embarrassing had Lawson Little not turned pro earlier that year. Little had accomplished the unique feat of winning the British and US Amateurs in both 1934 and 1935; a back-to-back double that not even Jones had achieved. Little's golf at Prestwick in the first of those years was particularly awesome. Aged 23, he destroyed Jack Wallace with a 66 in the morning round of the final, and was one over threes for the five holes in the afternoon. His record winning margin of 14 & 13 was also of Jonesian dimensions and is likely to remain unsurpassed.

To the surprise of most people, the debacle at Pine Valley was followed by a British victory at the tenth attempt in 1938. They won by three points and had the added satisfaction of holding on to the trophy for nine years until the Walker Cup was resumed in 1947. The British hosted it again then because post-war circumstances made it more difficult for them to travel.

The Second World War coincidentally brought down the curtain on the halcyon days of amateur golf, though after it there were several outstanding amateurs – particularly Americans like Bill Campbell, Frank Stranahan, Charlie Coe, Dick Chapman, Willie Turnesa, Harvie Ward and Deane Beman, now the US Tour Commissioner. The latter four won both major Amateurs, and Chapman also took the national titles of Canada, France, Italy and Portugal. Ward, Stranahan and Beman all turned professional eventually, the latter two having limited success on the US Tour after they made the transition.

These seven were not quite in the same class of the professional stars of the day, but several of the young US Amateur champions of the 1950s chose to seek the fast lane to fame and fortune. Some of them found it, notably Gene Littler, Arnold Palmer and Jack Nicklaus (who, as in so many respects, was the exception that proved the rule because he was a threat to the professionals even before he joined them). The route they took has been frequently followed, and if one mentions only Lanny Wadkins, Craig Stadler, Jerry Pate and Hal Sutton, that is because they are the ones who have gone on to lift major professional championships as well.

These days, the standard career path for the promising American player means that if he wins his national Amateur he is already likely to be benefiting from a university sports scholarship,

Scott Verplank, the amateur prodigy who beat the American professionals at their own game before he turned pro in 1986.

during which he will mature with a regular diet of competitive golf. He will probably play in one Walker Cup before turning pro. Scott Verplank, the 1984 US Amateur champion, could be described as a classic case, but he went one better by winning on the US Tour – at the 1985 Western Open – while still at college, the first time an amateur had captured a tour event since 1954. Some leading amateurs, such as Vinny Giles and Jay Sigel who have been champions on both sides of the Atlantic, do not look on their successes as a stepping stone to professionalism and are not tempted by the uncertain riches of life on the circuit, but they are in the minority.

Affairs in Britain, as might be expected, have been less ordered. Instead of the support of a university sports scholarship, many of the best prospects since the Second World War have been dependent on assistance from various voluntary organizations or charitable institutions, such as the Golf Foundation, and encouragement from wealthy individual benefactors like Gerald Micklem. Twice an English Amateur champion and four times a Walker Cup player, Micklem has occupied just about every important post at the R & A except honorary professional. In 1985 he was elected president of Sunningdale, and the choice of the beautiful old

Opposite **Many bright young British golfing prospects since the Second World War have been delighted to come under the watchful eye of Gerald Micklem.**

Joe Carr, from Dublin, won the Amateur Championship three times. Most observers reckon his first title was the most memorable. At Hoylake in 1953 he beat Harvie Ward of the United States, then commonly considered to be the best amateur in the world. Here Ward watches Carr get a drive away in the final, which he won 2 up.

Opposite
Congratulations from the captain. Michael Bonallack (right) with Dr David Marsh after the latter had secured Britain's victory in the Walker Cup at St Andrews in 1971.

Berkshire course as the first inland club in Britain to host the Walker Cup in 1987 was a tremendous thrill for him.

Micklem has rendered sterling service to the R & A for many years, and the R & A's present secretary did as much for British golf in the 1960s and 1970s. Michael Bonallack succeeded Ireland's Joe Carr, who won the Amateur Championship three times, as the foremost amateur in the British Isles. He established a record which would justify a less unassuming personality to claim himself to be the world's best post-war amateur, certainly of those who never became professionals.

He won the British Amateur on his five appearances in the final: in 1961, 1965 and 1968–70. That last flourish made him the only man to achieve a hat-trick of victories in either of the two main Amateurs. Like Little in the 1930s, he could boast of something Jones would have been proud of but had not accomplished. Bonallack also collected nine English Amateur titles at either matchplay or strokeplay. These included the comprehensive demolition of David Kelley by 12 & 11 in the final at Ganton in 1968 when he shot a 61, with just two tiny putts conceded, in the morning round. His striking that day was as repetitive as it was accurate. The quality of his putting was underlined by the fact that he did not miss once from inside four yards.

Bonallack was naturally in both Walker Cup teams that avoided defeat in the period he was at the top. In 1965 the British had seemed certain to clinch a momentous victory at Five Farms, but needing just two points from eight in the second

series of singles (18-hole matches had been introduced in 1963) they could manage only 1½. It was left to Clive Clark, now the BBC's roving reporter on the fairways, to square the contest by holing from 35 feet on the last green. Six years later Bonallack was the captain when Britain won six singles on the second afternoon to turn the tide in improbably dramatic fashion at St Andrews. Victory was secured when David Marsh found the heart of the treacherous 17th green with a 3-iron to go to dormie-1 up on Bill Hyndman. In a sequence which was wholly out of keeping with precedent, the British won all four singles that went to the 18th.

Americans continued to plunder the British Amateur even with Bonallack as guardian in residence. Among them, in 1967, was Bob Dickson. A few months later he earned himself a place in the exalted company of Hilton, Jones and Little by adding the US Amateur, which in an ill-fated experiment was conducted as a 72-hole strokeplay tournament from 1965 until it reverted to the traditional amateur game of matchplay in 1973.

Steve Melnyk lifted the British Amateur in 1971, two years after taking the American title. Another American, Dick Siderowf, won the British Amateur twice in the 1970s, as did two Englishmen, Trevor Homer and Peter McEvoy. The former suffered

cruelly in a brief, impecunious career as a professional, whereas McEvoy has remained loyal to the amateur game.

When Philip Parkin won in 1983, he became only the second Briton for 60 years (the other was Michael Lunt in 1963) to win the Amateur against the might of the American Walker Cup squad. That augured well for his inevitable move into the professional game, but of greater significance for golf in general was the nationality of his successor.

Jose-Maria Olazabal from Spain won the 1984 Amateur at Formby. That was the meat in a sandwich which was started with victory in the British Boys' Championship in 1983 and topped off with the British Youths' in 1985. In its own way that too, in a chapter littered with outstanding achievements, is something likely to remain in the record books. Olazabal was denied by three years the privilege of being the first continental winner of amateur golf's oldest championship – Philippe Ploujoux of France secured the honour at St Andrews in 1981 – but the Spaniard's stunning rookie season as a pro in 1986 emphasized that the Americans and the British no longer have the show to themselves.

This has been demonstrated in the World Amateur Team Championship, contested in the even-numbered years for the Eisenhower Trophy which was offered by the late American president 'To foster friendship and sportsmanship among the Peoples of the World'. It was put up at the instigation of the USGA and is operated jointly with the R & A. It was launched in 1958 and the Americans won it for the first of nine times in 1960 when Jack Nicklaus, who bestrode the amateur scene like a colossus for three seasons, burned up Merion (and how often that illustrious name appears in these pages!) in a total of 269 strokes. The format calls for four rounds of strokeplay for four-man teams, the best three scores each day to count. That usually plays into the hands of the United States, but the Australians have won twice, including 1958 when they beat the Americans in a play-off, and so has Great Britain, in 1976 thanks to Ian Hutcheon playing the last eight holes in four under par at Penina in Portugal.

The cosmopolitan character of the Eisenhower Trophy was underlined in 1982 when the Swedes finished runners-up to the United States with a team which forms the nucleus of their current professional strength. Japan won two years later and Canada took over in 1986, pushing the

Philippe Ploujoux, the first player from continental Europe to win either of golf's two major amateur championships. The key to his surprising success in 1981 lay in his mastery of St Andrews's huge double greens.

Americans into second place with a team which ironically included three players at American colleges. Canada apart, there were superb displays by individuals from a wide variety of countries, and if they too – like Britons such as Philip Parkin – have gained experience from their time at university in the United States, that is all to the good for the growth of the game around the world.

However, just as there is a huge difference between that calibre of player and the average club golfer, so there is a great gulf between the top level of the amateur game and the professional ranks. Some of the men discussed here have bridged the gap, others could have, but many make the move without realistically assessing their chances – no doubt often driven in the search for money by rules which mean that as amateurs they are not allowed to win cash or receive anything worth more than a set of golf clubs. More frequently they will get another toaster, a 27th kettle, or something similar. By forfeiting their amateur status to turn pro, the ultimately unsuccessful ones are consigning themselves to an uncertain future, dependent on the mercy of the R & A or USGA for reinstatement or else existing in the awful limbo of being neither professional nor amateur: simply a non-amateur.

Many golfers have learned what a tough transition that is to attempt. But then as an amateur it's not easy keeping up with the Joneses.

CHAPTER TWELVE

The Ladies: Belles of the Ball

Women golfers in Britain will not protest about the allocation of just one chapter out of 16 in this book to the distaff side of the game. They won't allege chauvinism or even ungallantry. They will acknowledge instead that it represents greater recognition than they are normally accorded.

British golf clubs have a reputation for treating women as they do domestic pets or soiled shoes. 'No dogs allowed' and 'No spikes in the bar' are common enough signs, and so are restrictions which order – in the best exaggerated traditions of apocryphal tales – 'No women on the course except after dark'.

Although no club has ever gone quite that far (surely?), the members who champion such forms of petty discrimination would not hear of women being given the same rights of access to the course as men if they paid the full subscription, rather than a reduced fee as is customary. They refuse to come to terms with the astonishing fact that some women now work in the week and haven't got time to participate in Ladies' Day, which is usually not a full day at all but a mid-week afternoon.

The use of the word 'Ladies' is widespread in golf clubs but it is generally patronizing rather than polite, as is the reasoning behind the absurd rules which permit men to wear golf gear in their own bar but prohibit it in the mixed. The only defence for insisting that men wear a tie, cravat or polo-neck sweater in mixed company is that someone somewhere down the line has objected to the prospect of women seeing anything as potentially offensive as a man's bare throat. The truth is that they are considerably more likely to be horrified at some of the ghastly colour combinations contrived by the men in their futile attempts to dress smartly: an ensemble of brown trousers, blue shirt, green tie and grey jacket perhaps.

It must be stressed that some clubs have adopted a significantly more enlightened attitude than the scenario depicted here, and recently a handful of women have been appointed female professionals at British golf clubs. Twenty years ago that would have been as preposterous an idea as a woman Prime Minister. It was just over 20 years ago, at the 1965 Ladies' British Open Amateur Championship (hereinafter referred to as the British Amateur) at St Andrews, that there occurred one of the most celebrated anecdotes in the long line of humiliations suffered by women golfers. A group of competitors were huddled in front of the R & A clubhouse (which was then, but is no longer, distinctly out-of-bounds to women), sheltering under their umbrellas from a dreadful storm, when a club official approached them. Their immediate hopes that he was about to do the decent thing and invite them in were cruelly dashed when instead he asked them to lower their brollies because they were spoiling the view of the Old Course enjoyed by the members, comfortably ensconced in the lounge.

It is, of course, a serious chap who does not have to suppress a chuckle at this story. Women may find it harder to laugh.

If some clubs treat women as not so much second-class citizens as a sub-species, it has to be said that the Ladies' Golf Union (LGU), the governing body in the British Isles, has not pleased many of its own members with its controversial decisions to take the 1984 Curtis Cup (the women's equivalent of the Walker Cup, between amateur golfers of Great Britain & Ireland and the United States) to Muirfield, and the 1988 clash to Royal St George's at Sandwich. Neither club allows women members, nor does the R & A. The neat circular argument in respect of the latter is that there are no women among the membership because there are no appropriate bathroom facilities for them; the reason there are none is that there are no women members to justify their installation.

The obvious rejoinder to those who complain at this kind of sexual apartheid is to suggest that women should form their own clubs if they don't like the way men run them. Some have. For instance, today England has separate ladies' clubs – as opposed to the usual ladies' sections – at Sunningdale, Formby and the Wirral. One of the pioneering British women professionals, Vivien Saunders, went one better in 1986 by buying her own club in Cambridgeshire. It is not female-only.

In the United States, golf began as a pastime in which the sexes were regarded as socially compatible. The few exclusively male clubs were coloquially called 'Eveless Edens'; most of the rest were country clubs and as such welcomed the family as a group. Nowadays there are several male-only American clubs where women are not allowed beyond the gates, much less into the clubhouse or on to the course. These include some of the best in the nation, as one poor woman discovered when she tried to match her husband's feat of playing the 100 top courses in the country as listed by the monthly magazine *Golf Digest*, the world's largest selling golf publication. Three of the clubs do not permit women to play, whatever the circumstances, and the most significant threat to the continued existence of these institutions as sanctuaries of male secrecy has not been the repeated complaints of ardent feminists but the prospect of withdrawal of their private club tax concessions.

Across a rather shorter stretch of water from the British Isles, golf on the continent is free of sexual prejudice, perhaps a relic of its aristocratic roots. But then in Britain the female game could scarcely have had a more distinguished role-model in its early days than Mary Queen of Scots, although she was not entirely an enviable example. She failed to survive the cut after being espied playing golf within 24 hours of the sudden death of her husband in 1567.

During the subsequent 300 years there were desultory references to women playing golf. The townsfolk of Musselburgh, near Edinburgh, were enthusiasts, and a Fish Wives' Society was formed there in the late 18th century. In the first part of the 19th century, women also played at St Andrews, although they risked being branded as near-harlots. One Miss A. M. Stewart later wrote: 'A damsel with even one modest putter in her hand was labelled a fast and almost disreputable person, definitely one to be avoided.' Try telling that to the Lady Captain!

Three centuries after Mary Queen of Scots lifted her head for the last time, the first ladies'

golf clubs were founded, at St Andrews in Scotland and, on 8 June 1868, in the south-west of England. The Westward Ho! and North Devon Ladies' Club had 47 full members (ladies) and 23 associates (men). The women had their own nine-hole course separate from the men and play was restricted to 'every other Saturday between 1st May and 31st October', a regulation which is often retained in spirit today.

One of the first ladies' golf clubs was the Westward Ho! and North Devon Ladies' Club, founded in 1868.

Long skirts and elegant coiffures were part of the female game in the last century, as this invitation makes clear.

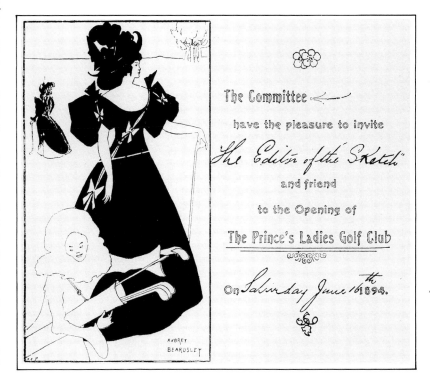

It is probable that Scottish women played a similar course to the men. Their English counterparts at Westward Ho! pursued a shorter form of the game; so short that it was considered reasonable to invoke a rule whereby a wooden putter was the only club allowed on the links. This tied in with the contemporary mores governing the way women played golf, as exemplified by Horace Hutchinson.

'We venture to suggest 70 or 80 yards as the average limit of a drive advisedly; not because we doubt a lady's power to make a longer drive but because that cannot well be done without raising the club above the shoulder. Now we do not presume to dictate, but we must observe that the posture and gestures requisite for a full swing are not particularly graceful when the player is clad in female dress.'

Despite this sort of overzealous anxiety for the ladies' welfare, which caused several clubs to limit their activities to the putting green, by 1900 there were about 130 women's golf clubs. One might guess from the comments of Hutchinson and Miss Stewart that women golfers wandered around like floozies. In fact, it was customary for them to be not so much dressed as bedecked. Restricted by the 19th-century corsets and girdles, and clad in a long dress which ensured that no man would glimpse anything of her flesh other than her face and hands, it was a wonder that a lady golfer could play a half pitch, let alone execute a full swing.

I shall return to the subject of changing fashions later, but it is pertinent here to remark on the privileged background which nurtured women's golf in England around the turn of the century. It was in such genteel surroundings that the movement for the enfranchisement of women was born and flourished, and golf did not escape the consequences of the bid for emancipation. Nobody sought martyrdom from the impact of Harry Vardon's follow-through in the way Emily Davison did when she threw herself under the King's horse at the Derby, but just down the road from Epsom racecourse a band of suffragettes did attempt to debag the Prime Minister, David Lloyd George, while he was playing at Walton Heath.

It was at Walton Heath in 1910 that a more conventional blow was struck for lady golfers. Cecilia (Cecil) Leitch, the young heroine of pre-war British women's golf, faced Harold Hilton in a 72-hole challenge match at Walton Heath and Sunningdale. Both players drove from the men's tees, but the fact that Miss Leitch was compensated for her relative lack of length by receiving a stroke every other hole from the great man did not detract from the delight of her vast throng of noisy supporters when she edged home by 2 & 1.

Three of the early heroines of women's amateur golf. Left to right: Lady Margaret Scott and May Hezlet, both three-time winners of the British title; and Dorothy Campbell (later Hurd), the first of only three players to win the British and American Ladies' Amateurs in the same year.

Miss Leitch won the first of her four British Amateurs in 1914. The tournament, like its male equivalent, was contested at matchplay. It had begun in 1893, the year the LGU was created by the members of Wimbledon Ladies' Club with the aims of holding a championship, promoting women's golf and establishing a handicapping system suitable for women. That first Ladies' Amateur was appropriately won by a lady: Lady Margaret Scott, whose title accurately indicates that she was not from a deprived family. In fact, her father had a course laid out in his private park.

Lady Margaret won the first three championships before suddenly retiring. The next dominant figure was May Hezlet, one of three talented Irish sisters, who became champion in 1899 at the age of 17. She won twice more, including 1907 when she defeated her sister Florence in the final, and was beaten at the last hurdle in 1904 by the irrepressible Lottie Dod, who had got tired of winning the Wimbledon Tennis Championships every year and so turned to golf in search of another sport to conquer.

Dorothy Campbell from North Berwick went over to the United States in 1909 following her triumph at Birkdale and became the first woman to win the British and US Amateurs in the same year. The American version had been inaugurated in 1895, the same year as its male counterpart. The first native female golfing star in the United States

was Alexa Stirling (a childhood friend of Bobby Jones), who won the American crown in 1916, 1919 and 1920, a sequence interrupted only by the First World War. In Britain Cecil Leitch did likewise, winning in 1914, 1920 and 1921, and she also collected the English Ladies' Amateur Championship in 1914 and 1919. She was an inspiration and something of an idol to her fans, who had never before seen a woman give the ball such a mighty thwack. The war cost her several opportunities to add to her considerable achievements, and when that was over Joyce Wethered cost her several more.

Cecil Leitch looks on as the great amateur, Harold Hilton, endeavours to sink a putt during their famous 'Battle of the Sexes' Challenge Match at Walton Heath in 1910.

Cecil Leitch (centre) with daintily dressed colleagues at Le Touquet in 1920 during the French Ladies' Championship.

Joyce Wethered. Her swing combined power with grace and, allied to a marvellously unflappable temperament, it made her one of the greatest golfers – man or woman – in history.

Opposite **Two of the finest women amateurs ever produced in the United States – Alexa Stirling (left), a childhood friend of Bobby Jones and winner of three successive American Amateurs, and Glenna Collett (later Vare), who emulated Miss Stirling's hat-trick of victories and went on to win her national title six times.**

Leitch, Miss Wethered is the only person to win the British Amateur four times. Their clashes in the 1920s popularized women's golf in Britain, and not just among women.

They met in five major finals. Miss Wethered won in three – at the 1920 English Amateur at Sheringham, despite having stood 6 down at one stage of the afternoon round, and in the British Amateurs of 1922 and 1925. Miss Leitch countered with both the British and French titles in 1921.

The 1920 English Amateur was the first remotely important competition Joyce Wethered entered. She had learned the game at Dornoch in the north of Scotland and had been driven on by the exhortations of her brother, Roger, himself a fine amateur golfer. Following her success in 1920, Miss Wethered participated in each of the next four English Amateurs and won the lot. From 1921 to 1925 she played in the British Amateur five times and was victorious on three occasions, twice when her last opponent was Miss Leitch. In 1922 they went into lunch all-square but Miss Wethered was rampant in the afternoon and by the 11th it was all over. Three years later, an epic enounter remained in the balance until Miss Leitch bowed the knee at the 37th.

With a record of eight wins and two seconds from 11 championship appearances, Miss

Miss Wethered brought an altogether more elegant action to the game, but the grace and fluidity of her swing belied a tremendous power generated by her easy rhythm and wide arc. Henry Cotton and Walter Hagen both paid effusive tributes to the quality of her play. Bobby Jones called her simply the best golfer, man or woman, he had ever seen – one in the eye indeed for male chauvinists. That's like Shakespeare saying someone could have made a better job of *Hamlet* than he did.

Joyce Wethered is, more than any other golfer of either sex, worthy of being compared with Jones. She too was a true amateur. Like him she displayed unfailing sportsmanship and warmth on and off the course and, had she been less modest, she could have pointed to her fantastic record of winning more often than she lost. It is to the credit of Cecil Leitch, who was the senior by 10 years, that she could consolidate her own reputation when her prime coincided with that of such a formidable adversary. Apart from Miss

The end of the morning round in the final of the 1929 British Ladies' Championship. This was the middle point of Miss Wethered's tremendous recovery against the American champion, Glenna Collett, in what is commonly regarded as the finest women's match ever played.

Wethered retired. She returned just once, for the 1929 British Amateur – largely because it was held at St Andrews – and made her way to the final. There she met Glenna Collett, the reigning American champion who had already won her national title in 1922 and 1925 and was by then embarked on a hat-trick of wins from 1928 to 1930. Miss Wethered was 5 down after nine holes but she rallied splendidly to cover the next 18 in 73 strokes in an era when 80 was acknowledged to be an excellent tournament score for even a top woman player. As she left the 9th green in the afternoon Miss Wethered was 3 up, and she held on to win by 3 & 1.

Two anecdotes concerning Miss Wethered are legendary. She is the source of the famous phrase 'What train?', a remark she made after journalists at the 1920 English final enquired if her concentration had been disturbed by a passing locomotive as she was putting on Sheringham's 17th green. And then there is the tale of the postman patrolling the streets of St Andrews in 1929, gloomily relaying the news 'She's five doon' as Miss Wethered reached her lowest point in the match against Glenna Collett. Of course, there weren't many folk listening. Most of the town was out watching.

Joyce Wethered's defeat of Miss Collett emphasized her pre-eminence in the game. In the words of Charley Price: 'She did not have to play in America to convince the Americans that she was perhaps the best female golfer who ever lived.' Miss Collett was the queen of the American scene and, following her marriage, she went on to collect a record sixth US Amateur under the name of Glenna Collett Vare. She lost twice in the final as well, once to Virginia van Wie, who emulated the hat-tricks of Mrs Vare, Alexa Stirling and Beatrix Hoyt by completing one of her own between 1932 and 1934.

There was no second comeback for Miss Wethered, assuming one discounts her regular subsequent appearances in the friendly ambience of the Worplesdon Mixed Foursomes, which she won a record eight times between 1922 and 1936. Her glittering career was conducted at the same time as Bobby Jones was establishing his place among golf's immortals and even in retirement the parallel between the two was maintained. Both quit at the age of 28. Both forfeited their amateur status in the 1930s to allow them, independently, to reap material gain from their reputations, though neither had any intention of competing as a professional. Miss Wethered, who took the title Lady Heathcoat-Amory on her marriage in 1937, was reinstated as an amateur after the Second World War. It was only fitting that she was. There will never be another amateur to match her or Jones.

But women's amateur golf in Britain did not wither without Wethered. Enid Wilson annexed the British Amateur from 1931 to 1933. Helen Holm managed to fit in a couple of wins before the war, as did Pam Barton. In 1936, aged 19, the latter repeated the performance of Dorothy Campbell (who, as Mrs Hurd, had won a third American title in 1924) by winning the British and US Amateurs in the same season. Tragically, she lost her life in a plane crash while serving in the WRAF. Jessie Anderson (later Valentine) succeeded Miss Barton in 1937 and won for a third time in 1958.

It was during the 1930s that the Curtis Cup matches between the two nations were started. The countries had met sporadically in friendly matches since 1905. Two of the Americans who took part in that first meeting at Cromer, in England, were the sisters Harriot and Margaret Curtis, later to be US Amateur champions once and three times respectively. They offered a cup to the USGA 'To stimulate friendly rivalry between the women golfers of many lands'. As with the Walker Cup, it actually started as Great Britain & Ireland versus the United States, and that is the way it has stayed.

Until 1986, the analogy with the Walker Cup could be as closely pursued to results as to origins. Of the 23 contests between 1932 and 1984, the Americans won 19. They lost twice in Britain,

THE CURTIS CUP

Year	Venue	Winners	Score	
1932	Wentworth, England	USA	5½	3½
1934	Chevy Chase, USA	USA	6½	2½
1936	Gleneagles, Scotland	tied	4½	4½
1938	Essex, USA	USA	5½	3½
1948	Birkdale, England	USA	6½	2½
1950	Buffalo, USA	USA	7½	1½
1952	Muirfield, Scotland	Britain	5	4
1954	Merion, USA	USA	6	3
1956	Prince's, England	Britain	5	4
1958	Brae Burn, USA	tied	4½	4½
1960	Lindrick, England	USA	6½	2½
1962	Broadmoor, USA	USA	8	1
1964	Porthcawl, Wales	USA	10½	7½
1966	Cascades, USA	USA	13	5
1968	R. County Down, NI	USA	10½	7½
1970	Brae Burn, USA	USA	11½	6½
1972	Western Gailes, Scotland	USA	10	8
1974	San Francisco, USA	USA	13	5
1976	Lytham, England	USA	11½	6½
1978	Apawamis, USA	USA	12	6
1980	St Pierre, Wales	USA	13	5
1982	Denver, USA	USA	14½	3½
1984	Muirfield, Scotland	USA	9½	8½
1986	Prairie Dunes, USA	Britain	13	5

tied once in their own country and – by way of a bonus for the British compared with their Walker Cup compatriots – there was also a tied match in Scotland.

The British lost the first match at Wentworth in 1932 by 5½ points to 3½, despite having Joyce Wethered, Enid Wilson, Wanda Morgan and Diana Fishwick in their line-up. Miss Wethered reaffirmed her status as the world's best woman golfer of the day by hammering Mrs Vare 6 & 4 in the top singles, but she and her colleagues could not overcome the burden of losing all three foursomes.

In 1936 the home team grabbed a share of the spoils at Gleneagles, thanks to Jessie Anderson sinking a putt of 20 feet on the last green of the match, but it wasn't until the seventh fixture, at Muirfield in 1952, that the British won; Elizabeth Price securing the crucial point. The 5–4 margin was repeated at Prince's four years later when Frances (Bunty) Smith made a five at the final hole to Polly Riley's six. To complete a decade of unparalleled joy for a British team against the Americans, the visitors retained the trophy with a tie in Massachusetts in 1958. Again the principals in the concluding drama were Mrs Smith and Miss Riley, and again the former was triumphant. Needing to halve the last to secure the tie, she won it.

It may seem that British successes have been overemphasized here, but American victories

The host team for the Curtis Cup match at Gleneagles in 1936. Jessie Anderson (later Valentine), who is standing on the extreme right of the photograph, holed from 20 feet on the last green to enable the British to secure a half. Other notable names shown here include Pam Barton (standing second from the left); Helen Holm (next to her); Doris Chambers (seated centre); and Wanda Morgan (seated on the right).

were the norm and hence hardly noteworthy. They won every encounter from 1960 to 1984, sometimes narrowly but usually with a great deal in hand. Then in 1986, in perhaps the biggest shock in amateur golf since Jones lost in the first round of the 1929 US Amateur, the British and Irish won in the fatiguing heat and humidity of a Kansan August with a team of reputed has-beens and no-hopers. Under the captaincy of Diane Bailey, they annihilated the Americans 13–5, an achievement put into its proper historical context when one considers that it was the first time the United States had ever lost a Ryder, Walker or Curtis Cup match on home soil.

Though the British relished their period of dominance in the 1950s, with the likes of Bunty Smith, Jessie Valentine, Elizabeth Price and Ireland's Philomena Garvey to the fore, it was by then doubtful that the leading women amateurs were any longer *per se* the leading women golfers. In America, women – no doubt to the posthumous chagrin and astonishment of Horace Hutchinson – were playing professional golf, and doing it very well.

The stage was set by Miss Mildred Didrikson, better known as Mrs 'Babe' Zaharias. As a 19-year-old athlete, she smashed world records and won two track-and-field gold medals at the 1932 Olympic Games. She then took up golf and was the nearest thing the women's game has had to a natural, to a Sam Snead. She drove the ball immense distances, and when asked how a woman of 5ft 7ins and weighing 10 stone could find such power, she would reply, in an answer guaranteed to have Hutchinson wincing as he rotated in his grave, 'I just hitch up my girdle and let it rip.' She made money by touring the country with top men professionals, demonstrating those booming tee shots. This made her a professional in the eyes of the USGA, but in 1944, having learned that there is more to golf than hitting the ball 250 yards or so, she was reinstated as an amateur.

The Babe wasted no time in making her mark. She won the US Amateur in 1946, and in 1947 at Gullane she became the first American to take home the British title. She then turned pro once more – this time properly, so to speak – and won 31 American tournaments, including the US Women's Open in 1948, 1950 and 1954. She won the latter by 12 strokes, and sadly it proved to be her epitaph. She never defended the championship. Her victory was a remarkable accomplishment because she had undergone cancer surgery the previous year. A recurrence of

The free-flowing, uninhibited action of Babe Zaharias, on her way to the British Ladies' title in 1947.

the illness prevented her from competing in the Open again and she died in 1956.

The US Women's Open is now the most prestigious championship in ladies' golf. It was first held in 1946 under the auspices of the fledgling Women's PGA of America. Though the Open ran continuously, the WPGA had a chequered five-year existence from 1944 to 1948. The moribund body was revived in 1950 under the banner of the Ladies' PGA, and the transmogrification from women to ladies apparently did the trick. Since it was chartered in 1950, the LPGA has expanded from an initial membership of 11 to some 275 tournament professionals. Purses have rocketed too, despite a serious financial hiccup in the mid-1970s. Commissioner John Laupheimer arranged a tour worth in excess of $10 million in 1986, compared with the $45,000 the father of the circuit, Fred Corcoran, rustled up in 1950.

The leading lights of the tour in its formative years, and the women who virtually played pass the parcel with the US Open trophy, were Zaharias, Patty Berg, Betty Jameson and Louise Suggs – all previous winners of the American Amateur Championship. A fifth figure, Betsy Rawls, won the Open in 1951 and then twice more in 1953 and 1957. Her second and third

THE MAJOR LADIES' CHAMPIONSHIPS – WINNERS

Year	British Amateur	US Amateur
1893	Lady Margaret Scott	–
1894	Lady Margaret Scott	–
1895	Lady Margaret Scott	Mrs C. S. Brown
1896	Amy Pascoe	Beatrix Hoyt
1897	Edith O. Orr	Beatrix Hoyt
1898	Miss L. Thomson	Beatrix Hoyt
1899	May Hezlet	Ruth Underhill
1900	Rhona Adair	Frances Griscom
1901	Miss Graham	Genevieve Hecker
1902	May Hezlet	Genevieve Hecker
1903	Rhona Adair	Bessie Anthony
1904	Lottie Dod	Georgianna Bishop
1905	Miss B. Thompson	Pauline Mackay
1906	Mrs Kennion	Harriot Curtis
1907	May Hezlet	Margaret Curtis
1908	Miss M. Titterton	Kate Harley
1909	Dorothy Campbell	Dorothy Campbell (GB)
1910	Grant Suttie	Dorothy Campbell (GB)
1911	Dorothy Campbell	Margaret Curtis
1912	Gladys Ravenscroft	Margaret Curtis
1913	Muriel Dodd	Gladys Ravenscroft (GB)
1914	Cecil Leitch	Kate Harley Jackson
1915	No competition	Mrs C. H. Vanderbeck
1916	No competition	Alexa Stirling
1917–8	No competition	No competition
1919	No competition	Alexa Stirling
1920	Cecil Leitch	Alexa Stirling
1921	Cecil Leitch	Marion Hollins
1922	Joyce Wethered	Glenna Collett
1923	Doris Chambers	Edith Cummings
1924	Joyce Wethered	Dorothy Campbell Hurd (GB)
1925	Joyce Wethered	Glenna Collett
1926	Cecil Leitch	Helen Stetson
1927	Thion de la Chaume (Fr)	Miriam Burns Horn
1928	Nanette Le Blan (Fr)	Glenna Collett
1929	Joyce Wethered	Glenna Collett
1930	Diana Fishwick	Glenna Collett
1931	Enid Wilson	Helen Hicks
1932	Enid Wilson	Virginia Van Wie
1933	Enid Wilson	Virginia Van Wie
1934	Helen Holm	Virginia Van Wie
1935	Wanda Morgan	Glenna Collett Vare
1936	Pam Barton	Pam Barton (GB)
1937	Jessie Anderson	Mrs Julius Page
1938	Helen Holm	Patty Berg
1939	Pam Barton	Betty Jameson
1940	No competition	Betty Jameson
1941	No competition	Elizabeth Hicks Newell
1942–5	No competition	No competition

Year	British Amateur	US Amateur	US Open
1946	Jean Hetherington	Babe Zaharias	Patty Berg
1947	Babe Zaharias (USA)	Louise Suggs	Betty Jameson
1948	Louise Suggs (USA)	Grace Lenczyk	Babe Zaharias
1949	Frances Stephens	Dorothy Germain Porter	Louise Suggs
1950	V'tesse de St Sauveur (Fr)	Beverly Hanson	Babe Zaharias
1951	Mrs P. G. MacCann	Dorothy Kirby	Betsy Rawls
1952	Moira Paterson	Jacqueline Pung	Louise Suggs
1953	Marlene Stewart (Can)	Mary Lena Faulk	Betsy Rawls
1954	Frances Stephens	Barbara Romack	Babe Zaharias
1955	Jessie Anderson Valentine	Patricia Lesser	Fay Crocker
1956	Margaret Smith	Marlene Stewart (Can)	Kathy Cornelius
1957	Philomena Garvey	JoAnne Gunderson	Betsy Rawls
1958	Jessie Anderson Valentine	Anne Quast	Mickey Wright
1959	Elizabeth Price	Barbara McIntire	Mickey Wright
1960	Barbara McIntire (USA)	JoAnne Gunderson	Betsy Rawls
1961	Marley Spearman	Anne Quast Decker	Mickey Wright
1962	Marley Spearman	JoAnne Gunderson	Murle Lindstrom
1963	Brigitte Varangot (Fr)	Anne Quast Welts	Mary Mills
1964	Carol Sorenson (USA)	Barbara McIntire	Mickey Wright
1965	Brigitte Varangot (Fr)	Jean Ashley	Carol Mann
1966	Elizabeth Chadwick	JoAnne Gunderson Carner	Sandra Spuzich
1967	Elizabeth Chadwick	Mary Lou Dill	Catherine Lacoste (Fr)
1968	Brigitte Varangot (Fr)	JoAnne Gunderson Carner	Susie Berning
1969	Catherine Lacoste (Fr)	Catherine Lacoste (Fr)	Donna Caponi
1970	Dinah Oxley	Martha Wilkinson	Donna Caponi
1971	Mickey Walker	Laura Baugh	JoAnne Gunderson Carner
1972	Mickey Walker	Mary Anne Budke	Susie Berning
1973	Ann Irvin	Carol Semple	Susie Berning
1974	Carol Semple (USA)	Cynthia Hill	Sandra Haynie
1975	Nancy Syms (USA)	Beth Daniel	Sandra Palmer
1976	Cathy Panton	Donna Horton	JoAnne Gunderson Carner
1977	Angela Uzielli	Beth Daniel	Hollis Stacy
1978	Edwina Kennedy (Aus)	Cathy Sherk	Hollis Stacy
1979	Maureen Madill	Carolyn Hill	Jerilyn Britz
1980	Anne Quast Sander (USA)	Juli Inkster	Amy Alcott
1981	Belle Robertson	Juli Inkster	Pat Bradley
1982	Kitrina Douglas	Juli Inkster	Janet Alex
1983	Jill Thornhill	Joanne Pacillo	Jan Stephenson (Aus)
1984	Jody Rosenthal (USA)	Deb Richard	Hollis Stacy
1985	Lillian Behan (Ire)	Michiko Hattori (Jap)	Kathy Baker
1986	Marnie McGuire (NZ)	Kay Cockerill	Jane Geddes

victories were especially painful for Jacqui Pung from Honolulu.

The Hawaiian golfer had won the US Amateur in 1952. The following June, having joined the professionals, she was decisively beaten by Rawls in a play-off for the Open in the first season it was administered by the USGA. But Pung appeared to have gained her revenge four years later when she handed in a card for 298 to pip Rawls by a stroke at Winged Foot. Soon after Pung returned her score, it was discovered that she had signed for a five on a hole where she had actually had a six.

She had attested to the correct total but had not checked the arithmetic. Whereas 11 years later Roberto de Vicenzo would deny himself the chance of a Masters play-off by signing for a *higher* score than he had taken, Pung was disqualified for her offence. She had won – and then she hadn't. She had finished first – and suddenly she had finished nowhere. The members of the host club organized a whip-round and raised $3000 for her; $1200 more than the first prize. It was a marvellous gesture but little consolation.

In 1960 Betsy Rawls added a fourth Open

medal to her collection, a tally since equalled by Mary Kathryn (Mickey) Wright. Just as Joyce Wethered was the greatest amateur to grace women's golf, and Babe Zaharias the perfect link between the two codes, so Mickey Wright is arguably the finest professional the female game has ever produced.

Her first US Open was, coincidentally, Zaharias's last, and the two were paired for the last day's double round in 1954. Wright turned pro the next season and from 1956, when she won her first LPGA event, until 1969 she won 81 tournaments. She notched up her 82nd triumph in 1973. Kathy Whitworth has since passed this total of career victories, and in the process become the 'winningest' professional in the history of American golf, but she has never matched the stranglehold that Wright had on her contemporaries. One might, mindful of an even more powerful grip exerted on the men's tour in the 1940s, say that Wright held her rivals in a half-Nelson.

A select sample of her records amply illustrates the point. In five years from 1960 she won 50 of the 130 tournaments she entered; twice in her career she won four back-to-back victories; in six seasons she was the leading tournament winner; five times she received the Vare Trophy for the lowest stroke average; on four occasions she headed the Money List. In 1963 she won 13 tournaments, and the 62 she shot in the 1964 Tall City Open has never been bettered.

She won four US Opens, four LPGA Championships, three Western Opens and two Titleholders' Championships. These constituted the four legs of the women's Grand Slam, giving her 13 major championships, one more than Patty Berg. Wright won three of the four majors in 1961, but Zaharias had gone one better by winning the only three on offer in 1950. Sandra Haynie later took the Open and LPGA Championships in 1974 during a period when the two other majors had fallen by the wayside.

As this lack of continuity suggests, the concept of the female Grand Slam carries less kudos than it does for the men. This is borne out by the fact that the Western and Titleholders' events have now been replaced by the Nabisco Dinah Shore tournament and the du Maurier Classic. These were recently accorded their exalted rating with retrospective effect and it has to be said that commercially sponsored majors do not have quite the same ring of authenticity.

It is also a curious fact that so many of the stars

of the women's game have never captured the crown they covet most – the US Open. Whitworth is one who has missed out; and so too, among others, have Judy Rankin, Nancy Lopez, Beth Daniel, Betsy King and Patty Sheehan. Since Wright's heyday, the tradition of multiple winners has been maintained: Susie Berning and Hollis Stacy three times each, and Donna Caponi and JoAnne Carner (née Gunderson) twice. The latter deserves far more extensive treatment than

Above left Mickey Wright, who dominated the LPGA Tour in the 1960s to the extent that she can justifiably be acclaimed as perhaps the best woman professional ever to play the game.

Above right Kathy Whitworth came on to the scene shortly after Wright but she has not similarly been tempted by the prospect of early, maybe premature, retirement from competitive golf. When Whitworth won the Rochester International tournament in 1984 it was her 85th victory on the LPGA Tour, one more than Sam Snead's record on the men's circuit.

JoAnne Carner has followed a fantastic amateur career with an equally outstanding professional record. She has established a firm reputation as one of the 'characters' of women's golf, although the jovial 'Big Momma' is no longer as big as she once was. Even athletes sometimes have to diet.

Pat Bradley, who enjoyed the most lucrative season in LPGA history in 1986. She was understandably less than delighted when sceptics suggested that her success was largely due to Nancy Lopez being at home having a baby. After all, a woman can't do much more than win three of the four legs of the female Grand Slam.

she can receive here. She won the US Amateur five times and was twice runner-up. Having threatened Glenna Collet Vare's record as an amateur she has gone on to establish herself as one of the greatest women professionals.

What the US Open has also done since Wright first hit the headlines is to provide a debut professional win for a startling number of players – Murle Lindstrom, Mary Mills, Sandra Spuzich, Donna Caponi, Jerilyn Britz, Janet Anderson (née Alex), Kathy Baker and Jane Geddes. The last four have all been champions in the past 10 years, yet by the end of 1986 they had only two other tour victories between them. Strange indeed.

To that miscellaneous gallery of names must be added spare details of two more. Nancy Lopez cast herself as the Arnold Palmer of the LPGA Tour when as a 21-year-old rookie this bright, attractive and vivacious personality won nine tournaments in 1978, five of them in a row. This stupendous achievement relegated Andy North's surprising triumph in the men's US Open to second golf story of the week. Lopez rejuvenated women's golf and, when she's not at home having kids, she still has the ability and enthusiasm to show her rivals who's boss, as she did in 1985 by topping the Money List.

Her successor as leading money-winner in 1986 was Pat Bradley, who won three legs of the Grand Slam (to give her a complete set of four) and

amassed nearly $500,000 to take over the lead on the LPGA Career Money List. These figures put Seve Ballesteros's earnings in Europe into the shade and reflect not only Bradley's talent but also the growth of the tour which now stages its own tournament in Japan, where the members of the JLPGA circuit also play for millions of dollars. The two tours meet annually in another of those interminable cup competitions, in this case the Nichirei Ladies' Cup.

Two Japanese players, Chako Higuchi and Ayako Okamato, have enjoyed the immense financial rewards to be gleaned on the LPGA tour, while ironically their domestic circuit has become almost the personal preserve of Ai-Yu Tu of Taiwan. Women's golf is indeed international these days, and Sally Little of South Africa, who lost the 1986 US Open in a play-off to Geddes, and Jan Stephenson of Australia, who won it in 1983, are confirmed among the elite in America. European golfers like Marta Figueras-Dotti (Spain), Anne-Marie Palli (France) and Pia Nilsson (Sweden) have elected to concentrate on the LPGA Tour and thus forsake the WPGA Tour in Europe.

The latter was inspired by the Ladies' European Open, which was staged by the LPGA at Sunningdale for some years under the guidance of David Foster, the perceptive chief executive of the Colgate company. He worked with the saviour and then Commissioner of the LPGA, Ray Volpe, to resurrect the fortunes of the American tour in such spectacular fashion in the 1970s. The WPGA Tour (for some arcane reason, female professionals are stamped as ladies in the United States but women in Europe) was initiated in Britain by Barry Edwards in 1978. By the early 1980s it was beset by internal squabbling and Colin Snape, the Executive Director of the British PGA, took control. He used the influence and connections of his organization to strengthen the circuit by taking it on to the continent. This move enabled the £1-million prize money barrier to be broken in 1987, an announcement made a few weeks after Snape had 'resigned' – in fact, been dismissed – over what was considered his dictatorial attitude. His legacy is a tour which has produced a genuine British star in Laura Davies, who appears to have the strength of game and character necessary to be more successful than predecessors like Jenny Lee Smith and Cathy Panton on her forays in America. Davies won the 1986 Ladies' British Open, which was inaugurated in 1976 but had been cancelled for one

season in 1983 when the organizers, the LGU, failed to find a sponsor.

Talk of the LGU takes us back to amateur golf. The burgeoning LPGA Tour meant that after the Second World War few prominent American amateurs were encouraged to retain their status. Most, like Beth Daniel and Juli Inkster, have followed the path taken by JoAnne Carner and converted their class into cash. Anne Sander (née Quast) was one who didn't. She won three US Amateurs and a British Amateur, the latter coming 22 years and three marriages after her first national title in 1958. Marlene Stewart, Barbara McIntire, Marley Spearman, Brigitte Varangot, Elizabeth Chadwick, Carol Semple and Michelle (Mickey) Walker – one of the first women club professionals in Britain – are other women of the era to have at least two victories in the major Amateurs under their belts.

The outstanding woman amateur since the war has probably been Catherine Lacoste of France. She won the British and US Amateurs in 1969 to become only the third person (after Dorothy Campbell in 1909 and Pam Barton in 1936) to do the double. In the former she ended the reign of her compatriot, Miss Varangot, who had ruled for three of the preceding

six years. But it was what Miss Lacoste did in 1967 that set the world alight and left several American professionals with red faces and hot tempers. As an unheralded 22-year-old, she won the US Open, the only amateur to do so. Miss Lacoste, now a Madrid housewife who can still knock the ball round in scratch, has the sort of sporting pedigree that would have an equine expert purring with satisfaction: in 1927 her mother became the first overseas winner of the British Amateur, and her father won the men's singles title at Wimbledon in 1925 and 1928. Miss Lacoste, Miss Varangot and Claudine Cros won the first of the Women's World Amateur Team Championships for the Espirito Santo Trophy, in Paris in 1964. Since then the United States has emphasized its superiority with nine wins in this event, being denied only in 1978 by Australia – with a team which included the brilliant stalwart of her country's amateur golf, Edwina Kennedy – and in 1986 by Spain.

No discussion of the modern amateur scene would be complete without mentioning Belle Robertson of Scotland. Aged 45, she seemed to have capped a distinguished career by at last lifting the British Amateur trophy in 1981, after suffering defeat in three previous finals. She did it the hard way too, letting slip a lead of 5 up with five to play against Wilma Aitken before prevailing at the second extra hole. But that was not the end of the trail for her. In 1986 she was

Opposite **Laura Davies, a prodigiously powerful striker of the ball who displayed all-round skills to win the 1986 British Ladies' Open at Royal Birkdale. She has the potential to become an international star, as she proved when finishing 11th on her debut appearance in the US Women's Open in 1986.**

Catherine Lacoste gave heart to amateur golfers everywhere and caused consternation among the American professionals when, as a totally unsung young amateur, she startlingly won the US Women's Open in 1967. Two years later this outstanding French golfer added the British and United States Amateur Championships to her record.

Women's golfing attire has altered somewhat since the Victorian era. Beth Boozer, one of the American competitors on Europe's WPGA Tour, is seen here modelling for a calendar in rather less inhibiting and more revealing clothing than the likes of Cecil Leitch carried on to the links in the 1920s.

among those British Curtis Cup heroines who managed to upset the odds and defy the experts by winning in Kansas.

Belle Robertson goes back a long way, but not far enough to have witnessed many of the changes in female attire in the 90-odd years that have elapsed since Lady Margaret Scott adorned the fairways dressed in a sailor's hat, a blouse with billowing sleeves and starched collar, and a skirt that brushed the ground. When Gladys Ravenscroft, who would later win the British and American titles, rolled up her sleeves on the course in the 1909 British Amateur at Birkdale, it nearly caused a scandal. And one might have thought the apocalypse was nigh when the exotically-named Gloria Minoprio arrived on the first tee for the opening round of the 1933 English Amateur clad in tight-fitting navy-blue trousers, with a matching sweater which did nothing to hide the contours of her body. She played with just one club, which she employed a caddie to carry along with a spare, and was beaten 5 & 4. Henry Longhurst filed his piece for the *Evening Standard* that night under the headline 'Sic transit Gloria Monday!'

The LGU immediately 'deplored any departure from the traditional costume of the game'. Those members would be appalled by subsequent developments. Thirty years later Marley Spearman, a former professional dancer, not only burst into the limelight with her golf but also popularized brightly coloured clothing on the course in Britain. It is doubtful that she could have envisaged the skimpy skirts, tight shorts and T-shirts that would become the norm. Even the most prescient early statesmen of the LPGA Tour would not have imagined the day that two Americans, Laura Baugh and Beth Boozer, would fail to win golf tournaments yet make fortunes by modelling for calendars and posters. Baugh, who aged 16 became the youngest-ever US Amateur champion in 1971, is the ultimate example of the marketing expertise of Mark McCormack. Another client of his, Jan Stephenson, is several steps higher up the ladder in terms of achievement and ability but she too has not been chary of capitalizing on her good looks and film-star figure. Stephenson has more than doubled her on-course income by being photographed in a number of suggestive poses, usually with all her clothes on.

And where does all this leave our stereotyped male club golfer? Maybe he'll ogle the latest Beth Boozer poster, dismiss as sheer nonsense the amount of money the women professionals play for, and ignore the sound advice that he would probably learn more by trying to copy the women tour pros rather than the men because the men are literally playing a game he will never be familiar with. He's content anyway, because the majority of lady members are happy with, or keep quiet about, the *status quo*, which means, in the words of Horace Hutchinson: 'If they choose to play at times when the male golfers are feeding or resting, no-one can object. But at other times – must we say it – they are in the way; just because gallantry forbids to treat them exactly as men.'

Such chivalrous intent often flies out of the window in a torrent of abuse if the man's partner dumps him in every bunker on the course during the mixed 'gruesomes', especially if she's his wife; and nobody is immune to impatience when his round is perpetually delayed by a ladies' fourball, zig-zagging across the fairway as if under sniper fire. It is on such occasions that all men succumb to the chauvinistic and outmoded attitudes outlined in this chapter and are forced to seek solace by remembering what we are out on the golf course for. As P. G. Wodehouse's Oldest Member once said: 'A woman is only a woman, but a hefty drive is a slosh.'

Jan Stephenson (left) and Nancy Lopez, two of the attractive women who in their different ways have helped to promote and elevate interest in ladies' professional golf in the 1970s and 1980s.

The perpetrators of the golfing story of 1986, the members of the Great Britain and Ireland team which removed the Curtis Cup from American possession over the course of two hot summer days at Prairie Dunes. Left to right: (back row) Mary McKenna, Elsie Brown (vice-captain), Lillian Behan, Patricia Johnson, Jill Thornhill, Belle Robertson; (front row) Karen Davies, Claire Hourihane, Diane Bailey (non-playing captain), Vicki Thomas.

'Captain driving off'. Old Tom Morris is teeing the ball for the captain of the R & A in 1894, the Rt Hon A. J. Balfour. Old Tom was Custodian of the Links at St Andrews from 1865 to 1903. Among his duties was the placing of the ball for the new captain to drive into office, a function which has since been assumed by the R & A's honorary professional. This painting depicts the club's members and the people of the town awaiting the start of the annual ritual.

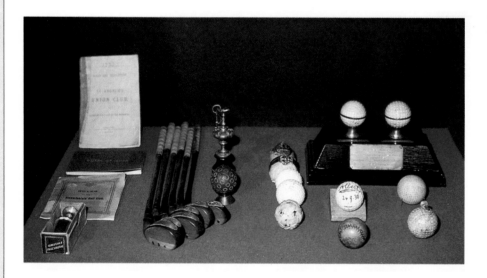

The R & A's museum contains old balls, clubs, artefacts and documents, and also houses its original trophies.

The Open Championship is a special affair. When it is held at St Andrews it is extra special. The town turns itself over to the occasion completely and unashamedly. The paraphernalia which accompanies the modern Open Championship – tented village, scoreboards, grandstands, etc – are evident from this photograph of the 1st, 17th and 18th holes.

A scene enacted for centuries – the sun going down on golfers at St Andrews. In the foreground players tackle the 17th, the Road Hole, perhaps the most fearsome par-4 known to man. In the distance is the grand but somewhat austere clubhouse of the R & A, which has stood there for less than 150 years but is now probably St Andrews's most famous landmark.

The 'auld grey toun' as seen from the tower of the medieval cathedral. The golf courses are situated upon the finger of land that thrusts out into the sea in the top right-hand corner of the photograph.

St Andrews at sunset. The flags in the foreground are on the 4th (white) and 14th (red) holes on the Old Course. This aerial shot gives some idea of the size of the vast greens – note in the distance the biggest of the doubles, that of the 5th and 13th at 49,000 square feet. The late evening light throws into sharp relief the number of fiendish bunkers and the capriciously undulating nature of the terrain. This also provides an excellent view of the 14th hole, with Hell bunker in the left-centre of the picture and the tee back in the corner beside the wall which separates the Old from the Eden Course. The New Course lies over the road to the right, while the sparkling blue waters of the Eden estuary, down by The Loop, form the backdrop against which most golfers expect to make their score before facing the rigours of the homeward journey.

CHAPTER THIRTEEN

St Andrews:
the Cradle of the Game

The most famous stretch of golfing ground in the world is the Old Course at St Andrews in Fife, on the east coast of Scotland. Famous is not the same thing as oldest (despite the extravagant bombast of Scottish historians down the ages) but that does not really matter. While it may not truly be the home of golf in the strict sense of the phrase, St Andrews is certainly its spiritual home, the cradle of the game. Although no documentary evidence will ever be produced to substantiate the oft-made claim that the Old Course is the oldest links in the world, it is widely regarded as the original golf course – the prototype from which all others are, directly or indirectly, copied.

The most famous golf club in the world is the Royal and Ancient Golf Club of St Andrews. Not even the most rabid St Andrean would suggest his town is home to the most senior club in golfdom, certainly not within the hearing of a member of the Honourable Company of Edinburgh Golfers, but the R & A is now indubitably paramount, sharing as it does the governance of the game with the USGA.

The influence and importance of the R & A has been a recurring theme throughout these pages and no purpose would be served by repeating all that has gone before. But the R & A is a vital part of any picture which attempts to portray the significance of St Andrews, and its emergence as a power in the game, inextricably bound as it is to the course, cannot be ignored here.

The R & A was granted its royal charter in 1834. It had come into existence some 80 years previously as the St Andrews Society of Golfers, but that itself was two centuries after the first written reference to golf being played at St Andrews. Nobody knows how long ago golfers had in fact been a regular sight on that now-hallowed tract of land, but the niceties of weighing the evidence have been overlooked by some respected researchers who have preferred to follow gut reaction rather than documentary proof and assert that golf was a popular pastime in

St Andrews centuries before it probably was. In fairness, they were commenting from the heart as much as the head, and without access to the subsequent material unearthed by Steven van Hengel and others, but that has not prevented their more recent disciples from espousing the same cause by applying the policy that if one says something often enough it will become accepted as the truth.

Whenever it was that the first golf ball took flight, or perhaps scuttled along the ground, at St Andrews, it was surely sometime before 25 January 1552, when the dignitaries of the town granted the public the right to use the links to 'play at golf, futball, schuting, at all gamis with all uther, as ever they pleis and in ony time'. Not only was the place a mêlée of sporting pursuits but rabbits were reared there too, and women hung up their washing to dry in the fresh sea air. These other diversions represented additional hazards for the golfer as he laboured to master the game with his rudimentary equipment. But they emphasize that, though the stipulation contained

St Andrews from above. This photograph from 1964 shows the old railway yard eating into the 17th fairway. The Old Course Hotel now stands on that site and trains no longer chug up and down the lines, but the scene in the 1960s had not much altered from centuries past and today little else has changed either. The Old Course occupies the land immediately to the right of the railway line and it winds its way out to The Loop by the estuary. To the left of the Old is the Eden Course, to the right the New, and by the sea the Jubilee Course, which is presently the subject of an ambitious improvement programme.

in the 16th-century licence ordering that nobody should 'plough up any part of said golf links in all time coming' has happily been adhered to, the course is laid out on common land. The point was rammed home to Lee Trevino during the third round of the 1970 Open. He was leading the championship when a dog barked just as he was about to hit a short putt on the 16th green. He missed. 'If I'd got to that dog it would have gone home with a putter in its head,' he averred later. 'I'm playing for the Open and I might blow it right there because some guy is out walking his dog.'

His annoyance was understandable, but St Andrews would not possess its unique atmosphere and fascination if the golf course was not so integrally connected with the life of the town.

St Andrews was originally a small fishing village. By the Middle Ages it had assumed an important role as a city of prosperity and learning and the university was opened in 1410. But over the next two centuries it became an unwanted focus for the murder and pillage that swept Scotland in the name of religion. The castle and magnificent cathedral were ravaged by looters. When man was finished with his dastardly deeds, fate took a hand and the region was beset by plagues which saw off many of those who had survived the man-made terror. The town's fortunes revived at the beginning of the last century when it came to be regarded as a superior holiday retreat. Since then, most of the tragedies have been confined to the tumbling terrain of the golf course.

Throughout centuries of fluctuation, the course has remained a constant – not only in being hardly

A familiar sight at St Andrews down the ages. The boys of the town sample the delights of golf in the middle of the last century. The threesome in the foreground are playing the 18th on what is now known as the Old Course.

altered but also in simply being there. As Horace Hutchinson wrote in *The Badminton Library* in 1890:

'All the great mass of golfing history and tradition – principally, perhaps, the latter – clusters lovingly within sight of the grey towers of the old University town; and, to most, the very name St Andrews calls to mind not a saint nor a city, nor a castle nor a University, but a beautiful stretch of green links with a little burn, which traps golf balls, and bunkers artfully planted to try the golfer's soul.'

The little burn and artfully planted bunkers are reinforced by plenty of hidden hazards, and others – like roads and stone walls – which are frighteningly visible. Then there are the blind drives and approach shots, and the huge double greens with contours so severe that Robert Trent Jones (no relation to Bobby; instead, a savant among American golf course architects) said of the 7th and 11th green: 'I feel that at no other place but St Andrews would such a slope be countenanced.' And not even an architect as innovative as Jones would dare to present a client with a plan for a par-72 course featuring just two par-3s and two par-5s. As he himself opined: 'The Old Course is only right at St Andrews.' It has served as the inspiration to countless course designers, and many of its facets – the undulations of a green, the shape of a hole, the location of a bunker – have been copied in isolation elsewhere in Britain, the United States and the world over. To attempt to reproduce it in its entirety would be sheer folly; yet it has been tried, at considerable loss of money and face, in Japan.

The singular mysteries of the Old Course are what Bernard Darwin was referring to in the first sentence of this passage from *Golf Courses of the British Isles*. It is a typical example of the master's brilliance. He describes how the people, the course and the town came together as one in a manner which would gladden the heart and soul of the most fervent Zen Buddhist.

'There are those who do not like the golf at St Andrews, and they will no doubt deny any charm to the links themselves, but there must surely be none who will deny a charm to the place as a whole. It may be immoral, but it is delightful to see a whole town given up to golf; to see the butcher and the baker and the candlestick maker shouldering their clubs as soon as his day's work is done and making a dash for the links. There he and his fellows will very possibly get in our way, or we shall get in theirs; we shall often curse the

crowd, and wish wholeheartedly that golf was less popular at St Andrews. Nevertheless it is that utter self-abandonment to golf that gives the place its attractiveness. What a pleasant spectacle is that home green, fenced in on two sides by a railing, upon which lean various critical observers; and there is the clubhouse on one side, and the clubmaker's shop and the hotels on the other, all full of people who are looking at the putting, and talking of putts that they themselves holed or missed on that or some other green. I once met, staying in a hotel at St Andrews, a gentleman who did not play golf. That is in itself remarkable, but more wonderful still, he joined so rationally, if unobtrusively, in the perpetual golfing conversation that his black secret was never discovered. I do not know if he enjoyed himself, but his achievement was at least a notable one.'

Darwin's book was published in 1910 but the sentiments are equally true in the 1980s. The place is hopelessly devoted to golf. While visitors may be seduced for a while by the grand, graceful grey town, with its three spacious main streets (North, Market and South), or be lured to the ruins of the castle or drawn to the old graveyard with its shrine to Young Tom Morris, in due course they will join the residents out on the links 'shouldering' their clubs. Trolleys are not permitted.

It is no longer free to play the Old – the charge was £16.50 for a round in summer 1987 – but nobody will ask you for a handicap certificate or letter of introduction. Over 40,000 rounds a year are played on it by pilgrims from all over the globe, although never on a Sunday. As Old Tom Morris is reported to have told one eager golfer: 'The Old Course needs a rest on the Sabbath, even if you don't.' Well, almost never on a Sunday. The Open Championship and Dunhill Cup have demonstrated that the game's elite are, as in so many respects, exempt from the restrictions imposed upon the rest of us.

One of the great joys of golf is that it is played on natural terrain, and is not subjected to rigid rules governing the dimensions of the field of play which pertain to the majority of ball sports. The

The double green on the 7th and 11th holes on the Old Course is of typical St Andrews dimensions, but it is canted more severely than most. The huge bunker in front of the 7th green is called Cockle, while the deep pit to the left is Strath, the chief guardian of the 11th hole.

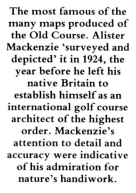

The most famous of the many maps produced of the Old Course. Alister Mackenzie 'surveyed and depicted' it in 1924, the year before he left his native Britain to establish himself as an international golf course architect of the highest order. Mackenzie's attention to detail and accuracy were indicative of his admiration for nature's handiwork.

Old Course epitomizes the game in a genuinely natural environment. It has been changed less than any other great golf course, though it has not been immune to progress since the day in 1764 when William St Clair played its 22 holes in 121 strokes, an act of sacrilege which resulted in modifications eventually leading to 18 holes becoming standard everywhere else as well. For instance, new tees have been constructed to increase its length in the face of the development of the club and ball, and the condition of the course has been improved immeasurably from the days that meant James Durham's round of 94, which won him the St Andrews Society's Silver Club in 1767, stood as a record for 86 years.

What has not been altered, though, is the essential nature of the Old Course, with shared fairways and greens being the norm rather than the exception. They came about because the configuration of the narrow strip of land available for recreation compelled the early golfers to play over the same ground going 'out' and coming 'in' – which in itself probably explains the origin of those terms. Then the fairways were a meagre 40 yards wide, which made a call of 'fore' a mandatory accompaniment to every shot. They have since been increased to around 100 yards, and the greens similarly widened so they remain nearly as broad as the fairways.

The two most distinctive features of St Andrews are its bunkers and its greens. Of what he called 'the artful planting of the bunkers', Hutchinson said: 'Not, of course, that they were planted by any but Nature's hand; but planted by nature, one would say, with an obvious artistic eye for the golfer's edification.' There are few golfers, either distinguished or humble, who have

emerged from one of St Andrews' ubiquitous and pernicious bunkers feeling particularly edified. Many of those satanic orifices contain just enough room 'for an angry man and his niblick', to quote Darwin's memorable expression. Some were created by sheep sheltering from the wind, others by foxes chasing rabbits, and yet more by man, although St Andrews owes less to the ingenuity of the latter than any course in the world. There are reckoned to be 110 bunkers on the Old Course, but don't take that figure as gospel. There could be a couple more lurking somewhere, less conspicuous perhaps than the one close to the 12th tee into which a senior naval officer tumbled while distracted by a fair damsel who had strolled on to the links. It was promptly christened 'Admiral's Bunker'. Some of the other traps have some fairly intriguing and occasionally evil names: 'Principal's Nose', 'Mrs Kruger', 'Ginger Beer', and 'The Beardies' fall into the former category; 'Lion's Mouth', 'Coffins', 'Hell' and 'Grave' decisively fit into the latter.

The apparently random and illogical siting of several bunkers is not simply because they owe their genesis to the whims of refuge-seeking sheep. It used to be common procedure to play the course backwards, a novelty only possible because of the unique shared fairways and greens. This practice had the obvious pleasure of providing a different challenge, and the considerable advantage of allowing the parts of the course which suffered the most wear and tear to recover from the incessant hammering of club on turf. If one were to start from the first tee and play to the 17th green, and so on, such bunkers become relevant rather than redundant. It would also make St Andrews more fun for the average hacker possessed of a slice. The regular way of playing the course is to tack down the righthand side of those massively wide fairways, out and back, leaving the Old Course open to the accusation of breeding more hookers than Soho.

While the first awareness of a bunker's existence will often coincide with the sight of one's ball in it, it is impossible to miss the greens which they guard so menacingly – at least with the naked eye, if not with a 3-iron in your hand. Only the 1st, 9th, 17th and 18th holes have single greens. The rest share seven monstrous putting surfaces – from the 2nd and the 16th nearest the clubhouse, out to the 8th and the 10th at the far end of the links by the Eden estuary, where the stretch of shortish holes from the 7th to the 12th, 'The Loop', is known by the locals to be the place to build a good score. The largest green, about an acre, is that of the 5th and 13th. Bobby Jones is reputed to have once birdied the long 5th with a putt of 40 yards. Lee Trevino took three putts from much the same place in the final round of the 1970 Open. He had committed the cardinal error of aiming for the wrong coloured flag. The greens at St Andrews are tormenting enough without such mistakes. Most are upraised on plateaux, and

no course is more demanding of the pitch or chip-and-run shot. Their very size means that three-putting can sometimes be a reason for congratulation, not commiseration.

If some of the fire has been extracted from the course since the installation of a sprinkler system in 1969 – which has fuelled allegations that it is now too heavily watered – St Andrews is still manifestly no pushover. Its greatest protector is the wind, which can be sufficiently capricious to be against on the outward journey and then switch just in time to be against coming home. The Old Course is vulnerable in the absence of a stiff breeze, or preferably something stronger. It needs the wind to keep the golfer alert and mindful of the hazards it brings into play. Whatever the weather, St Andrews remains a supreme test of golf for the club player. Although the professionals carry the power to bludgeon it into submission on a calm day, the record Open total of 12 under par 276, set be Seve Ballesteros in 1984 in largely benign conditions, is proof that the Old Course is not outdated. Its timeless quality was reinforced by a statistical survey conducted by the PGA European Tour in 1986 which showed that its 11th, 14th and 17th holes were

The old and the new at St Andrews: the Old Course and the new champion. Seve Ballesteros crosses the ancient bridge over the Swilcan Burn after hitting his final drive in the 1984 Open. When Ballesteros birdied the 18th it gave him a two-shot victory over Bernhard Langer (walking behind him) and Tom Watson and set a new low for a St Andrews Open of 276. Note also the Old Course Hotel, which has replaced the original railway sheds.

respectively the toughest 11th, 14th and 17th holes on the circuit that season. Competitors in the Dunhill Cup learned that St Andrews is no less valid an examination today than it was for Allan Robertson and the Tom Morrises, with their hickories, featheries and gutties, a century and more before Ballesteros was born.

Those three holes are, by common consent, the best at St Andrews. The course contains several others of outstanding merit, but as one stands on the first tee there is no hint of why it has come to be regarded as the golfing equivalent of Mecca. To an American raised on emerald fairways, water hazards, a plethora of sand bunkers and an abundance of trees, it is a disorientating experience to see none of these things and be assured that what looks like a field is indeed the most revered golf course in the world. Sam Snead, who won the Open there in 1946, gained the first impression that it was 'an old abandoned sort of place'. He twisted the knife further with the opinion that it 'was so raggedy and beat up I was surprised to see what looked like fairway among the weeds. Down home we wouldn't plant cow beets on land like that.'

The immediate prospect is of the joint widest fairway in the world, a distinction the 370-yard opening hole shares with the 354-yard last since they occupy the same ground. There is no rough and no sand, and only a player afflicted with a chronic slice or capable of perpetrating a foozle of Wodehousian proportions can get into trouble off the tee. The critical shot is the approach to the green over the narrow gully of the Swilcan Burn, the 'little burn' of which Hutchinson spoke. Although there is no danger over the back of the green, countless great golfers have contrived to dump their second shots into the Swilcan's shallow waters. Doug Sanders did it on the first hole of the 1970 Open and took six. Seventy-one holes later he took five on the 18th, another ostensibly simple affair, and squandered the title. In an incredible sequence at the 1895 Amateur Championship, Leslie Balfour-Melville won his quarter-final, semi-final and final at the first extra hole after his three opponents, who included John Ball in the final, had all found the burn with their second strokes.

Apart from illustrating that the first can be a formidable 19th, those incidents reflect the way in which one is following in the footsteps of the millions who have gone before when playing a round on the Old Course. The links is alive with the phantoms of the game's early practitioners. Each hole is stalked by the ghosts of champions past; haunted by memories of 23 Opens and innumerable important amateur championships and international matches. This intangible thrill may provide initial compensation for one's inevitable inability to grasp the finer points of nature's architectural genius, as one encounters the hidden bunkers, hanging lies and sidehill stances for the first time. The splendid subtleties of the design are not revealed until the golfer returns, as he will surely try to, but eventually he will appreciate that St Andrews is a magnificent test of strategic golf. One is generally safe in driving to the left, but the approach to the green will invariably be harder from there. The reward for taking the brave line from the tee is always the pleasure of being confronted by a much more straightforward angle into the flag.

There is no room here for a hole-by-hole summary of the Old Course, but a few highlights are in order, particularly from the homeward half where the holes are more stirring and, once The Loop has been left behind, all head back towards the clubhouse.

The 11th measures 172 yards and is one of only two par-3s, the 8th being the other. As Robert Trent Jones observed, the green is severely canted and the golfer putting down from the back to a

The beginning of perhaps the most eagerly awaited journey in golf. A fourball sets off down the first fairway of the Old Course. This view from the balcony of the R & A clubhouse also highlights the depth and contours of the Valley of Sin on the 18th green. The first and 17th greens are visible in the distance, as are the Swilcan bridge, the Old Course Hotel and the outline of the Swilcan Burn.

hole cut at the front will do well to keep his ball on the green, especially if the wind is off the estuary behind him. This problem arises from the temptation to be strong with the tee shot because there are two punitive bunkers to clear. 'Strath' usually acts as custodian to the flag, which is situated right behind it during tournament play. It thus becomes the job of 'Hill' bunker to the left to swallow up many a ball struck with caution in mind. Hill is some 10 feet deep and must have dwarfed the diminutive Gene Sarazen when he wandered into it during the 1933 Open. He took three in there and six on the hole. That same week he visited Hell, on the 14th, and left the green with an eight on his card. He finished the championship a stroke behind the winner, Denny Shute.

The 12th and 13th are respectively a short and a longish par-4. The 12th fairway is infested with bunkers which are out of view from the tee, while the 13th green is similarly invisible from the spot where a perfect drive will finish. In short, they are classic St Andrews holes.

The 14th goes under the simple sobriquet of 'Long', and that it certainly is at 567 yards from the championship tee. From the very back markers the drive at the 14th is fraught with danger, and the worries are exacerbated if the wind is unfavourable. A low stone wall delineates the out-of-bounds which awaits the slice, while the cluster of the four Beardies bunkers threatens a pull or a hook. The haven of the fairway, known as the 'Elysian Fields', seems a mile away, and once there the formidable prospect of Hell

bunker, the one that did for Sarazen, looms in the distance for those contemplating the direct but risky route. The Beardies and Hell combined to force an eight out of Bobby Locke in the 1939 Open, while the out-of-bounds helped the 1981 Open champion, Bill Rogers, to compile a 12 in the opening round of the 1984 championship. In 1970 Tony Jacklin, having launched a breathtaking defence of his crown by playing the first 13 holes in eight under par, arrived on the 14th with every chance of smashing all Open scoring records in the unusually calm conditions that rendered the Old Course virtually defenceless. As if the Gods decided it was all too

Strath bunker still baffles the best, as Greg Norman discovers here. Strath is the prime protector of the flag, which here is in its usual location for tournament play. The bunker has a voracious appetite and many of the balls it fails to gather end up in Hill, its companion bunker out of sight to the left.

Hell has claimed a star-studded roll of victims over the years, too. Its fear-factor and its sheer size are summed up by the tale of the anxious golfer who asked his caddie: 'Can I carry all that sand?' 'I doubt it,' came back the reply. 'It weighs about 22 tons.'

The Road Hole at tournament time in 1957 and 1984. In the latter Open Tom Watson was too strong with his approach to the 17th green in the last round. He was then faced with an awful shot from under the wall across the road and when he took five his hopes of catching Ballesteros had evaporated. In both photographs the dreaded bunker is conspicuous. Bernard Darwin wrote of it 'eating its way into the very vitals' of the green.

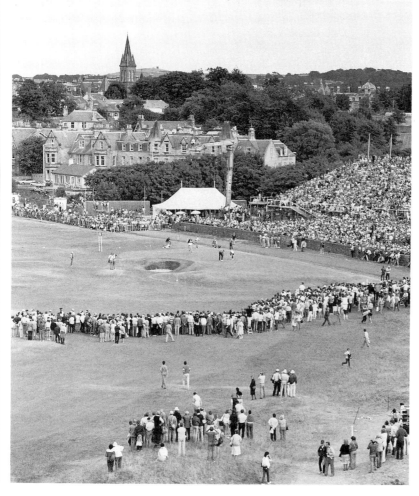

much, a violent storm caused the suspension of play just after Jacklin had carved his second shot under a bush. He returned the next morning to find the magic had gone and by the Saturday evening so had his hopes of retaining the trophy.

The 16th is a marvellous example of the St Andrews philosophy of 'what you play is what you get'. It is 382 yards on the card, but will play significantly longer if the golfer elects for prudence off the tee and aims to the left of the collection of three bunkers known as the Principal's Nose. He will then have to carry the 'Wig' bunker, which eats into the front of the green, with his approach. If instead he opts for the adventurous driving line, between the bunkers and the out-of-bounds fence on the right, he will, if successful in his endeavours, have an easy pitch left.

All the holes on the Old Course are named, and the 17th is 'Road'. It is simultaneously the most respected and feared, admired and loathed golf hole in the world. Seve Ballesteros is speaking for generations of golfers, of all standards, when he calls it the hardest hole he has ever played.

At 461 yards it is not a short par-4, but length is almost the last concern. Many old hands unashamedly play it as a par-5, with a drive well to the left of the out-of-bounds in the grounds of the Old Course Hotel, which was originally the site of a railway yard. The safe second shot is to the right of the green and short, thus avoiding the

ST ANDREWS: THE CRADLE OF THE GAME 153

siren depths of the awesome 'Road' bunker to the left and the awful fate of playing the next stroke from a pitted and uneven road, which is the punishment for being too aggressive. The road is a designated hazard, so the club cannot be grounded. Legions of golfers have bumbled the ball back towards the flag only to see it disobediently return to their feet off a bank which elevates this wide but thin green on to a ledge. The other obvious problem is that the bunker will gather in an over-ambitious recovery. Once in that pit it is distressingly easy to fritter away a few more strokes before emerging too strongly back on to the road or – worse – up against the stone wall which lies just beyond it. This heartbreaking pantomime can be endless, and keeping score difficult.

The cup during a championship is always cut on the narrow shelf between the bunker and the road. The only way to get close to the hole is to fire the drive over the out-of-bounds and then draw an iron in along the green. Tom Watson tried to do that on the last afternoon of the 1984 Open, but he grossly misjudged his second shot and it finished under the wall. He did extraordinarily well to salvage a five, but by then Ballesteros had made a typically audacious par on the hole just before him – his first four of the week there – and had holed his winning birdie putt on the 18th, a moment he greeted with an unabashed exhibition of matador-style salutes. David Marsh brought off the desired shot in similar circumstances to climax Britain's sensational Walker Cup triumph in 1971, but the tales of the 17th are more often of disaster.

They go back over 100 years, to the unfortunate David Ayton who got caught between the road and bunker in the 1885 Open. By the time he had finished skimming from one to the other he had taken 11. He ended the championship two strokes adrift of the victor, Bob Martin, a fellow-St Andrean. J. H. Taylor once took 13 on the hole, which was four more than Tommy Nakajima managed in 1978. The Japanese paid the penalty incurred by many of those who play safe in two. He putted into the bunker for three. After that experience it was perhaps no great shock that he needed four blows to get out. His nerves were probably not soothed by the recollection that three months previously he had registered a 13 at Augusta's 13th in the Masters. He was no doubt grateful for the small mercy that he had escaped without achieving such ignominious symmetry at St Andrews. To move right up to date, Richard

Zokol of Canada also took four swipes in the Road bunker in his match against America's Mark O'Meara in the 1986 Dunhill Cup. It cost him the lead and his country the chance of making further progress in the competition.

No man has ever played a bolder shot from that bunker than Doug Sanders in the final round of the 1970 Open. His look of anguish as he realized he was in the trap was soon replaced by a smile of jubilation as he exploded the ball to within a foot of the hole to save his par. That should have been the shot that won the Open. Instead, Sanders pitched too clumsily to the last in his anxiety to get over the 'Valley of Sin', the huge swale which forms the front left side of the 18th green, and his three putts had a sad inevitability about them. Sanders had deserted the traditional Scottish running shot at the precise moment he should have stayed loyal to it, and the silent spirits of the Old Course were not prepared to tolerate such craven treachery. The wickedly curling three-footer that eluded Sanders when he stood on the threshold of realizing the dream of 'this one for the Open' turned his fantasy into a nightmare.

St Andrews has produced great champions as well as great championships. Up to the First World War, eight St Andreans won the Open – the two Tom Morrises, Andrew Strath, Tom Kidd, Bob Martin, Jamie Anderson, Hugh Kirkaldy and Willie Auchterlonie. Since then there has been just one other, Jock Hutchison,

Willie Auchterlonie, the 1893 Open champion and honorary professional to the R & A from 1935 to 1963, outside his shop at St Andrews in 1899.

who had become a naturalized American by the time he beat Roger Wethered by nine shots in a play-off in 1921. Wethered, an amateur, was distracted anyway. He wanted to get back to England for a cricket match.

Since it joined Prestwick and Musselburgh on the championship rota in 1873, only four men – Martin, J. H. Taylor, James Braid and Jack Nicklaus – have taken two Opens over the Old Course. Several of the championships will be talked about for as long as the game is played. Some have been detailed here, others in Chapter 4, but the 1960 Open, won by Kel Nagle of Australia, deserves a special mention. It was the Centenary Open, and the man who came second was to change the course of Open history. He was Arnold Palmer, and though he never won the title at St Andrews he contributed more to the event than many winners could ever hope to do.

An Open at St Andrews is a little apart from one at another venue. The players freely confess they would prefer to win there than anywhere else. The public converge on the town in record numbers, and so does the world's media. One American magazine applied for 19 press passes to cover the 1984 Open, 15 more than it had requested for Birkdale 12 months previously. The greedy optimism inherent in such an application was crushed by an official who explained that he couldn't see how the championship had become nearly five times as important in one year.

The affection and esteem in which the golf course at St Andrews came to be held during the first half of the 1800s partly accounts for the restoration of the town's image as a salubrious resort, and for the consolidation of the position of the R & A. In turn, of course, the increased stature of the latter did no harm to St Andrews' claims to be hailed as the home of golf.

The R & A's status as golf's ruling body outside North America has its roots in the instability of the Honourable Company of Edinburgh Golfers some 150 years ago. By the middle of the last century the R & A's supremacy was unchallenged and in 1854 it published 22 Rules of Golf, a recodification and revision of past practices and new regulations. The very act of this promulgation reinforced the authority of the R & A. By the end of the century it had stipulated the size of the hole and legislated for the provision of defined areas from which to drive, as opposed to the previous procedure of teeing up the ball within eight club lengths of the hole that had just been completed. The R & A assumed responsibility for formulating the Rules of Golf in Britain in 1897, three years after the USGA had been created across the Atlantic, and in 1919 a meeting in Edinburgh of the most prominent British clubs passed a motion which moved: 'believing that in the best interests of the game the time had now arrived when there should be a supreme ruling authority for the management and control of the game, to further this end the Royal and Ancient Golf Club be asked to accept the management of the Amateur Championship and the custody of the cup.'

The R & A took over the Open at the same time, and later the Boys', Youths' and Seniors' Amateur Championships followed into the fold. In recent years the R & A has helped the LGU with the costs of running the Ladies' British Open, a gesture of largesse made possible because of the profit the club derives from the gigantic operation that is the modern Open Championship. The money-spinning success of golf's oldest tournament helps the R & A to meet the expense of staging national amateur events and international fixtures like the Walker Cup, and enables it to support worthy causes like the Ladies' Open or coastal erosion prevention schemes at other great links. It should be added, though, that the R & A does not handle every aspect of golf administration. For example, the complex and controversial men's handicapping system applied in the United Kingdom is the work of the Council of National Golf Unions (which represents the four countries of the British Isles) rather than the R & A, whereas this sensitive

Ken Nagle won the Centenary Open in 1960 by a stroke from Arnold Palmer. The vast crowds watch as he sinks the final putt.

subject is within the ambit of the USGA's authority in America. But despite such minor discrepancies, the chief function of both organizations is to protect the integrity of the game in a changing world, whether it be by amending the Rules, reviewing the latest developments in golf ball technology, or monitoring infringements of the strict laws governing amateur status.

From the time that King William IV acceded to the blandishments of Murray Belshes in 1834 and agreed to bestow the title Royal and Ancient upon the St Andrews Society of Golfers, the R & A has had a distinguished line of patrons, from William himself, to his widow Queen Adelaide on his death, and then Queen Victoria. Its captains have included two Princes of Wales and a Duke of York, who later became respectively the Kings Edward VII, Edward VIII and George VI. In 1908 Horace Hutchinson was nominated the first English captain of the R & A, and two Americans have also been accorded the highest honour in the club – Francis Ouimet in 1951 and Joe Dey in 1975. One of the great British golfing traditions, in a land famed for its love of pomp and ceremony, is the driving into office of the new captain of the R & A at 8 a.m. on the final day of the Autumn Meeting each September.

The club's honorary professional is presently Laurie Auchterlonie, who took over from his father, the 1893 Open champion, after his death in 1963 and who has maintained the family's reputation as master clubmakers. Custom dictates that he tees up the ball on the appointed morning and the captain-elect drives it into those empty acres of the 1st and 18th fairways. The act is instantaneously followed by the firing of a cannon which stands beside the 1st tee. A sizeable number of caddies compete for the glory of retrieving the ball, and the lucky one is rewarded with the gift of a gold sovereign from the fresh incumbent. Ouimet varied this aspect of the rite by handing over a gold $5 coin. Needless to say, the entire nerve-wracking ritual is replete with horror stories of air shots, tops and skiers, and wildly uncoordinated swings sending the ball scuttling between the legs of the hapless captain.

The R & A's clubhouse, surely the most photographed in the world, has presided over activities on the first tee and the last green since 1854 and it now welcomes some 1800 men – but no women – to enter its portals as members. About 40 per cent are those from overseas. Although it is the most famous building at St

Andrews it is not the only clubhouse, and it is often forgotten that there are also five other clubs, including two exclusively for ladies. Nor is the Old the only golf course, even if it is the one invariably referred to when people talk about St Andrews.

The New Course was opened in 1894, the Jubilee in 1899 and the Eden in 1913. All are 18-hole public courses, in addition to which there are the nine-hole Balgove layout, which dates from 1972, and the aptly named Himalayas putting course which is older than any except the Old itself. The right of public access to all of the courses was enshrined in the St Andrews Links

Captains away.

Above Lord Balfour drives in to office in 1894 to a round of applause from a white-bearded Old Tom Morris.

Below Fifty-seven years later, Francis Ouimet (holding driver) became the first non-British captain. He is seen receiving his ball from the caddie who caught it, Arthur Spaight, under the amused gaze of Willie Auchterlonie.

Act, passed by Parliament in 1894, which granted the R & A exclusive use of the Old Course for four weeks of the year (during which it fits in its Spring and Autumn Meetings). In return, the club was charged with the upkeep of the Old Course and the construction and maintenance of the New. The funds necessary for the adequate performance of these functions had reached a low ebb by the end of the last war, so in 1946 the Town Council permitted an annual fee to be levied on St Andrews residents for the first time. Since 1974 the Links Management Committee, which comprises representatives of the Town Council and the R & A, has assumed responsibility for the care of the courses.

The last word on St Andrews and the Old Course belongs properly – not incongruously – to an American, Bobby Jones. He hated it on his first visit for the 1921 Open. After taking 46 strokes to reach the turn in the third round, he suffered a double-bogey six on the 10th and found that five shots were insufficient to get him into the hole on the short 11th. He picked up his ball in fury and frustration. He quit in competition. Forlorn and remorseful at what he had done, the 19-year-old Jones, who in his early teens was known for throwing both clubs and tantrums to self-destructive effect, resolved he would never do anything so demeaning again and would henceforth be a model sportsman. From the moment he made that promise until the day he died, he never failed in his goal.

Jones was back in 1926 as a champion, no longer an unfulfilled prodigy. He trounced Cyril Tolley by 12 & 11 in his Walker Cup singles, and as he began to appreciate the charm of St Andrews so the townsfolk started to take to him. The affinity was confirmed when Jones was mobbed after winning the Open there the next summer, and the love affair was consummated in May 1930 when he survived a couple of alarms against Tolley and George Voigt before going on to beat Roger Wethered in the final of the British Amateur, thus securing the first leg of the Impregnable Quadrilateral.

Jones returned in 1936 for a friendly round while *en route* to the Olympic Games in Berlin. Word soon spread and 2000 people watched his progress. His golf was as good as ever on the front nine, which he covered in a four-under-par 32, and on the 8th he was offered a compliment he cherished forever. His boy caddie saw him strike an imperious tee shot and then said: 'My, but you're a wonder, sir.'

Jones was created an honorary life member of the R & A in 1956. In 1958 he returned again, by then being horribly crippled with his spinal disease, to captain the American team at the inaugural Eisenhower Trophy match. The tournament was overshadowed by the evening when Jones accepted an invitation to become a Freeman of the Burgh of St Andrews, only the second American to be so honoured. (Benjamin Franklin was the first.) Jones never exercised newly-earned prerogatives like drying his washing on the 1st and 18th fairways of the Old Course, but he did use the platform to pay tribute to St Andrews and its people. 'I could take out of my life everything except my experiences at St Andrews and I'd still have a rich, full life,' he said, a feeling rather echoed in 1984 in a thoughtful and moving speech delivered by Jack Nicklaus, in many ways Jones's heir apparent, when the town's university conferred an honorary degree of Doctor of Laws on him in the same Younger Hall that Jones had addressed. Today the university is one of several bodies which participate in the transatlantic cultural and scholarship exchanges dedicated to Jones.

When Jones finished his remarks on that unforgettable occasion some 30 years ago, he

Bobby Jones outside
R & A headquarters with
the Open trophy in 1927,
cheered to the echo by
the people of the town
who grew to love him as
he did them and their
course.

clambered into the electric golf cart which he relied upon to get about. As he motored slowly down the aisle, the packed congregation broke into a spontaneous rendition of the traditional Scottish song 'Will Ye No' Come Back Again?' He never did.

His audience, choked with emotion, took several minutes to wipe the tears from their eyes and clear their throats to speak. They were not to know that Jones had 13 more years of physical pain to endure. He died in December 1971. In May 1972 the R & A held a memorial service for him. In that same year he was accorded the privilege that would have delighted him the most. The 10th hole, previously nameless, was christened 'Bobby Jones'.

The 18th is called Tom Morris, but no other holes have been named in recognition of individuals. Those two reflect the contributions to golf of two men – one British, one American; one a professional, the other amateur; one from the 19th century, the other of the 20th; but both great champions.

Jones adored St Andrews as surely did Morris. In the course of his eloquent comments that evening in 1958, he summed up the eternal appeal of the cradle of the game.

'The more I studied the Old Course the more I loved it, and the more I loved it the more I studied it.' He likened it to a woman – a 'nice old lady, whimsically tolerant of my impatience but ready to reveal the secrets of her complex being if I would only take the trouble to study and learn.' And, finally, he captured the essence of its fascination and attraction as a place to play golf. 'There is always a way at St Andrews, although it is not always the obvious way.'

The ultimate accolade.
Jones receives the
Freedom of the Burgh of
St Andrews – the first
American recipient since
Benjamin Franklin 199
years previously – in a
moving ceremony in
1958.

CHAPTER FOURTEEN

The Architects: the Men who Make it Possible

'Nature is really a wonderfully good architect, when she is in a painstaking mood', wrote Bernard Darwin just after the turn of the century. He was referring to Royal Ashdown Forest, in the heart of the beautiful Sussex countryside, a course unblemished by sand bunkers or any other features which are unsympathetic to the natural environment, but the essence of Darwin's comment has a far wider application than the peaceful rural setting of south-eastern England.

It pertains in particular to the links courses where golf began in Scotland; to places like St Andrews. These stretches of sandy ground along the British coastline were bequeathed by the receding seas following the last Ice Age. The wind blasted the sand deposits into the shapes we now know as dunes and generally ensured the land was undulating rather than perfectly flat. This was then fertilized by the guano of indigenous or migrating birds and eventually many strains of grass took root. These came to provide the fine, firm turf on which links golf established itself; they were the origins of the sward upon which the first recognizable golf courses were created and upon which millions of disciples proclaim the game is best enjoyed. Eventually heather and gorse found a home there too, alongside the marram which today inhabits many of those areas of a links familiar only to the errant golfer and his lost ball.

It has taken one inadequate paragraph to describe centuries of evolution, and it would have taken several centuries more for Mother Nature to learn to prepare greens and plant flagsticks all over the Scottish countryside. That was where man stepped in. Golf was initially a kind of non-equine point-to-point. Man developed the links land by cutting holes and excavating bunkers, but on courses like St Andrews, Leith, Musselburgh, Montrose, Dornoch, Carnoustie and North Berwick the types and locations of hazards were generally dictated by the natural flow of the rolling ground. The greens were sited

in spots which were again suggested by the terrain, perhaps on raised plateaux as are found notably at St Andrews and Dornoch. Nature did such a good job at the former (as has already been discussed at length) that Bobby Jones declared that if he was confined to playing just one course for the rest of his life it would be the Old Course, while Dornoch was both a revelation and inspiration to Pete Dye, one of the most famous American golf course architects of the current generation.

Dye was a neophyte when he first went to Dornoch, on the Sutherland coast of north-east Scotland, in 1963. He returned home professing a fascination for its unspoilt qualities, its 'ageless aura'. His comment, 'when you play it you get the feeling you could be living just as easily in the 1800s, or even the 1700s' should not be taken as implying that the course is outdated. Dornoch, like St Andrews, is essentially a timeless classic. The only major concession to the march of the years is that it has had to be lengthened – first to cope with the gutty and later to contend with the rubber-cored ball – to enable it to remain a valid test. The increasing distance the ball can travel is no less a factor today and it has affected far younger courses than Dornoch.

Nature not only provided – unprompted – the land upon which man began to play golf but it is reckoned that, until golf course architecture became a profession about 100 years ago, she also made a better job of shaping it than did most of her human contemporaries. Dr Alister Mackenzie, one of the greatest golf course architects, declared in 1920: 'I believe the real reason St Andrews Old Course is infinitely superior to anything else is owing to the fact that it was constructed when no one knew anything about the subject at all, and since then it has been considered too sacred to be touched.'

The desire to appear 'natural looking' was as important 100 years ago as it is now. Mackenzie recited the tale of one contractor's solution to the

Dr Alister Mackenzie, who represents the architectural amalgamation of the old world and the new. A Scotsman by birth, it was in the United States that he made his most lasting impressions.

The old-fashioned virtues of Royal Dornoch are by no means outdated. This photograph of the short 10th exemplifies its devilish bunkers and plateau greens.

problem of making the contours and slopes of his greens seem God-given rather than man-made. He told his rival that the dilemma was easily resolved – he simply employed the biggest fool in the village and told him to make them flat.

The earliest architects tended to treat as sacrosanct the ground they were given to work with, which was fine for Old Tom Morris when he laid out Lahinch in Ireland but was a totally useless attitude when the planner was confronted with the heavy, clay-based soils often encountered inland. Great vision was necessary; so too was the ability to harness the horsepower (and not much else) that the architect had at his disposal in his attempts to mould the countryside to the best effect.

Old Tom was one of the eminent greenkeepers/ professionals of the day, and in his era the post of greenkeeper was more prestigious than that of professional. He took to golf course design in a simplistic and rudimentary fashion. He travelled to Westward Ho! to build the links there, although to say he built it is generously over-emphasizing his primitive plans which had 12 holes criss-crossing one another. But he was a Scot, and as such regarded as an expert. In fact, he subsequently refined his craft and imaginatively avoided the traditional concept of nine holes out, nine holes back when he designed Muirfield in Scotland and Royal County Down at Newcastle in Northern Ireland. His sophisticated routing on

both courses called for the holes to tack at different directions for two separate loops of nine, not only eliminating the tedium of playing in the same direction and in the same wind conditions for nine consecutive holes but also offering the advantage of two possible starting points.

Despite this touch of ingenuity on what are established as two of the great links of the world, Morris and the early pioneers were frequently guilty of including such integral St Andrean features as stone walls and hidden bunkers on courses where they appeared as anachronisms and excrescences, not the natural hazards their

Old Tom Morris laid out Lahinch in Ireland, and Mackenzie was called in later to remodel it. One hole he was not permitted to touch was the 6th, where the green is totally blind from the tee. Blind holes such as this, and those at old Scottish courses like Prestwick, have become increasingly scorned by course architects.

Willie Park Jnr – son of the first Open champion and twice winner of the Open himself, and perhaps the first real golf course architect.

Harry Colt (on the left) on site at St Cloud, Paris. This master British architect built scores of wonderful courses, St Cloud being one of those abroad and Swinley Forest (right) being one of his most notable achievements at home. This is the par-3 10th, where the large bunker well short of the green still traps many a weak tee shot today.

proponents had envisaged. But they did their work cheaply and thereby enabled course construction to flourish and more people to take up golf. The prevailing philosophy was summed up by Horace Hutchinson: 'The laying out of a golf course is a wonderfully easy business, needing very little special training.' The late years of the 19th century were dubbed the 'dark ages of golf architecture' by Tom Simpson, who was one of the men to do something substantial about altering that sad state of affairs. Alister Mackenzie was equally harsh in his indictment of the practices of some of his predecessors.

'Golf on a good links is, in all probability, the best game in the world, but on the late-Victorian type of inland course, where there is a complete lack of variety, flat fairways, flat unguarded greens, long grass, necessitating frequent searching for lost balls, and mathematically placed hazards consisting of the cop or pimple variety, it not only offends all the finest instincts of the artist and the sportsman, but it is the most boring game in existence.'

Denunciations of the game from an enthusiast are seldom as explicit as that. However, salvation was at hand with the realization that the best turf for golf courses was that which was least suitable for farming. The characteristics of the arable land which Mackenzie deplored – thick grass on impervious loam – were replaced by fine close-cropped turf and fast-draining soil on the heathlands to the south and west of London. The sandy subsoil of the region was a heaven-sent gift for golfers, once the heather and bracken had been cleared, and it spawned a new breed of golf course architects. They were called amateurs, because they had not earned a living from playing the game as their forerunners had, but they were really the first professionals in the field.

To the fore were men like Willie Park Jr., John Abercromby, Harry Colt and Herbert Fowler. Park, son of the first Open champion and twice winner himself, was a genuine innovator who has since been acclaimed as the first proper, capable golf architect. His book *The Game of Golf*, published in 1896, represented man's initial effort at putting into words the theory behind the profession.

A sample of the credentials of these four and their successors will have to suffice here. Park laid out Sunningdale and Huntercombe and began work on Worplesdon. That task was completed by Abercromby, who also built Coombe Hill and The Addington. Colt's first job was to design Rye, a superb English links on the Sussex coast. His expertise in the use of the sandhills there was so well appreciated that he was able to quit his reluctant vocation, the law, to realize his ambition to become a golf course architect. He accepted the position of secretary at the newly-opened Sunningdale club in 1901 and was responsible for planting the hundreds of pines which today adorn that beautiful course. When Park had laid it out it was largely a treeless site.

Colt was a master. He later designed Swinley Forest (which he called 'the least bad course' he ever built), Stoke Poges, St George's Hill, both courses at Wentworth and the New Course at Sunningdale. The fact that he was chosen to lay out the Eden Course at St Andrews is an indication of the esteem in which he was held. He did other admirable work too, including the extensive revision of both courses at Royal Portrush in Ireland and the building of Le Touquet in France, Kennemer in Holland, Falkenstein at Hamburg and Puerta de Hierro at Madrid.

Herbert Fowler's most renowned creations are at two 36-hole golf clubs near London, Walton Heath and the Berkshire. Nobody had a surer sense than he of making the best use of the land available. It was said that at Walton he simply followed the plans mapped out by nature. James Braid was appointed the club's professional when it opened in 1904, and he and his fellow-members of the Great Triumvirate followed in the footsteps of the professionals-cum-architects of the 19th century. They made a fair fist of things too. Braid remained true to his Scottish roots with his commitments at Gleneagles, Carnoustie, Blairgowrie and Dalmahoy. J. H. Taylor collaborated with Fred Hawtree in a huge number of remodelling projects, notably Royal Birkdale, and they energetically promoted the cause of public courses and the welfare of artisan golfers. The third of this great trio of pre-war championship golf, Harry Vardon, was less prolific, though Ganton in Yorkshire and Little Aston in the English Midlands were two clubs to benefit from his sagacity.

Tom Simpson became a prominent figure in the field after the First World War. He joined forces with Fowler and left his mark by altering existing heathland courses like Sunningdale New and New Zealand (which is in Surrey, not the southern hemisphere); improving the glorious links of Cruden Bay in Scotland; and designing magnificent courses in France at Morfontaine, Chantilly, Deauville and Hossegor. Simpson employed as an apprentice Philip Mackenzie Ross who, after the Second World War, joined forces with Cecil Hutchinson and resurrected Turnberry from an airfield into an Open Championship venue. Hutchinson was earlier in partnership with Sir Guy Campbell (whose first project produced the beautiful West Sussex Golf Club and whose later plans led to the breathtaking original course at Killarney in Ireland) and Colonel Stafford Hotchkin. The latter purchased a remarkable tract of land at Woodhall Spa in Lincolnshire – a sand-based property of fine turf, rolling terrain and an abundance of assorted trees and heather in a landscape largely distinguished by its lack of distinction – and on it he laid out what is indisputably one of the finest inland courses in Europe.

Hotchkin later emigrated to South Africa, where the outstanding Durban Country Club was his *pièce de résistance*. He and Simpson were just two of the Britons who followed the example set by Willie Park, Herbert Fowler and Harry Colt by displaying their expertise overseas. They were all men who appreciated the qualities of the pine and birch country in which they built their early masterpieces. They recognized how to use nature and when to reject or improve what she had

given. They had an eye for aesthetic values and as a result they created features which were in empathy with the surroundings: greens and hazards of subtle patterns and contours rather than hideous geometric shapes which only looked right on a drawing board. In short, they elevated what had generally been a crude pastime into an art. Three of Colt's associates, Charles Alison, John Morrison and Alister Mackenzie, also took their talents abroad. Mackenzie left the imprint of his genius in several places but, though he was a Scotsman, it was in the United States that he was to make his most seminal impression.

The first American golf course that looked like one was Shinnecock Hills on Long Island, New York. It was built by one of those *émigré*

The 6th tee at Woodhall Spa. This is arguably the finest inland course in the British Isles – a landscape reminiscent of Sunningdale transported 200 miles north from Berkshire into the otherwise open flatlands of central England.

Down to the south-west and St Enedoc in Cornwall. This imposing sandhill on the 6th hole is, not surprisingly, called 'Himalayas'.

The early days of golf course construction. Labour-intensive activity (above) at Royal Mid-Surrey, near London; and the employment of the primitive scraper (below) in the United States to create mounds and undulations.

Scotsmen, Willie Dunn, who did so much to establish golf in the United States at the end of the last century. Another, Tom Bendelow, resigned his job on the *New York Herald* in 1895 and joined A. G. Spaldings Bros under the grandiose and flattering title of 'design consultant'. This was like calling a dustman 'an environmental enhancement officer'. Bendelow's sole qualification was his Scottish accent. His courses were known euphemistically as 'Sunday Specials' (and something ruder with hindsight) because a weekend afternoon was all they took to stake out – one stake for the tee, another for a simple rectangular cross-bunker, a third for a pile of dirt-covered stones, known in the vernacular as 'chocolate drop mounds', and finally one for the green, which would invariably be flat. The only element of intrigue and curiosity on these Bendelow courses was whether the greens would be round or square.

Bendelow perpetrated 600 of these abominations across America. His limited vision, not to say blindness, was allowed to go unrebuked simply because few of his clients had ever seen a proper course. But he was also limited by a budget of $25 for nine holes, and like the novices in Britain he did provide plenty of playgrounds – if hardly great courses – on which the public were able to become acquainted with golf. He and his ilk at least deserve credit for that. In later life Bendelow raised his sights and in the 1920s he unveiled the No. 3 course at Medinah, Illinois, which will hold its third US Open in 1990.

Of more permanent impact than Bendelow's rough and ready endeavours were the Chicago Golf Club, the Myopia Hunt Club near Boston and the Garden City course on Long Island. The former was the first 18-hole course in America. It was built by Charles Blair Macdonald and staged numerous national championships in its early years. Proof of its longevity, and testimony to the enduring quality of the revisions undertaken by Seth Raynor, was provided by the USGA as recently as November 1986 with the announcement that it will be the venue for the Walker Cup in 1993, the club's centenary.

Myopia benefitted from the continual devotion of Herbert Leeds. When, as a nine-holer, it hosted the 1898 US Open, it attracted widespread praise for the quality of its greens, a facet of golf course design and maintenance which has increasingly occupied minds, research and hours of conversation throughout this century. The third course, Garden City, was the brainchild of Devereux Emmet and was extensively revised for the better by Walter Travis, the great amateur.

The most influential pre-war course in America was none of these. It was instead the National Golf Links of America. The typically immodest nomenclature indicates the identity of its arrogant author, Charlie Macdonald. It also belies its actual status as one of the country's most exclusive and under-played clubs. But the suggestion of some sort of model which is also inherent in the title is not misleading. The National showed up the standard Bendelow course for what it was – a field with holes in it.

Macdonald conceived the idea in 1901 after reading an issue of the British magazine *Golf Illustrated*, which conducted a survey of leading golfers to ascertain their opinions on the best holes in the British Isles. Seldom can such a pleasant exercise have had such profound consequences. The article caught Macdonald's fancy and he travelled extensively in Britain to see and learn from those holes the panellists had selected. He took some features from them all but copied none absolutely. Two famous par-3s, the 11th (Eden) at St Andrews and 15th (Redan) at North Berwick, were among the famous British holes adapted to the meticulously chosen site he had obtained on Long Island. Macdonald repeated them on other courses, such as Yale, where he spent an astronomical $450,000 of the owner's money. Other cognisant architects followed this lead and also learned from Macdonald's underlying philosophy that the player, no matter how good or bad he is, should have to make a decision before hitting the ball; whether to go left or right, aim for the pin, or clear a bunker.

Macdonald spared no expense in acquiring the best expert advice and in altering the natural terrain to enable him to sculpt 18 exemplary holes. There were to be no weak links on the National. When it was opened it was greeted with gasps of envy and incredulity by his American rivals and unreserved admiration from knowledgeable British observers. This was the ultimate accolade. The techniques which Macdonald perfected at the National – for moving earth and experimenting with different strains of grass, for example – were later exported to Britain, along with other Americanisms like the tee peg (patented by a New Jersey dentist, William Lowell, in 1920), new terms like 'birdie', and bastardizations of old English words like 'bogey', the meaning of which was changed from par to one over by its first transatlantic crossing.

Though the British were belated beneficiaries of Macdonald's brilliance, it was in the United

States that golf course architecture boomed, leading to the Golden Age of Golf. In their comprehensive book, *The Golf Course*, Geoffrey Cornish and Ronald Whitten highlight what they call the 'Pennsylvanian Influence'. The father and son team of Henry and William Fownes conceived and nurtured Oakmont, near Pittsburgh, the epitome of the penal school of course architecture. 'A shot poorly played should be a shot irrevocably lost' was the guiding principle behind Oakmont's design, and an absurd total of 220 bunkers converted the theory into practice. The family Fownes were determined to make theirs the toughest course in the world. A fiendishly shaped rake which left

The National Golf Links of America – Charles Blair Macdonald's legacy to generations of his country's course architects. The land along the shore of Long Island was not dissimilar to the links of Britain which inspired him.

Palmer at prayer. The great man hopes for a successful recovery from the famous 'Church Pew' bunkers at Oakmont, the most notorious of the many sandy hazards on the course.

One of the most famous and historic holes in the world is the 11th at Merion. It is where Bobby Jones clinched the Grand Slam by winning the US Amateur in 1930. It is also characteristic of Hugh Wilson's skill in turning a small, gentle parkland plot into a great golf course. The Baffling Brook guards the entrance to the green, an apparently innocuous water hazard which in the 1934 US Open cost Gene Sarazen the championship (see page 70) and Bobby Cruickshank a cut skull (see page 201). Note too the now unique wicker baskets instead of flags, an idea Wilson 'borrowed' from Britain.

grooves in the bunkers, a network of drainage ditches which were designated hazards, and lightning fast and unreceptive greens were essential ingredients in this recipe for excess.

Two sons of Philadelphia, George Thomas and Albert Tillinghast, were responsible for several marvellous Californian courses. Thomas bequeathed Riviera and the North and South Courses at the Los Angeles Country Club to the film star city. Tillinghast built the San Francisco Golf Club, a worthy companion to his superb north-eastern layouts which included both courses at Winged Foot and Baltusrol and others like Five Farms at Baltimore and Ridgewood in New Jersey.

Yet two more Philadelphians left their individual marks upon golf course design. The first was Hugh Wilson, an insurance broker who built Merion in the Philadelphia suburb of Ardmore. It was of necessity a compact affair, having to be squeezed into 126 acres. From the 7th to the 13th there isn't a hole over 375 yards, and only two are par-3s, but Merion has withstood the rigours of time and advances in equipment to the extent that it has been awarded more national championships by the USGA than any other club. The course reflected ideas Wilson had picked up on a seven-month visit to Britain – the ambience of an English parkland course, with Scotch

broom in the bunkers and wicker baskets instead of flags atop the pins – but Merion is certifiably an original, not a copy. The flair Wilson demonstrated in conjuring up this perplexing blend of extremely stiff long holes and equally difficult short ones was immense. Merion is not only a triumph of routing and subtlety but a reason to mourn the fact that Wilson never undertook another project of anything like the same significance.

And then there was George Crump. This millionaire Philadelphia hotelier disappeared into the pine-clad sandhills of neighbouring New Jersey in 1913 and, bar four holes which were completed by Hugh Wilson and Harry Colt along the lines he had ordered, by the time of his death in 1918 he had produced the most daunting golf course in the world. He called it Pine Valley. This beautiful course is still the supreme test, relentlessly demanding of every shot. The reward for excellence is all the greater for realizing the consequences of failure. It is often heralded as the greatest inland golf course in the world, a fitting epitaph to Crump's perseverance and his belief in the scheme into which he poured so much of his own money. He, like Wilson, was genuinely an amateur architect, just following his spirit. Pine Valley was his only excursion into course construction. He achieved what Macdonald attempted with the National, a golf course with 18 faultless holes.

Pine Valley ties in two themes. The first is the emergence and success of the amateur architects in the early 1900s, a point emphatically underlined when Jack Neville, a real estate salesman, finished the spectacular Pebble Beach on California's Monterey Peninsula in 1919. He, like the Fowneses, Wilson and Crump had no pedigree and nor was he to add a host of further credentials to his *curriculum vitae*. Unlike the other three, Neville was blessed with a site which even Bendelow at his worst could not have totally ruined. Nevertheless, it took considerable skill to incorporate the sea views and the rugged clifftops to the best advantage and a strong nerve to handle the pressure of knowing he was working with a property of such awesome potential that there would have been plenty of critics had he fouled it up. Neville did not crack. Though Pebble is not a links (the turf on the bluffs above Carmel Bay is not the right stuff), it is not short of advocates who hail it as the finest seaside course anywhere.

Perhaps what set these men apart was the absence of other projects from their portfolios. That permitted them time to lavish all the attention necessary to erect monuments; not mere golf courses but veritable Taj Mahals on green grass rather than in white marble.

The second theme reinforced by Pine Valley was the continuing vogue for penal course architecture which Oakmont had already

espoused so religiously. Two men in particular – both Scottish expatriates – changed the trend.

The first was Donald Ross. In the 1920s, Ross's name on the blueprint of a golf course was as coveted as any designer label today. He had learned his craft at Dornoch. In his formative years in the United States he benefited from his heritage in the same way as Bendelow had. Not averse to doing a few 'quickies' himself, Ross was involved with hundreds of American courses, though only peripherally with most. Those to which he earnestly devoted his time were landmark courses and are of the highest calibre. In

'Hell's Half Acre', the unraked desert which dominates the 585-yard 7th hole at Pine Valley. This awesome Sahara stretches for over 100 yards, and so strategic is its positioning that no man has ever reached the green in two shots.

The magnificent 18th at Pebble Beach, with the tee at the far end of the promontory. The manner in which Jack Neville shaped the hole along the Pacific coast is typical of the flair and imagination with which he made the best use of the land at his disposal.

Donald Ross, who took his talent from Dornoch to the United States and with it produced such gems as Seminole in Florida. This is its 6th hole, which Ben Hogan once described as 'the greatest par-4 hole in the world'.

an eight-year spell from 1919, six Ross courses were selected for the US Open (Brae Burn, Inverness, Skokie, Oakland Hills, Worcester and Scioto), but it is two others for which he is chiefly renowned.

The No. 2 course at Pinehurst in North Carolina was opened in 1925. Ross's *tour de force* complements perfectly the grand scale, grace and tastefulness of the plush resort. It is a particularly searching examination of the short game, and the manner in which the greens tend to repel anything less than a good shot is reminiscent of Dornoch. Four years after completing Pinehurst, Ross unveiled Seminole in Florida. It represents a stirring example of strategic design, the alternative school to the penal philosophy. The latter contends that a mistake should be punished mercilessly. The former stresses the positive rather than the negative by presenting a number of options on each tee and fairway. It rewards the brave or confident golfer who successfully executes a more difficult stroke, but allows the less audacious or less gifted player the opportunity to play the hole safely. Those who bite off more than they can chew are penalized in proportion to the gravity of their error, not irretrievably damned to run up double figures on the hole.

The rise in popularity of strategic theory helped to make golf a game for everyone, not just for supermen. It also eliminated the high costs incurred in maintaining the myriad of bunkers on the penal courses, though that has never been a problem at Pine Valley where the sandy wastes are deliberately left untended. But then Pine Valley is one of a kind – its unique appeal means that what would be undesirable eccentricities elsewhere are instead its hallmarks. For the rest, the return to the strategic values upheld through the ages by St Andrews was long overdue. The clinching factor was Augusta National, built by Alister Mackenzie with the help of Bobby Jones.

Like Harry Colt, Mackenzie renounced his original profession, in his case medicine, to turn to course architecture. Two English courses, Alwoodley and Moortown at Leeds, established his reputation. He enhanced it with his modifications to Lahinch, of which he said (with an uncomfortable echo of Charles Macdonald): 'Lahinch will make the finest and most popular course that I, or I believe anyone else, ever constructed.' Mackenzie did as much as anyone to prove that statement wrong by following up with the West Course at Royal Melbourne in Australia and Cypress Point in California, next door to Pebble Beach, where three oceanside holes, the 15th, 16th and 17th, are among the most photographed in the world. When Jones was surprisingly knocked out in the first round of the 1929 US Amateur at Pebble, he took his clubs down to Cypress for a game and was so impressed by what he saw – who wouldn't be? – that Mackenzie became the man Jones sought for the job at Augusta shortly after his retirement from competitive golf. Ironically, Mackenzie only received the commission at Cypress Point when the club's first choice, Seth Raynor, died.

Mackenzie certainly made the optimum use of his chance at Cypress and again at Augusta. The Augusta National had a profound influence on golf course architecture. Its special attributes have already been noted in Chapter 6. With its wide fairways, dearth of bunkers and huge greens it was the ultimate exposition of strategic design, and no hole more so than the 13th, that 465-yard dog-leg left par-5. Does one play safe off the tee, to the right side of the fairway, and ensure a safe five, bearing in mind that too far right lands you in the trees? Or does one cut the corner and risk tangling with the tall pines? And after an adequate or even perfect drive, is it worth attempting to carry the creek in front of the green?

Among Alister Mackenzie's finest creations is Cypress Point in California. This is the 16th. It measures 233 yards and is – obviously – almost all carry. For the average player the only way to tackle it is to attempt the shorter journey to the headland to the left and then rely on a pitch to the green. Even for the cream of professional golf, the 16th is a formidable obstacle. The annual statistics invariably confirm it as being the hardest hole on the US PGA Tour.

That hole, and the entire course, follows the tenor of the principles enunciated by Mackenzie in his codification of 13 of 'the essential features of an ideal golf course' which were listed in his book *Golf Architecture*, published in 1920, and are reproduced opposite. Mackenzie and Jones not only created the most radical departure from the hitherto popular penal style but they also refused to be hidebound by conventions, like those that dictate a par-4 has to be a hole measuring between 251 and 475 yards, with a par-3 being anything below and a par-5 anything above those limits. The 13th offends the dogma on one side while the 10th (a majestic downhill par-4 of 485 yards) goes the other way. Shot values and judgement were what Mackenzie and Jones were concerned with, not strict adherence to a card par.

In subsequent years, too many architects imitated Augusta's greens on the misconceived premise that big was beautiful. The strategy seldom worked elsewhere but at Augusta it was exactly right. There was also a sad footnote. Mackenzie, like Crump, did not live to see his course in play.

The appearance of Augusta National coincided with the Great Depression, when most courses built in the United States were municipal layouts funded by generous government programmes. Considering the fact that they were geared for

Mackenzie's 'essential features of an ideal golf course'

1 The course, where possible, should be arranged in two loops of nine holes.

2 There should be a large proportion of good two-shot holes, two or three drive-and-pitch holes, and at least four one-shot holes.

3 There should be little walking between the greens and tees, and the course should be arranged so that in the first instance there is always a slight walk forwards from the green to the next tee; then the holes are sufficiently elastic to be lengthened in the future if necessary.

4 The greens and fairways should be sufficiently undulating, but there should be no hill climbing.

5 Every hole should have a different character.

6 There should be a minimum of blindness for the approach shots.

7 The course should have beautiful surroundings, and all the artificial features should have so natural an appearance that a stranger is unable to distinguish them from nature itself.

8 There should be a sufficient number of heroic carries from the tee, but the course should be arranged so that the weaker player with the loss of a stroke or portion of a stroke shall always have an alternative route open to him.

9 There should be infinite variety in the strokes required to play the various holes – viz., interesting brassy shots, iron shots, pitch and run-up shots.

10 There should be a complete absence of the annoyance and irritation caused by the necessity of searching for lost balls.

11 The course should be so interesting that even the plus man is constantly stimulated to improve his game in attempting shots he has hitherto been unable to play.

12 The course should be so arranged that the long handicap player, or even the absolute beginner, should be able to enjoy his round in spite of the fact that he is piling up a big score.

13 The course should be equally good during winter and summer, the texture of the greens and fairways should be perfect, and the approaches should have the same consistency as the greens.

mass consumption, their quality was uniformly high. But overall, more clubs closed than opened in the States during the 1930s and 1940s. Augusta apart, most of the few top-class courses of this epoch – like Southern Hills and Prairie Dunes – sprang from the fertile drawing board of Perry Maxwell.

The Second World War represents an appropriate juncture to take stock. The premier American architects had shown a capacity to grasp the same fundamentals as Park, Colt and Fowler: the need to find or manufacture gently rolling terrain where possible; to maintain a balance in the types of shot required; and to create an intriguing and visually appealing test of golf, preferably one which appeared – even if falsely – to be virtually untainted by the hand of man. The Americans hastened the demise of blind holes, or what Prince Charles might have called the 'carbuncles' of golf course architecture. This process had been started by the first leading British exponents of the art and it was decisively embraced by men such as Hugh Wilson, whose Merion has only three holes where the green is not visible from the tee. He and his learned contemporaries recognized that the likes of Prestwick's 5th (Himalayas) and 17th (Alps) holes were best left to their natural home on the Ayrshire coast and not copied out of context. Instead the fashion was for bunkers to be honest,

not hidden. Decorative hazards like trees, shrubs and bushes were also encouraged.

In some respects, the post-war successors to the great American architects may have gone too far, so that a player nowadays regards a blind shot as one where the whole of the flagstick is not in view. The differences between the game on the two sides of the Atlantic have in fact generally been heightened, despite the initial cross-pollination of ideas caused by the pilgrimages to Britain of Macdonald and Wilson and the migration to America of Ross and Mackenzie. For instance, the greens in the United States tend to be so heavily protected that the only method of attacking the pin is through the air. The lusher American grasses frequently preclude the traditional Scottish chip-and-run shot anyway, but many Americans regret the way their architects have removed some of the options from the game.

By the 1950s the United States had emerged from its economic trough. Its golf course architects had two paramount advantages over their British rivals – finance and property – and they did not squander their superiority. They dominated their field as comfortably as their professionals did the tournament scene. If the earlier 1900s have received the majority of attention here, that is because it was the period when standards of excellence were set. Any comprehensive ranking of the top 50 courses in the United States is bound to favour the pre-war era, especially at the top end of the list. The same is true of the British Isles, but there the bias is frankly disturbing. When the UK magazine *Golf World* published such a survey in November 1986, only three of the 50 courses were of post-war origin, and one of those was built by an American.

That last course in question, the New at Ballybunion in Ireland, is testimony to the skill of Robert Trent Jones. He was born in England in 1906 but moved to the United States with his parents at the age of five. Perhaps the simplest way to salute his significance is to quote again from *The Golf Course* by Cornish and Whitten. The authors call Jones 'the man who had the greatest impact on the profession of golf course architecture, and upon the game of golf itself'.

That's a pretty effusive and unequivocal tribute, but Jones has certainly been the influential post-war figure in a profession which for him was never anything other than his intended vocation. He even devised his own syllabus for his studies at Cornell University. When he graduated he walked into a world of affluence, with scores of people eager to supply the land on which they wanted a first-rate golf course and the money with which to build it. Trent Jones was happy to oblige. He was lucky to have qualified at a time of great prosperity in the United States, when the golf craze was getting into full swing, and to have had the incalculable benefit of a practical education from a mentor like Stanley Thompson, the man responsible for several of Canada's finest courses. But fortune wasn't half of it. Talent and an appetite for work were Jones's prime assets.

He is as esteemed for the courses he has revised as for those he has built. The former group includes Oakland Hills, which Ben Hogan called the 'monster' at the 1951 US Open, Augusta National and Baltusrol. Trent Jones teamed up with Bobby Jones not only at Augusta but also at Peachtree in the latter's home-town of Atlanta, where the length of the tees (around 40 yards) and the size of the greens (averaging 8000 square feet) are extraordinary. Long tees became almost a patented Trent Jones trademark. They allow the high-handicap golfer to enjoy his game off the front markers while keeping the professionals in check off the back, and the hazards come into play for both categories. The course can thus be stretched from around 6000 to 7500 yards and yet be a valid test at either end of the range. Jones also

propounded the notion that every hole should be a tough par but an easy bogey. His big greens can play easily or severely, depending on their pace and the location of the flag.

In addition to the above, Trent Jones put forward a third theory of architecture: the heroic theory. It was not a revolutionary concept because Macdonald had done something like it at the National, but Jones widely promoted the idea of offering alternative routes for the player, always threatening the most rewarding line with a horrific bunker, a water hazard or something similarly unpleasant. It was almost a composite philosophy between the penal and strategic schools. The deficiences of penal design were amply demonstrated when Jones was called in to remodel Oakland Hills for the 1951 US Open. He discovered the existing bunkers were largely redundant. He had to open up new ones because the top pros were able to blast the ball past all the old traps. Furthermore, he had to go back and do it again for the 1985 Open. Johnny Miller proved the same point at Oakmont in the 1973 US Open with his 63. It is no threat to have a plethora of bunkers if they are in the wrong place. As Jones once remarked, that is the essential truth that elevates Pine Valley. There the problem is not confined to making the carries; trouble is alongside every fairway so you have to be straight as well. Advances in equipment have taken their toll on other courses, which have had to be modified or lengthened or else risk being rendered obsolete.

Among Jones's original American courses are those at superb resort destinations like Dorado

Robert Trent Jones, golf course architect *extraordinaire*, and two of his masterpieces on different continents.

Opposite page The 13th hole on the New Course at Ballybunion, a modern links with all the glories of its most distinguished ancestors.

Below The 3rd hole at Spyglass Hill, another of the marvellous layouts along California's Monterey Peninsula.

Beach on Puerto Rico, Mauna Kea in Hawaii, and Cotton Bay in the Bahamas. They catered for the boom in demand for luxury golf holidays and they are not out of place beside Jones's mainland accomplishments such as Peachtree, Spyglass Hill in California and Firestone in Ohio.

Jones has not been without his critics, and often vehement ones. When Tony Jacklin won the 1970 US Open at Jones's Hazeltine, the runner-up, Dave Hill, was fined for saying that all it lacked was 80 acres of corn and a few cows. 'They ruined a good farm when they built this course,' he said.

Other critics have alleged that his courses are too expensive to maintain (though Jones claims the very opposite); look too much alike because he has accepted too many assignments; and rely too heavily on water as a hazard in an exaggerated attempt to counteract the golfer's increasing proficiency with the sand wedge. His publicists have also been guilty of advertising every new Trent Jones development as 'a championship course', thereby turning a meaningful compliment into a meaningless blurb. The venue for the 1987 Buckinghamshire Girls' (Harewood Downs, if you're interested) is more accurately described as a championship course than is a newly-opened 7000-yard multi-million dollar complex which will never stage anything more earth-shattering than a pro-am.

Robert Trent Jones Jnr sculpted the beautiful Bossey course from some unpromising terrain above Geneva on the French/Swiss border. It is a prime instance of how a big budget and enlightened planning can enable a golf course to be built even without nature's co-operation.

The degree of credibility one attaches to each of these points is purely subjective. It may be that Jones's best work has been achieved outside America. The New Course at Ballybunion is a stunning triumph, a worthy companion to the magnificence of the Old. Jones handled with care and delicacy a piece of land every bit as compelling as that which confronted Jack Neville at Pebble Beach. At Ballybunion Jones realised a lifelong ambition to build a genuine links. He came up with a masterpiece.

Jones has had several successes on the continent too, including Sotogrande, for many people the jewel of Spain's Costa del Sol; I Roveri, a parkland gem in Turin; Troia, a controversial quasi-links near Lisbon; and Pevero, dramatically blasted out of volcanic rock on the Mediterranean island of Sardinia. Altogether Jones has designed over 400 courses in 25 countries.

Jones did not have the 1950s and 1960s entirely to himself, however. Another man who spent the best part of two decades sifting through a mountain of mail was Louis (Dick) Wilson, no relation to Hugh but coincidentally another man who perpetuated the Philadelphian dynasty with some exemplary projects, primarily in America and notably in Florida. His protégé, Joe Lee, continued to carry the torch, and the flame of American golf course architecture has been kept burning by scores of practitioners, including family partnerships such as the Fazios and the Maples.

It would be pointless to list them all here, but a handful of names and details are in order. Trent Jones's two sons, Rees and Robert Jnr (Bobby), have embarked on the task of trying to emerge from the shadows of a famous father. They have managed it well and both sons have also shown a yearning to spread their wings beyond the United States. Bobby's course at Bossey in France, overlooking Lake Geneva, is proof too of the way the art has become a science. An immediately suitable site is no longer a pre-requisite: given a big budget, a golf course can be laid out anywhere. Bossey is halfway up a mountain, which usually means a tedious series of uphill holes. Jones has avoided that with some judicious and ingenious planning. By extending a few of the walks between green and tee, he has ensured that Bossey is played almost on the level, or even downhill.

Another man to utilize modern technology to the utmost effect is Paul (Pete) Dye. He has now joined his compatriots in exploiting the vast potential of Europe but it is in and around the United States that he established a reputation which has carried around the world. His breathtakingly beautiful holes at Casa de Campo, beside the Caribbean surf of the Dominican Republic, epitomize his inventiveness and ability to harness the machinery and implement the research which now makes it possible to drain marshes, irrigate deserts and replace a wilderness with paradise. The golf course architect today has to be an expert in agronomy, botany, chemistry, geology and civil engineering, or have access to someone who is, and combine these practical qualifications with the eye of an aesthete.

Controversy and admiration have followed Pete Dye's career in approximately equal measure. His Tournament Players' Club at the US Tour's headquarters in Florida caused an uproar when the professionals first played it. They complained the greens were convex and therefore threw the ball off them, even when a shot was struck perfectly. Amendments were made, but water and huge sandy wastes are still apparent in abundance, as is Dye's signature – the use of railroad ties, or sleepers, an idea he stole from Scotland and took to America for inclusion on great courses like Harbour Town at Hilton Head in South Carolina. Across the nation in California, a new Dye course, PGA West, has already been allocated the 1991 Ryder Cup. This former desert is now a glorious golfing oasis, but an oasis without respite. Lee Trevino took one look and said: 'I know some courses which are easier than the practice ground here.'

Dye has been in the vanguard of his country's movement towards a return to small greens and good old punitive pot bunkers, as opposed to the commonplace American fairway traps which the rawest novice can blithely wander into with a 4-wood. Even grass bunkers are making a comeback. This is part of a transformation colloquially termed the 'natural look', though it can paradoxically be an expensive exercise and there may be more than a shred of validity in the assertion that British architects are more content to leave the land in its pristine state rather than disturb everything as many of them allege the Americans are prone to do. Sceptics suggest the natural look in the United States involves digging up the site and then putting things back again as they were. This is denied by the converted who preach that their manoeuvrings reduce maintenance costs and that less manicured courses are desirable and inevitable. In truth, 'natural' in

Two stunning examples of the malevolent genius of Pete Dye, from the spectacular Casa de Campo along the ocean to the controversial PGA West in the desert.

No expense has been spared by the owners, Hermon and Martin Bond, in enabling Jack Nicklaus to build the new course at St Mellion. This is the heavily guarded 12th green. Few British architects have been entrusted with that sort of capital, but equally few people can complain that Nicklaus's work on this project is not of the highest quality.

America is occasionally and confusingly equated with 'Scottish'. Jack Nicklaus has designed two courses, Grand Cypress and Loxahatchee, whose characteristics and hazards resemble a Scottish links at first sight, but whether the flatlands of Florida is the right place to recreate Dornoch is a matter for debate.

Nicklaus is the foremost professional golfer turned course architect. One would expect no less of him. Several other pros have also taken the plunge but without producing anything of the quality to be found at Nicklaus's Muirfield Village (venue for the 1987 Ryder Cup), Glen Abbey (regular home of the Canadian Open) and Shoal Creek (site of the 1984 USPGA Championship and slated in again for 1990). He has additionally undertaken work in Australia, Japan, continental Europe and Britain, where his debut effort, the marvellous St Mellion course in Cornwall, was officially opened in the summer of 1987. Arnold Palmer and his partner, Ed Seay, have been similarly peripatetic, leaving their mark in China, Japan, Ireland – at the spectacular Tralee course in Co. Kerry – as well as in North America.

The amount of money spent on St Mellion has been a popular guessing game for some time in Britain. Nicklaus's thoroughness, which is legendary and does not come cheap, extends to a clause being inserted into his contracts specifying that one of his staff must supervise the course's maintenance for a number of years after completion. And Nicklaus is not afraid to test the size of his client's wallet. Hall Thompson, the owner of Shoal Creek, once said: 'I gave Jack an unlimited budget and he exceeded it.'

That sort of tale is sour news indeed to British architects, who have to fight the legacy of all those great courses built in the last century or early 1900s where the clubs actually have the freehold to their land. These men have to battle to overcome the resultant view that golf club subscriptions and green fees should be as low as possible. It is clearly not easy for them to build new courses in Britain of the calibre we have been discussing when people are not prepared to pay the vast sums for their golf that they are overseas. The situation is even harder to bear when the prestige projects in Britain are entrusted to foreigners who have made their names in a far more favourable climate, both economically and weather-wise, and in a country with an almost boundless supply of land available for the purpose. The contrasting circumstances on either side of the Atlantic are not restricted to the insistence on a variety of clubhouse amenities in America and a dogged devotion to faster-running fairways in Britain.

But the British have not been moribund. The lack of land and the financial constraints at home may have led to precious few other courses of the quality of Southerness, St Pierre, Woburn and The Belfry adding to the enjoyment of the British golfer since the last war, but approaching 400 courses have been built since 1970, 40 per cent of them being municipal layouts. And architects from Britain have continued to export their skills in the wake of Colt, Simpson and other crusaders, in particular to the European continent where property and cash are seemingly quite plentiful.

Fred Hawtree, whose father had been associated with J. H. Taylor, designed Royal Waterloo in Belgium and St Nom-la-Bretèche near Paris. He even retaliated to the transatlantic challenge by laying out Mount Mitchell in North Carolina. Ken Cotton produced Olgiata in Italy, while Frank Pennink numbered Halmstad in Sweden, Noordwijk in Holland and Vilamoura in Portugal among his most impressive performances. These two formed a company with Charles Lawrie, and St Pierre and both courses at Woburn are part of their British collection. Though all three are now dead, the firm continues to prosper at home and overseas with Donald Steel, who is also a distinguished golf correspondent, at the helm. The late John Harris was another Briton who worked abroad extensively.

English-speaking architects have not had a monopoly. Bernard von Limburger from West

Germany was responsible for scores of courses all over Europe, including the superb Club zur Vahr at Bremen, and Spain's Javier Arana completed 11 layouts in his home country. One of them, El Saler near Valencia, is arguably the finest course on the continent. The development in the east which was stimulated by the British (notably Charles Alison) was nourished by the emergence of native architects like Kinya Fujita in Japan.

American golf course architects have occupied the bulk of this chapter. In the past half century they have been the major trend-setters and the midwives to the majority of great new courses. They will probably be the names who are remembered in another 50 years time. In addition to the reasons already referred to, that is because the growth of the game on inland ground and away from coastal links has logically led to the American influence being propagated. Even recent British inland layouts – like the Duke and Duchess Courses at Woburn and Letham Grange near Arbroath in Scotland (the loving creation of an entrepreneur called Ken Smith) – resemble classic American designs rather than the traditional British courses exemplified by Sunningdale and Walton Heath.

Obviously, most new courses have no pretensions to represent a watershed in design or to become a regular tournament stop. They cost nearer £200,000 than £2 million. They are intended simply to please and satisfy those who play them. But every course, of whatever stature, is dependent upon the skill of the greenkeeper. A good man will show it off to the best effect; a poor one will have the golfers on temporary greens at the first sign of winter.

And then there are the committee men and club captains anxious to leave their mark. As someone is reported to have said of Lindbergh's first solo flight across the Atlantic: 'It would have been more wonderful if he'd done it with the aid of a committee.' The architect may be permitted to finish his course in peace but there will be 100-plus amateur 'experts' in every club who would love to interfere or tamper with it – and some actually do the whole lot from scratch themselves. There is a bit of architect in every golfer, and sometimes Mr Hyde makes his escape and wreaks havoc. The awful consequences can be seen at some appalling courses throughout the world, and nowhere more than in the British Isles.

Golf course architects have contributed massively to our pleasure over the past 100 years, perhaps more than any other single body of people involved in the game. They are the men who make it possible to be seduced by its infinite temptations and attractions – the splendid solitude of Pine Valley and Swinley Forest, the tranquil beauty of Sunningdale and Woodhall Spa, the gorgeous scenery of Augusta National and Pebble Beach, the ancient charm of St Andrews and Dornoch, the rugged majesty of Birkdale and Ballybunion, and so on. But even in a less romantic setting, surrounded by a housing estate or close to factories and offices, the golf course provides the reason for our affection and fondness for the sport. The glory of golf lies in being out there. That is what it's all about.

Above The view from behind the 3rd green on the Duke's Course at Woburn, near Milton Keynes in the heart of England.

Below The renowned 6th hole at Vilamoura, on Portugal's Algarve coast. Vilamoura illustrates that the British are still able to follow the traditions established by the likes of Harry Colt and build some excellent courses overseas.

CHAPTER FIFTEEN

La Crème de la Crème: Classic Courses

The final paragraph of the last chapter leads us conveniently into this one. As well as being a conclusion it serves as a kind of introduction to the 24 courses featured here.

If you will forgive the grammatical solecism, this is a random selection, certainly far more arbitrary than the system used to arrive at the 30 Household Names in Chapter 3. It takes in eight courses from the British Isles – including the Republic of Ireland – eight from the United States and eight more from as many different other countries (in that order by alphabet). It does not pretend to be a ranking of the top 24 courses in the world. How could it when there is no St Andrews, no Augusta? Those two giants have been covered extensively elsewhere in this book, hence their exclusion now, and there are at least a couple of dozen other courses which could justifiably claim a place in an equally auspicious alternate listing. Royal St George's at Sandwich

and Royal County Down at Newcastle, Northern Ireland, are two links that fall comfortably into that category; Merion and Woodhall Spa are among the most magnificent and beautiful inland courses in the world; while El Saler and Vilamoura combine some of the qualities of both terrains. That's just six for starters.

What these 24 courses do illustrate is golf at its best and at its most cosmopolitan, at its heights of excellence and at its most exotic. They all deserve their inclusion here and they all demonstrate why many of us are prepared to swear that golf is the greatest game there is.

BALLYBUNION
Co. Kerry, Republic of Ireland

Herbert Warren Wind called the Old Course at Ballybunion 'the finest seaside course I have ever seen'. Robert Trent Jones described the property at his disposal for the building of the New as 'the

The 15th on the Old Course at Ballybunion displays all the virtues of links golf – a great hole, rugged sandhills, a visible (albeit tough) target and the ocean in view.

The Queen's Course at Gleneagles is rather overshadowed by the reputation of the King's. It may not be quite such as stern a test as its neighbour but it yields to nowhere in terms of natural beauty.

finest piece of linksland that I had ever seen'. One must assume that both these eminent Americans are telling the truth, so which is right? Well, Wind was speaking before Trent Jones, with the considerable assistance of nature, sculptured the New Course in the 1980s, so there is no dilemma as such. The sensible attitude is to follow the club members' lead and declare Ballybunion to be the proud and lucky possessor of the best 36 holes of links golf in the world. Tom Simpson recognized the Old for what it was when he was called in to revise it substantially for the 1937 Irish Amateur Championship. He moved just three greens and inserted one bunker. Part of Simpson's genius lay in his ability to acknowledge that even he could not improve on what God had done.

GLENEAGLES
Auchterarder, Perthshire, Scotland
When a visitor returns from his first visit to Gleneagles he will inevitably wax lyrical for hours on end about the breathtaking beauty and tranquility of the surrounding hills and the opulent splendour of the famous adjoining hotel. The quality of the golf will be an after-thought, or may be even ignored altogether if the spell has captured him completely. That is not to cast aspersions on the four 18-hole courses at Gleneagles; rather it stresses the seductive powers

of the setting. The pick of the courses is the King's, with the Queen's not far behind. They are both superb Scottish golf courses, but not golf links. The dramatic rural amphitheatre of Gleneagles has more in common with the ambience normally associated with other Scottish pursuits such as salmon fishing and whisky drinking, but the golf is no less enjoyable for that.

KILLARNEY
Co. Kerry, Republic of Ireland
Killarney's reputation as the Irish Gleneagles is an obvious analogy, but such comparisons can be demeaning and indeed meaningless. Killarney is capable of happily standing on the basis of its own merits. It boasts two 18-hole layouts, Mahony's Point and Killeen, but there are many who claim that Killarney had more to brag about when it had just one course. That was designed by Sir Guy Campbell in collaboration with Henry Longhurst and the owner of the idyllic countryside around the shores of Lough Leane, the Viscount Castlerosse. Commercial considerations have caused the original to be split into two, and the best 18 holes at Killarney are probably Campbell's 18, but there is no need to shed any tears at the prospect of now having to play 36 holes to sample them all. There are a million worse places to spend a day than in this lakeside paradise.

One of the most distinctive clubhouses in British golf is that at Royal Birkdale, from where the members have watched the conclusion of six Open Championships.

MUIRFIELD
Gullane, East Lothian, Scotland

Despite the misgivings and insults which greeted its arrival on the Open Championship rota in 1892, Muirfield is today regarded as the fairest links test in tournament golf. The vituperative comments of Andrew Kirkaldy and other staunch St Andreans (see page 54) have been replaced by a common accord that Muirfield is a classic examination of skill. It represents a blend of two schools of thought, with the traditionalists being delighted at the sight of this fabulous stretch of genuine links beside the Firth of Forth and the modernists enraptured by the lack of blind shots, hidden hazards and irregular bounces. Like all links Muirfield is the better for having a breeze blowing across it, but its touchy greens and the apparently magnetic properties of its deep bunkers provide adequate defence even in calm conditions. Muirfield's impressive roll of Open champions – which includes Hilton, Vardon, Braid, Hagen, Cotton, Player, Nicklaus, Trevino and Watson – does not flatter it one bit.

ROYAL BIRKDALE
Southport, Lancashire, England

Birkdale is another course which has something for everyone. It looks exactly as a traditional links should, with towering sand dunes which make it the first stadium golf course built by God. From the point of view of catering for the thousands of spectators who attend the Open these days, Birkdale is the best championship venue. And, it should go without saying, the course itself is no slouch. Like Muirfield it is eminently fair, with flattish fairways which welcome rather than repel the accurate drive. Birkdale has only been on the Open rota since 1954, and George Lowe's original layout had by then been substantially revised by J. H. Taylor and Fred Hawtree. The latter's son continued his father's good work in the 1960s. The club's second Open was also the second for Arnold Palmer, and the scene of the great American's first win. A plaque on the 16th hole commemorates the spot from where Palmer dramatically extricated himself from some typically severe Birkdale rough *en route* to a thrilling one-shot victory over Dai Rees.

The wicked slopes of Muirfield's greens and the perils of its cavernous bunkers are both apparent from this shot from behind the short 13th.

Gleneagles is Scotland's premier inland golf venue, as renowned for the magnificence of its surroundings as for the quality of its four courses. The pride of Gleneagles, the King's Course, is caught here in a rare moment without a soul in sight.

The contrast between this photograph and the one on page 177 is startling. Sunningdale in the autumn is glorious proof of the efficacy of Harry Colt's tree-planting programme at the club. The 5th hole on the Old, and the 6th beyond it, are two of the finest holes on a marvellous golf course.

Right The 18th on the Mahony's Point course at Killarney, one of Sir Guy Campbell's original 18 and one of the most beautiful holes anywhere. It measures 202 yards and Henry Longhurst called it 'the best short hole in the world'. Longhurst may have been somewhat biased since he was involved in the design of the course, but thousands who have played it would not disagree with his opinion.

Far right Another dramatic short hole where water comes into play even more. The 12th at Muirfield Village is only 158 yards long but to err on the short side is to commit a very costly mistake.

The 17th at Cypress Point is, at 376 yards, one of the world's great par-4s. The choice from the tee is obvious – to risk the big carry over the rocks and the waves in the hope of an easy pitch to the green, or to play safely to the left of the gnarled trees.

Above One of the most fearsome shots in golf is the approach to the 8th at Pebble Beach. The players on the horizon have to decide whether to go for the flag across the chasm of the Pacific coastline or, as at Cypress Point, aim to the left and be happy to make a bogey five.

Far left The 14th at Pine Valley – 185 yards of potential torture. This idyllic setting was the scene of disaster for one hapless performer who took 44, and more modest double-figure scores are commonplace.

Left The golf course and the hotels are American-style. The topography is unmistakeably that of Rio de Janeiro. The Gavea Golf and Country Club in Brazil is expensive, exclusive and indubitably blessed with an enviable location.

Above Royal Melbourne is generally regarded as the top course in the southern hemisphere. The Championship Course takes 12 holes off the West and six from the East. This is the 176-yard 5th, a hole which does not suffer from a shortage of sand.

Surely the best hole at the Durban Country Club. The 3rd is a par-5 of 506 yards, with dense bush and large bunkers making the narrow ribbon of fairway an elusive alley indeed.

ROYAL DORNOCH
Dornoch, Sutherland, Scotland

A trip to Dornoch has become the golfing equivalent of the search for the Holy Grail. The place has acquired an almost mystical reputation, rather like a modern Camelot, an impression largely due to Dornoch's remote geographical location. It has been established that golf was played there at least as early as 1616, making it the third-oldest known course in the world after St Andrews and Leith. But it was the replacement of six weak holes after the last war which upgraded its quality, a fundamental alteration enforced on the club because the RAF had requisitioned part of its land for an airstrip. Dornoch is characterized by upraised plateau greens which make it unsurpassed as a links in its demands on the accuracy of the approach shot. Being 90 minutes drive north of Inverness, Dornoch is generally uncrowded and is probably the easiest great golf course in the world on which to get a game.

SUNNINGDALE Berkshire, England

Sunningdale is generally acclaimed to epitomize inland golf in Britain. On a summer's evening the birch, pine and heather conspire to create an intoxicating environment. The view from the 5th tee, with the 4th green in the foreground and the next two holes stretching out to the horizon between a gracious avenue of trees, has frequently been captured on film and canvas and it adorns

clubhouse walls throughout the world. The panorama from the 10th tee is equally exhilarating. Sunningdale relies on subtlety, not length, and two par-4s are under 300 yards, yet it remains a thoroughly valid championship venue. The most famous score over it was Bobby Jones's 66 in a qualifying round for the 1926 Open, an almost unheard-of achievement in those days. The Old Course, to which the foregoing refers, now has a worthy companion in the New, which may suffer by comparison in visual beauty but compensates for it by being marginally tougher.

A myriad of humps and hollows and greens set upon knolls are the essence of golf at the venerable links of Dornoch, as typified by this shot of the 4th green.

The view from behind the 4th green at Sunningdale Old Course, with the 5th and 6th holes in the distance, before the trees grew. The occasion was the London Amateur Foursomes in 1911, one of many distinguished events to grace this gracious course.

WALTON HEATH
Tadworth, Surrey, England

As its name implies, Walton Heath personifies heathland golf, and at the highest level too. It is close to Sunningdale, both on the map and in people's hearts. For every man who declares Sunningdale to be the superior another can be found to vouch for its rival. Walton Heath has hosted the Ryder Cup, Sunningdale the Walker Cup. They stage the European Opens in alternate years. They are both that good. Among the members at Walton there is a different debate – is the Old Course better than the New or vice versa? The Old is usually favoured; indeed, it supplies 15 holes to the New's three when important events are held over a special composite course, but there is very little in it. Probably no inland course anywhere is so amenable to play during all four seasons. The only problem of golfing at Walton Heath in winter lies in finding time to squeeze in a game on both wonderful courses.

CYPRESS POINT *Pebble Beach, California*

Public awareness of Cypress Point is almost confined to three of its holes – the 15th, 16th and 17th, all of which are played to the accompanying sound of the Pacific breakers on the rocks below. That is unfortunate, if understandable. They are three of the finest holes on earth and are a major part of the reason why the course has been hailed as 'the Sistine Chapel of Golf'. It is a magnificent amalgam of the best elements of links, woodland and heathland, and the holes among the cypress trees and the dunes are worthy companions to their dramatic successors alongside the ocean. Cypress is an ultra-exclusive club, although it does open its gates to the public once a year when it plays host to the stars of the US Tour. Those who see the course then understand why so many people have said that if they were restricted to playing only one course from here to eternity, Cypress Point would be it.

MUIRFIELD VILLAGE *Dublin, Ohio*

This is the definitive version of the course that Jack built. In recent years Jack Nicklaus has attempted to step out of his own shadow as the greatest professional golfer of his and maybe all generations to take on the golf course architects. Muirfield Village was only opened in 1974 yet already there are many experts who unhesitatingly award it a position among the top 10 courses in the United States, and there is no shortage of competition for that accolade. The indefatigable Nicklaus has succeeded again. The course is built on the outskirts of his home town of Columbus and is named in honour of the Scottish links where he made his Walker Cup debut in 1959 and won his first British Open in 1966. It demands every shot in the bag and is invariably in immaculate condition. But that is no surprise. Jack Nicklaus has never accepted anything less than excellence in himself, either when playing courses or when building them.

Like Sunningdale, Walton Heath relies on pine, heather and sand to trap the wayward golfer. The protection afforded to the flag on the 11th hole on the Old is a case in point.

The 15th at Cypress Point measures a mere 139 yards but it is devoid of neither danger nor scenic distraction. In quality course design, one can have strength without length.

The sanctuary of the clubhouse beckons but it takes considerable skill to negotiate the hazard-strewn route to the 18th green at Muirfield Village.

The 7th at Pebble Beach is just 120 yards from tee to green, but hitting the target with a wedge is no formality and if the wind is off the Pacific a 3-iron might be needed to get up.

PEBBLE BEACH
Monterey Peninsula, California

Given their proximity to each other, comparisons between Pebble Beach and Cypress Point are inevitable. Much the same may be said about Rome and Venice because they both happen to be in Italy. Like those two great cities, the courses have differences and similarities but they are unquestionably united by brilliance. Robert Louis Stevenson described Carmel Bay, which the best and most spectacular holes at Pebble Beach overlook, as 'the finest meeting of land and sea in the world'. That sets the appropriate tone. It may be that Pebble has more mundane holes than its equally illustrious neighbour but it probably possesses more holes of genuine championship quality and its greater length means that it is able to test the best far more rigorously than Cypress can. In 1972 Pebble Beach became the first public course to stage the US Open. Jack Nicklaus was the winner. Ten years later Tom Watson thwarted the Golden Bear in a thrilling finale. No doubt Pebble Beach will produce a champion of similar calibre at its third attempt in 1992.

PINEHURST *North Carolina*

There are now seven courses at Pinehurst and, given the way new ones are springing up all over this pine-clad sand belt, there could be one or two more by the end of the century. Even if there are, none will eclipse Donald Ross's masterpiece. The No. 2 course is synonymous with Pinehurst as surely as the Old Course is with St Andrews. Tribute has already been paid to Ross's work in the previous chapter. No. 2 exemplifies his ability. It would not win a beauty contest against Cypress Point or Pebble Beach but, as with many of the outstanding Scottish courses where Ross learned his craft, it constantly puzzles the golfer by the decisions it demands and baffles him with its insidious undulations. It will succumb to great golf and 62s have been recorded in professional tournaments. The players that have achieved those scores will cherish them forever because they enhance their reputations rather than detract from Pinehurst's. Tommy Armour summed up No. 2's appeal when he said: 'The man who doesn't feel emotionally stirred when he golfs at Pinehurst . . . should be ruled out of golf for life.'

The No. 2 Course at Pinehurst does not bludgeon the golfer into submission but instead beguiles him with its subtlety. This is the 4th, one of a quartet of par-5s.

The end in sight – the last hole at Pine Valley. One man once stood on the tee having taken 79 strokes for 17 holes and confidently expecting to win a large bet that he couldn't break 90. It took him 13 to hole out.

PINE VALLEY *Clementon, New Jersey*

One disheartened American professional called Pine Valley 'a 184-acre bunker'. An awestruck English visitor once stood on the 2nd tee and asked: 'Do you play this hole or do you photograph it?' That sums up Pine Valley. The emerald fairways and greens are generous enough but the penalty for missing either is so severe that one is intimidated into doing exactly that. Thousands of courses afford plenty of opportunities to lose balls. At Pine Valley one can lose count. People have even lost their playing partners. The rough isn't rough, it's jungle in a desert. Horror stories are legion – a man taking 44 on a par-3, the club championship being won with a 33 over par total of 173, and much more. But Pine Valley is also beautiful, both to behold and in the indescribable pleasure to be gleaned from courting all that disaster and still pulling off the intended shot. One day a leading amateur, Woody Platt, played the first four holes in six under par. He knew that sort of thing couldn't last so he retired to the bar. Pine Valley has driven many golfers to drink, but the place is so bewitching that none would wish to stay away for long.

Nobody could ever accuse the 4th, 5th and 6th holes at Seminole of being short of sand.

SEMINOLE *North Palm Beach, Florida*

Seminole is a thinking man's course and a rich man's course. Palm Beach is one of the most exclusive winter playgrounds in the United States and the club reflects the Florida season by closing during the hot and humid summer. For the other six months of the year it provides the best golf in the Sunshine State, albeit that only members and their guests get the chance to enjoy it. Seminole is not your average Florida resort course. It is said to be the only one of the hundreds of Donald Ross designs that he actually campaigned for; for the others he was sought out. He was doubtless attracted by the echoes of Scotland in the closeness of the ocean, the sea breezes and the fine, firm turf. It has other attributes that bear no resemblance to Ross's native country – such as warm winter air, beautiful palm trees and over 200 gleaming white sand bunkers which Ross created in harmony with the rolling Atlantic surf – but its class transcends frontiers. Ben Hogan, who is hardly free and easy with compliments, once said: 'If you can play Seminole, you can play any course in the world.'

The panorama from the clubhouse at Shinnecock Hills. Its hilltop vantage point commands a view over one of the most natural-looking settings in American golf.

SHINNECOCK HILLS
Southampton, Long Island, New York

This selection of eight American courses includes only two which have held the US Open. Pebble Beach is one and Shinnecock Hills the other. Add Augusta to the list of non-hosts and one can see that the United States is well endowed with fabulous courses which do not need/want the honour/hassle of staging their country's national golf tournament. Shinnecock went without it for 90 years between the second US Open in 1896 and its second in 1986 because it was considered not to have the extraneous facilities necessary for a modern major championship. But the USGA eventually decided to defy the sceptics and return to America's first great golf course. It is still great. Ben Crenshaw, the 1984 Masters champion and an enthusiastic student of the game, remarked when he heard the news: 'At the US Open the golfers will have the *privilege* of playing Shinnecock.' They did, and Raymond Floyd had the privilege of winning the title.

TOURNAMENT PLAYERS' CLUB
Sawgrass, Florida

This was the original stadium golf course. It merits inclusion in this august company as an example of contemporary course architecture at its best and at its most controversial. Pete Dye's design is ingenious; many would say disingenuous. One writer has alleged 'there are enough bad lies to blow the circuits of a polygraph'. There are 77 greenside bunkers and water, water everywhere, nowhere more than on the 17th, a 132-yard par-3 consisting of a green, a pot bunker and a lake. Machiavelli could not have devised anything more penal. When Jerry Pate won the first Tournament Players' Championship over the layout, he lived up to his promise and threw Dye and Tour Commissioner Deane Beman into the pond at the 18th. A few of the watching professionals were heard to mutter something hopeful about alligators but Dye escaped unscathed and his magnificently fiendish creation survives too, and is now copied elsewhere across the nation.

The fiendish 17th at the original Tournament Players' Club.

It would be hard to imagine a more spectacular site for a golf course than Banff. The huge building at the foot of Sulphur Mountain, by the way, is the Banff Springs Hotel – not the clubhouse.

BANFF *Alberta, Canada*

All descriptions and tales of Banff Golf Club relate to the sheer beauty and grandeur of its location. The course is surrounded by majestic firs and two swelling, swirling rivers, the Bow and the Spray. Overlooking the whole scene are the rugged snow-topped peaks of the Canadian Rockies. Stanley Thompson redesigned the course in 1927 and, to use the inelegant Americanism, he shifted a lot of dirt in the process. One would never know it without being told – the course is perfectly in empathy with its setting. The fact that it is Banff's visual beauty that one hears of should not be permitted to give the illusion that the course is a mere holiday track. It contains 6700 yards of exacting and exhilarating golf, though the altitude of 5000 feet means it plays shorter than the card suggests.

DURBAN COUNTRY CLUB
Natal, South Africa

It is widely recognized that Durban Country Club is the best course in Africa. It presents an intriguing mixture of parkland golf in a seaside environment, with the wind off the nearby Indian Ocean a constant factor. Several holes are reminiscent of a traditional British links, such as the par-4 17th where the humps and hollows would do justice to Prestwick. The course is always impeccably groomed and, while there are reminders of Britain in the atmosphere, the Durban Country Club resembles many top American courses with its verdant appearance and true, quick greens. But it is also distinctly African. The inclination of the mischievous monkeys to pelt the golfer with nuts from the safety of their treetops leaves no doubt as to which continent this course is on.

GAVEA *Rio de Janeiro, Brazil*

South America is not extravagantly endowed with golf courses, and consequently has very few outstanding layouts. One of the most distinguished is the Gavea Golf and Country Club in Brazil. As the name implies it is modelled on American lines but the deep blue ocean, long golden beaches and 'sugar loaf' mountain outcrops surrounding the course are

The 18th at the Durban Country Club is perhaps the shortest closing par-4 on a genuine championship course anywhere in the world. It is 276 yards long but still no simple four.

Torakichi Nakamura driving from the first tee during his historic individual win in the 1957 Canada (World) Cup competition at Kasumigaseki. Japan won the team title too, thus completing a superb week for them.

unmistakeable evidence that one is in Rio de Janeiro, one of the world's most alluring cities. The course occupies two entirely different terrains – the higher, hilly ground inland for the front nine and the flatter land near the shore on the homeward half. For mere mortals Gavea's par of 69 is a tough target to pit one's handicap against, though Gary Player had a 59 there in the 1974 Brazilian Open. But then that season saw Player at his best. He won the Masters and the British Open. Gavea could not be expected to resist that sort of form.

KASUMIGASEKI *Tokyo, Japan*
It was at Kasumigaseki that the Japanese team produced a shock win in the 1957 World Cup with no less than nine shots to spare over the crack American duo of Demaret and Snead. That ignited the golf explosion in Japan and did nothing to harm the venerability of Kasumigaseki in the eyes of the golf-mad public. The East Course is the better known of the two 18s. Kinya Fujita's layout was stiffened by the British architect Charles Alison, who installed several deep bunkers. Ever since these awesome and hitherto unfamiliar hazards to the Japanese have been quaintly called 'Arisons'. The course is

marked by one uniquely Japanese practice. There are two greens on each hole, one sown with bent grasses and the other with korai, a specially developed eastern strain which can withstand the intense summer humidity. Having discovered the game, the Japanese are not prepared to allow their climate to stop them enjoying it the whole year round.

Morfontaine is one of continental Europe's truly great courses. The 9th is typical – not awesomely long but claustrophobically tight.

The start of the season at Royal Calcutta in 1894 as a group of British expatriates gather to celebrate the annual ritual of opening day.

MORFONTAINE
Mortefontaine, Nr Paris, France

No man did more to provide the French with golf courses of the highest order than Tom Simpson. Morfontaine was reputedly his first project across the Channel and it may well be the best. At 6600 yards it is considered too short for men tour professionals, but that's their misfortune. For the rest of us it is paradise, and no pushover. Pines, heather and sandy scrub are the chief problems; its flawless condition and ethereal quiet are among the many pleasures. To Britons it will recall Woodhall Spa, to Americans Pine Valley. Morfontaine is in that league. Henry Longhurst called it 'the most attractive course in France', and he could safely have cast the net wider than that. In addition to its superlative 18-hole course, Morfontaine has a marvellous par-35 nine-holer, where several greens have contours that make those at Augusta National seem gentle.

ROYAL CALCUTTA *West Bengal, India*

Royal Calcutta is the oldest golf club outside the British Isles. It was founded in 1829 and received the Royal charter in 1911. Today it is a splendid, if anachronistic, monument to the lost days of the British Empire. The grand clubhouse and superbly maintained golf course present an uncomfortable contrast to the squalor of the city. The course itself is a parkland design decorated by hundreds of beautifully coloured trees, and water hazards (known as tanks because they are used for storage) are far more prevalent than sand bunkers. Golf in Calcutta is not only a reminder of a colonial past. It has left a legacy to other courses in the tropics. By successfully nurturing the dhoob grass indigenous to the region, the pioneers of Royal Calcutta demonstrated from the outset that golf in the intemperate climes could be enjoyed on grass, and need not be endured on sand.

The 2nd hole at Royal Melbourne. This superb course combines the physical elements of the great British heathland courses with the coastal climate of the southern United States.

ROYAL MELBOURNE *Victoria, Australia*

Some of the most respected experts on the subject reckon that the sand belt of Melbourne has spawned as great a concentration of excellent golf courses as any other area of comparable size in the world. The pick of an unquestionably outstanding bunch is Royal Melbourne. There are two layouts – the West (by Alister Mackenzie) and the East (by Alex Russell) – but when authoritative voices proclaim that the club has one of the finest courses in the world they are referring to a composite 18 which relies on 12 holes from Mackenzie's design and six from Russell's. Indeed, two eminent professionals have declared it to be the best in the world, period. One is Greg Norman, who may be biased, and the other is Ben Crenshaw, who isn't. The course demands length and finesse, and an ability to plot one's way round and to handle the fearsome pace of its greens. It is also a glorious sight, a compelling blend of heathland and links to delight every golfer.

SOTOGRANDE *Costa del Sol, Spain*

The southern coasts of Spain and Portugal are now long-established destinations for vacationing golfers from northern Europe. They arrive on the Mediterranean and Atlantic shores in search of sun and golf and nowhere are their desires more agreeably fulfilled than on Robert Trent Jones's Mediterranean marvel of Sotogrande. It is a resort course, but much more than that – a quality design in anyone's judgement. The American upbringing of its author is evident throughout: long tees, big greens, a multitude of ponds and lakes and bright white sand traps. The course is manicured to the highest American standards, though the cork trees and distinctive mountain ranges mean its Spanish heritage can never be in doubt. Sotogrande was completed in 1965. In the intervening years more fine courses have been opened along the Costa del Sol, but for many people Sotogrande still has no peer.

Among the pines and palms, olives and almonds of the Costa del Sol, Sotogrande is arguably the best course on the Mediterranean. The approach to the 7th green is evidence of its American heritage.

Golf Around the Globe

This book has shuttled between the British Isles and the United States like a transatlantic airliner for the preceding 15 chapters, almost to the exclusion of anywhere else. Occasionally it has been hijacked to Australia, Africa or some other destination, but it has tended to concentrate on the development, impact and importance of the game in its twin strongholds.

Such bias is easily justified. The United States is comfortably the world's biggest golfing nation with 17.5 million people whom those who collate statistics are glad to call 'golfers', and that number will be out of date within the year. The United States has had a far more profound influence on golf than any other country in the past 60 or 70 years, whether one is considering advances in equipment, the construction of golf courses (around 62 per cent of the world's 25,000-plus courses are in North America or its surrounding islands), or the rearing of the majority of the top players. There is a downside too, of course: modern equipment has included the advent of the golf cart; some American architects have

encouraged the notion that new courses cannot be built without a seven-figure budget and wholesale rearrangement of the topography; while the heroes of the pro tour have lugubriously cultivated the impression that four hours represents a quick round and that no putt can be hit without at least 30 seconds of preliminary gazing and pacing.

The rise in the ascendancy of the American star meant something had to give. Consequently the former dominance of the British has waned considerably since the end of the First World War, even though the old country has enjoyed sporadic periods of renaissance and on several fronts it is by no means in the doldrums or a distinctly poor relation to its cousin across the ocean. It was the British who took golf around the globe, but as with soccer and cricket they are no longer the masters of that which they taught to the world. Nevertheless, they deserve universal gratitude for spreading the gospel, an end accomplished thanks to the dedication and devotion of Britons abroad, who were anxious to enjoy the game in their strange surroundings, and to the enterprise of desultory expeditionary forces.

The first international golf tour was conducted in 1903 by the intrepid gentlemen of the Oxford and Cambridge Golfing Society (formed in 1898) when they crossed the Atlantic for a 10-match, 39-day foray of the United States. Their successors in the society inaugurated the President's Putter at Rye in Sussex in 1920. This annual January reunion of university 'old boys', a marvellous tribute to the legendary eccentricity of the British, is about fun and conviviality against a background of chilly but competitive golf. The 1987 event represented a watershed, not because snow caused the conclusion to be delayed until March – not an unprecedented occurrence – but because a woman, Fiona Macdonald, took part. She qualified by being selected to play for Cambridge in the 1986 Varsity Match, though she could not help her team to victory.

No, not a bunch of lunatics – just the members of the Oxford & Cambridge Golfing Society enjoying their annual reunion for the President's Putter at Rye.

Not surprisingly, there were no female golfers in the party that set sail for America in 1903. That trip was, with hindsight, a truly historic occasion. It was the precursor of the international contests of the modern age and its timing was coincidentally appropriate, for within a few years Open Championships began in several of those countries which inherited the game from the envoys of the British Empire. Just as the original Open had sparked interest in Scotland and England, so fledgling championships nourished the game in Australia and Canada (started in 1904), New Zealand (1907) and South Africa (1909).

Among the most fortunate golfers in the world are those of Australia and New Zealand where it is reckoned that there are between 250 and 300 players per course, a generous ratio compared with elsewhere. As with South America, Africa and Asia, golf prospered in the Antipodes most spectacularly during the Golden Age, that glorious 20-year span between the wars. New Zealand has few top-notch courses, but in addition to the 36 holes at Melbourne Australia can point proudly to other distinguished Royal clubs at Adelaide, Canberra, Hobart, Queensland and Sydney. The Australian Golf Club, also in Sydney, was founded in 1882 and Alister Mackenzie and Jack Nicklaus are two of the architects to have modified it down the ages.

Canada too has received relatively short shrift in this book, but then in golf as in much else it finds it hard to emerge from the massive shadow of its neighbour to the south. Royal Montreal, Glen Abbey and Banff have already been mentioned within these pages and there are a dozen more golf courses of that calibre. On the opposite side of the United States, Mexico is by no means bereft of good courses, but there is a scarcity of quality in South America. The Dick Wilson-designed Lagunita at Caracas, Venezuela, is one exception: it was considered sufficiently demanding to be selected as a venue for both the men's and women's World Amateur Team Championships in 1986. Alister Mackenzie built the 36-hole Jockey Club at Buenos Aires in Argentina, but by his standards it is a lacklustre affair.

South Africa dominates the game on its continent, a legacy of the days when relations with Britain were more harmonious than is the case now. There are about 400 golf clubs in the country, more than 80 within a 60-mile radius of Johannesburg. The gold capital of the world is the

The Australian Open Championship has encouraged the game 'down under' by treating the public to the sight of the best golfers in the world. Golfers do not come any better than Jack Nicklaus, seen here producing a combination of strength and skill to escape from a troublesome spot during the 1971 Australian Open at Royal Hobart, Tasmania. He landed the ball on the green and went on to win the tournament.

golf capital of the southern hemisphere and it possesses several outstanding layouts. South Africa has also produced some fine golfers to fly its shell-shocked flag in the wake of Locke and Player. Nick Price holds the single round record (63) at the Masters and was very close to claiming the 1982 Open at Royal Troon until he faltered to let in Tom Watson. Price's compatriot, Mark McNulty, has proved himself one of the most consistent tournament winners anywhere. He won five times in succession on two continents in late 1986, including the controversial Million Dollar Challenge at Sun City where the organizers are talking of a winner-take-all first prize of $1 million for 1987. McNulty, incidentally, won what may have been the world's first genuine stadium golf tournament – on a nine-hole course, complete with sand and water hazards, set up at the Ellis Park rugby ground in Johannesburg.

There are a handful of championship tests in other African countries like Zimbabwe, Kenya and Zambia. In the far north, Royal Dar-es-Salam at Rabat in Morocco and El Kantaoui at Sousse in Tunisia have staged European Tour events, which is indicative of the need for a late winter overflow for Ken Schofield's circuit rather than a geographical identity crisis for the two countries.

Above The swing's the thing when there's no golf course to play on for these boys at Abidjan in the Ivory Coast.

Below The 18th brown at Dubai Country Club, as seen from the clubhouse. Note the sand 'bunker' guarding the front-left edge of the putting surface.

'Browns' also serve as putting surfaces at the Dubai Country Club in the desert of the United Arab Emirates. Them apart, the course is one huge sand bunker. The eager golfers carry a strip of Astroturf on which they place the ball to hit it from tee to green, except when it strays beyond the stakes which delineate the sand that is rough as opposed to the sand that is fairway. Then it is played as it lies. All very confusing, but just one of the many instances of how man will not permit mere trifles such as the lack of grass to prevent him from practising his favourite sport. One of the oil barons of the region, Sheik Mohammed Bin Rashid Al Maktoum, has recently had an all-grass course, called The Emirates, constructed in this Arabian wasteland. It is a feat of engineering that emphasizes a point made in Chapter 14. With an unlimited budget literally anything is possible, and pockets don't come any more bottomless than the Sheik's. He is one of the multi-millionaire Arabians who have breathed fresh life into British horseracing while simultaneously reinforcing its image as the business of tycoons rather than the sport of kings. In Dubai he owns the desalination plant which in summer pumps 1.25 million gallons of water per day to keep The Emirates' pastures green.

Both these courses are green, but that is not always the case in this near-equatorial area. Instead of greens, many courses have 'browns', a rolled mixture of compacted sand and oil. They are generally receptive to an approach shot, and easy to putt on because they are flat and true. There is no borrow on a 'brown'. That was undoubtedly a factor in enabling Peter Tupling from England to shoot 255, a world record total for 72 holes over a full-length course, at the Ikoyi club, Lagos, in the 1981 Nigerian Open.

Water is as precious a commodity as oil in the Gulf States. There's plenty of the latter on Das Island, which sounds an exotic spot but is, on the

Sam Snead during one of the toughest rounds of his career, at the opening of the Caesarea course in Israel.

contrary, a sand covered rock, less than a mile square, in the middle of the Persian Gulf. Civilisation, in the shape of Abu Dhabi, is 150 miles away. The island has an oil refinery, an airport and a nine-hole grassless golf course. The workforce has to endure 42-day shifts without any female company but there is the inestimable compensation of golf. It may not be much of a layout but at least it is a course and the men thoroughly appreciate it.

The same could not be said for some of the Arabs' political adversaries in Israel. Israel's first golf course at Caesarea, north of Tel Aviv, was opened in 1961 by an exhibition match between Sam Snead and British Ryder Cup player Harry Weetman. A sizeable crowd had assembled, but their collective knowledge of the sport was roughly equal to that of a retarded amoeba. As Snead prepared to drive from the first tee, the incessant jabbering of his audience reached an excited pitch of anticipation. How were they to know that they were supposed to remain quiet? Snead stared at the gallery with distaste and disbelief and they in turn stared back, perplexed by his inactivity.

Patrick Campbell, the aristocratic wit and raconteur, described the subsequent events beautifully. 'I was able to identify enquiries in English, French and German as to whether he had already, perhaps, done it and if so where had it gone, and if he hadn't what was he waiting for and would it be possible for him to get on with it now? Snead then made a suggestion which some of the stewards carried out in part, waving their arms and asking politely for silence. This had the immediate effect of redoubling the noise, people asking one another in genuine bewilderment how silence on their part could possibly contribute to whatever Snead was trying to do.'

Eventually relative peace was secured and Snead unleashed a corker, miles down the fairway. Having never seen a golf ball hit before, the crowd had no idea what to expect and never saw it. They dutifully stayed silent. Snead's already frayed temper was not improved when Weetman's tee shot, a fast duck-hook, was observed throughout its dismal flight and was accordingly treated to a loud burst of applause. Later poor Sam tried to execute a wedge shot while surrounded by three old men, clad in traditional Jewish garb, who were intrigued by what he was doing. Thus golf came to the Holy Land.

The game has conquered almost the whole of Asia, despite the kaleidoscope of cultures and climates encountered in that vast land mass. It is even established in the Himalayas, with the course at Gulmarg, in the Indian state of Kashmir, standing 8700 feet above sea level. Some form of golf has reportedly been played even higher on 'the roof of the world', over 16,000 feet up in Tibet, but there are no courses as such in those far reaches of the atmosphere.

China used to embrace the royal and ancient game before the People's Revolution of 1949. The prevailing doctrine then decreed that golf was a bourgeois pastime and the existing courses were ploughed up to be replaced by paddy fields. Chairman Mao preferred other pursuits to golf, like swimming (down the Yangtze River) and shooting (dissidents). But now the Bamboo Curtain has been pierced again. In August 1982, Arnold Palmer and Ed Seay began to build the Chung Shan Hot Spring Golf Club, less than an hour's drive from the old Portuguese colony of Macau. It duly became China's first new course since the Revolution and it is worthy of the honour. More are in the pipeline, and a handful of others have already been completed.

Another communist stronghold, North Korea, has fallen to the sport. Japanese contractors were responsible for its first course being opened near the capital, Pyongyang, in April 1987. Capitalist South Korea, host country to the 1988 Olympic Games, has been converted for a long time, as have the Philippines, Singapore, Indonesia and the other nations involved in the Asia Tour. But without question, the golf bug has never proved more infectious than in Japan.

For most Japanese, 'gorufu' is not played on a course. It is experienced on a driving range. The Japanese Golf Association estimates there are getting on for two million golfers in the country, which is similar to the British figure if the term is defined as someone who plays on a golf course, albeit only once or twice a year. But Japan has 16 million enthusiasts who are proud to call themselves golfers. The huge discrepancy between those statistics arises because the majority never get beyond the driving range.

Japan exemplifies the idea of golf as a rich man's game. Entry fees at some of the 400 clubs are set at around £35,000, while at Tokyo's plushest club, Koganei, membership dues approach £1 million. And having forked out anything from the cost of a Mercedes car to a Mayfair apartment for the privilege of joining, the members still have to pay anything between £20 and £150 for a green fee to get on to the first tee. That's if all the starting times haven't already been reserved. Green fees for guests are higher still, and it is no exaggeration to say that the annual subscription at some excellent British clubs is less than the expense of a day's golf in Japan once the price of a caddie and lost balls have been taken into account. The caddies are frequently young girls in colourful native dress, who double up as greenkeepers by replacing and resoiling the copious divot holes, while equipment is marked up beyond the bounds of extortion in British eyes.

The ingenuity of the Scots. These scenes depict the makeshift nine-hole course on Green Island, Mirs Bay, off the Chinese mainland north-east of Hong Kong in 1902. Members of the Royal Navy's China Squadron played a rudimentary game among the rocks and shrubs and thereby helped to establish golf in China.

The game is so indecently expensive because of the nature of the country's terrain. The flatter land which would be much cheaper to develop for courses is needed for agriculture, so golf has to be banished to the hills where construction costs are exorbitant. Architects glibly toss around sums in excess of £20 million as being necessary to blast the site into shape. The completed product will resemble a show garden, with phenomenal attention paid to topiary, flower arrangements, rockeries and fountains. It is therefore no wonder that it costs a fortune to get on a proper course and it also explains why the Japanese play the game so slowly. Every moment on the course is one to be savoured. A six-hour round is logically more enjoyable than one which lasts for five hours. To ensure they don't get it over with too quickly, many Japanese take tea breaks, a meal or even a bath (or all three) at various stages of the round. It is not known how many of them deliberately take more shots in order to obtain better value for money.

Money is synonymous with golf in Japan. Golf club memberships or concessions are the ultimate business perk, and company credit cards take care of most of the bills. The affluent individual country club members enrol their children at birth, pass on their membership as an inheritance or buy and sell it as they would deal in stocks and shares. The relatively lowly have to get up in the small hours of the morning and queue for a round on one of the few and enormously crowded municipal layouts. It's either that or a lifetime on the driving range and a lunchtime putting session on the little course on the rooftop of the office or local department store.

The prospect of practising forever, without much likelihood of being able to take the results on to a golf course, would be anathema to most westerners, but the Japanese are lured on by this half-golfer existence. They have an insatiable appetite for magazines, books and newspaper articles on the subject. They flock to watch the stars of the Japanese Tour who have followed in the wake of Nakamura and Ono, those heroes of the 1957 World Cup, and to pay homage to overseas players like Seve Ballesteros – who is hailed as a king in Japan – when they descend on the tour each autumn. Ballesteros is just one top name who has a wide range of business deals in Japan, from clothing endorsements to course architecture. The income which he and other golfers can earn from tapping the potential of this golf-crazy country is due to the way its inhabitants are hopelessly besotted by the game and by the reputations of its leading exponents.

It is sad that such unashamed love of the sport can seldom be rewarded by something so simple as a round on a golf course. But since the Japan Open was inaugurated in 1927 golf has captured the imagination of the public in fantastic fashion, a process fuelled by that World Cup victory 30 years later. Their imagination is as near as some Japanese ever get to a real course, and hence they genuinely regard a visit to places like St Andrews as a pilgrimage. The comparative informality and ease of arranging a game in Britain is sheer bliss for them, though often sheer purgatory for the people held up by a cheerful bunch of Orientals who intend to relish every second of their day. A Japanese on a golf course is as happy as a Russian with a pair of faded denims.

Back in their homeland, there may be hope for those envious and frustrated hackers who would like to join the elite relaxing in one of the grand eastern temple-inspired clubhouses while reminiscing about a particularly galling on-course experience. The Japanese have formed an alliance with an American company to market a luminous ball which will enable golf to become a 24-hour recreation. Some cynics have deplored the development, suggesting that this is a classic case of the light at the end of the tunnel being an oncoming train, but if there is one person who would be prepared to give the night game a go it is the Japanese golfer. It might get him, at last, on to a golf course. The land of the rising sun could also be the place where it doesn't matter when it sets.

Fanatical though the Japanese are, the biggest growth area of golf anywhere in the world is now Western Europe. That has been evident for several years, and at the beginning of 1987 Jack Nicklaus acknowledged the fact by announcing his intention to expand his course architectural interests on mainland Europe. His move, like the majority of Nicklaus's decisions, has to be a sensible one. The increasing concentration of European Tour events outside the British Isles both confirms and helps the burgeoning popularity of the game on the continent.

Spain is generally considered to be in the forefront of the boom in Europe. It has produced by far the greatest number of outstanding players, including four members of Europe's winning team in the 1985 Ryder Cup. That represents a remarkable turnround from the dark days after the Spanish Civil War when only seven professional golfers remained alive in the country and they had to issue an appeal to Britain for clubs, balls and other equipment in order to play the game again.

Seve Ballesteros waged an almost solitary war for many years in an effort to convince his countrymen that golf could be as fun as football and bull-fighting. They are now getting the message, although municipal courses are still a comparative rarity and membership is not cheap at clubs like Puerta de Hierro in Madrid, El Prat in Barcelona and the Real Club at Pedrena, where Ballesteros and his brothers learned their skills. All three are superior establishments with courses to match.

The Iberian Peninsula, however, earned its reputation through its resort courses. Many of these have since become private clubs which demand astronomical green fees. Sotogrande, Torrequebrada, Las Brisas and La Manga are among the many fine courses which grace the Costas. The trend of converting high-class holiday playgrounds into exclusive clubs has gained currency across the border in Portugal, too. Quinta do Lago, Vilamoura and Penina are the pride and joy of the Algarve. Further north around Lisbon there are more excellent courses like Estoril, Quinta da Marinha and Troia.

The boom is to be welcomed, but one doesn't have to be an impractical aesthete to complain that many of the layouts along the Atlantic and Mediterranean coastlines are hemmed in by holiday homes and condominiums. The course is financed by the property, and blatantly so. A wayward shot at Vale do Lobo on the Algarve can constitute a danger to somebody taking a dip – not only in the swimming pool but also in their bath. Another side effect is to put more bandits on the

Vale do Lobo in Portugal. Don't miss the fairway – you might commit a trespass with your ball.

streets of the main towns than there are on the golf courses. Instead of carrying hugely inflated handicaps, this lot hawk glossy literature, spurious incentives and cheap plonk in their attempts to sell timeshare apartments.

It was on Spain's premier golf course, El Saler, that Bernhard Langer fired the most impressive round of his life; and it's not as if there haven't been many superb ones. His closing ten under par 62 to clinch the 1984 Spanish Open demonstrated that a great course will yield to great golf. The day provided a memorable meeting between a brilliant continental golf course and a brilliant continental golfer.

Langer has been the Pied Piper who has encouraged his fellow Germans to follow him into golf. They have done so with typical Teutonic stoicism. In no other country in Europe would wealthy novices pay between £1000 and £8000 in entry fees to a golf club and then willingly accept that they cannot actually venture on to the course until they have a certificate from the pro to say they are competent enough. Professionals in West Germany are in some respects in the same position as the first pros in America 100 years ago. A British accent can be a passport to a rich pay-packet.

Langer has been an inspiration to his compatriots. Swedish golfers like Ove Sellberg, Anders Forsbrand and Mats Lanner may well emulate Langer's successes and be instrumental in raising the standard of golf in Sweden as Bjorn Borg did for tennis. Indeed, there are signs that that process is already underway.

The analogy with tennis is especially appropriate when it comes to golf in France. That country, above all, is ripe for exploitation. The game has drifted away from its upper-class base and started to break out among the masses. The contagion will surely reach epidemic proportions.

At present there are about 160 golf clubs to cater for 70,000 golfers. The equivalent British figures, with a similar population of 55 million, are 2000 and 2 million, yet France is over twice as large as Britain. But now some 40 new courses are scheduled for completion by 1990 and experts reckon golf will explode in France in much the same way as tennis did in the early 1970s. The predictions are for a million French golfers by the end of this century.

The up-market image associated with golf in France has not been assiduously cultivated but it is a basic fact that most clubs are privately owned by the members who have to purchase a share when

joining. That made golf the preserve of the well-heeled and until recently there were only 6000 players with a handicap better than 15. Today public courses – as well as several expensive, exquisite designs – are springing up throughout the country, and this trend shows no signs of abating. When Willie Dunn was cornered at Biarritz by the founders of Shinnecock Hills in 1890 and enticed over to the United States, he wasn't at all certain he was doing the correct thing. He and other Britons had a feeling that the future of golf lay in France, not America. He took

Golf was a fashionable affair in France in the 1920s, as exemplified by the illustration above. There is no lack of style in the cross-Channel game either. The photograph below shows La Bretesche in Brittany, but it should be pointed out that the clubhouse is the elegant building with the open courtyard rather than the grand chateau on the lake.

Splendid clubhouses are a frequent sight on continental Europe. Villa d'Este in Italy, near Lake Como, has a course of the same calibre as its striking headquarters.

a chance and was amply rewarded. His original hunch has taken nearly a century to come to fruition, notwithstanding that a course has been established at Pau since 1856.

Other European countries are not far behind either. Italy has great potential, not least because of the astonishing fact that there are no 18-hole courses on its Mediterranean coast south of Tuscany and none at all – by the sea or inland – south of Albarella, near Venice, on its Adriatic side. These omissions will surely be remedied. Switzerland and Austria have courses with glorious mountain views, and Pete Dye and Jack Nicklaus will soon be adding to them.

Golf is almost invariably a family pursuit on the continent, with women and children, and maybe dogs and cats, taking a vibrant part in the life of the club. The atmosphere is relaxed and informal and the buildings and surroundings would put the majority of British clubs to shame. Having said that, it is one of the undeniable pleasures of the game in Britain that golf clubs are meant for golf. The clubhouses tend to be functional rather than architecturally adventurous – Moor Park, Stoke Poges and a few more excepted – but they are by no means all drab or unpleasant. They often have an understated sense of style and a warm, clubby ambience.

If the continentals have a penchant for castles and stately homes, the Americans are not averse to the grandiose when it comes to clubhouses. Olympia Fields, near Chicago, was obviously the work of someone who had a sideline in cartography – it is massive. Not far away from Olympia, the clubhouse at Medinah is nothing less than a Byzantine palace. A thousand and more miles to the south-east, Seminole's gracious golf course is fronted by a large but elegant hacienda.

Returning to Europe, one should not entirely discount the countries behind the Iron Curtain. It has not exactly been rent asunder by golf but there also the British influence lingers on and the Warsaw Pact nations have not been immune to penetration.

King Edward VII introduced golf to Czechoslovakia shortly after the turn of the century. Although subsequent political developments have not been conducive to its widespread growth, course construction is gradually on the increase. Eighteen-hole layouts already exist at Karlovy Vary, Marianske Lazne and Ostrava, and not all date from the days of the Austro–Hungarian Empire. Ostrava was opened in 1968, a year more commonly remembered in Czechoslovakia for the Prague spring and the sinister rumbling of the Soviet tanks.

The Russian Revolution killed off golf in the USSR, where Moscow and St Petersburg (now Leningrad) were formerly enthusiastic centres. His Imperial Highness, the Grand Duke Michael of Russia, even exported the game and founded the Cannes Golf Club at Mandelieu on the French Riviera in 1891. But since 1917 golf has hardly been a major platform for party propaganda. Then, in 1974, Robert Trent Jones (who else?) was asked to design Tovarich Hills, near Moscow, the first course in the country since the Czars departed. As yet it is uncompleted, but the project has recently been resuscitated with a view to an opening by the end of the decade.

Since the last war Russia has bullied and dominated the other Warsaw Pact nations and the Kremlin has not been keen to promote golf in any of its satellites. The authorities ripped up courses in Bucharest and Budapest, though the game has been haltingly revived in each capital with the nine-hole Diplomatic Club (surely an American resort developer will steal that title?) in Rumania and the five-hole Kek Duna (Blue Danube) Golf Club in Hungary.

Yugoslavia, always the least loyal of Russia's allies when it comes to adhering to social discipline, has one course, at Bled. It's a scenic

delight, surrounded by mountains. Donald Harradine, the British course architect, unveiled it in 1974, and it is featured in many tourist brochures. Like Karlovy Vary and Marianske Lazne, Bled is a spa town, but it is unusual for the locals to settle for a couple of bottles of mineral water to drown their post-golf sorrows or celebrate their post-round glee. East European countries manufacture some desperately potent spirits, and Czechoslavakia and Yugoslavia are no exceptions.

Neither communism nor the extremes of geography have been able to repulse the golf enthusiast. The highest course in the world is at the Tuctu Golf Club in Morococha, Peru. It stands 14,335 feet above sea level. At that rarified height even moderately long drivers can seriously imagine they are Greg Norman. The drawback, of course, is that any sort of undulation could cause air sickness, so a good caddie will pack you a parachute and oxygen mask. Next door to Peru, in Bolivia, the La Paz Country Club has the highest 'green' golf course in the world at an altitude of 10,886 feet. It used to be sited a further 1500 feet up but the members shifted from their original location because grass wouldn't grow there. The course, situated in jagged mountainous terrain *below* the Bolivian capital, has 18 perfectly acceptable holes and demands several terrifying carries.

At the opposite end of the scale, the low point of the game worldwide is to be found at Furnace Creek in Death Valley, California. The enervating desert heat dictates an early morning start at this inhospitable spot some 280 feet below

Bled Golf Club in Yugoslavia, the Iron Curtain's most popular golf destination for westerners, lies in the foothills of the Julian Alps.

Opposite **You won't want to be short of the green with your tee shot to the long par-3 12th at La Paz.**

The La Paz Country Club provides positively hospitable golfing ground compared to a few other locations, such as the makeshift nine-hole layout on the frozen surface of Lake Weissensee in Austria; the noisy 17th green at Glyfada in Greece; and this bunker in Beirut. In Lebanon, of course, the word 'bunker' takes on a rather more sinister meaning.

sea level. The Sodom and Gomorrah Golfing Society's nine-hole layout along the northern shore of the Dead Sea at Kallia, near Jericho, was even more of a test of endurance at 1250 feet below sea level, but it is now defunct.

Those are golf's highs and lows. The respective top and bottom are Golfklubber Akureyrar in Iceland, 55 miles south of the Arctic Circle, and the Port Stanley club on the Falkland Islands. This collection of trivia is open to dispute, depending on how one defines a golf course and on the progress the game makes in pushing ever more upwards, downwards, northwards and

southwards. Accordingly, no correspondence will be entered into.

The most improbable areas of the globe are populated by folk who know the difference between the interlocking grip and Vardon's overlapping grip; who can tell a genuine Ping putter from a fake. What would Vardon's great contemporary, J. H. Taylor, have made of it all? When the British team sailed to the United States for the first Ryder Cup match in 1927, his comments in the columns of *PGA Journal* suggested that he for one was not revelling in the consequences of Britain's munificence in giving the game to the world.

'Professional golf in this country has been overshadowed with the dark cloud of foreign superiority, for, like and admire them as we undoubtedly do, and as their merits deserve, our American friends are foreigners,' he wrote. 'I will admit that we do not look upon them with the same suspicion and distrust we perhaps would if they came from the far corners of the earth, or if their skins were not as white as our own, but they are foreigners nevertheless.'

One suspects that the Race Relations Board today might be a little perturbed to read that in a respectable publication. One also wonders how alarmed and shocked Taylor might have been at the way golfers from the far corners of the earth (like Peter Thomson and Roberto de Vicenzo) and of different coloured skins (Isao Aoki and Calvin Peete) have been treated as celebrities in Britain; and what he would have thought of players like Ballesteros and Langer being regarded as Britons in all but nationality.

Times have indeed changed. To return to my initial theme in this chapter, the divergence in the paths taken by golf in Britain and the United

States was exacerbated by the Second World War. The British economy was ravaged; in America it flourished. In golf this was manifested by the amount of money flowing into the American pro tour. The circuit attracted it through the performances of men like Nelson, Hogan and Snead, which in turn aroused more interest and generated more cash. This made life on the tour an agreeable and lucrative prospect for many aspiring professionals. The standards of play were thus raised and, in order to win a tournament, excellence became not so much a virtue as a necessity. It was a kind of delicious circle when it came to emphasizing superiority over the British, so that by 1951 Henry Longhurst was jestingly moved to toast the forthcoming Ryder Cup confrontation at Pinehurst with the words: 'May the best team lose.'

The torrential supply of dollars pouring into professional golf in the United States has become a deluge. Japan and Europe aren't impoverished but they cannot compete with statistics like these: Fuzzy Zoeller collecting $370,000 for beating Jack Nicklaus, Arnold Palmer and Lee Trevino in the hyped-up 18-hole Skins Game in November 1986, an event so meaningless that television didn't bother to show its conclusion; Australia's Bruce Crampton topping the US Senior Tour Money List for that year with $454,299; Bob Charles and Amy Alcott – who each earned

around $250,000 from the regular season Senior and LPGA Tours respectively – splitting $500,000 for winning a 12-team mixed tournament in Jamaica just before Christmas 1986; and schedules for 1987 that offered $10 million prize money for the Seniors (and business for the over-49s is so brisk that they have hived off the over-59s into a Super Seniors division), a million more than that for the LPGA, and a staggering $30 million for the men, including the Nabisco Grand Prix of Golf where 30 players shared $2 million and the winner received $360,000. It is tempting to describe that purse as a world record prize fund, but whatever new marks are set in 1987, some of them, maybe all, will surely be broken in 1988.

American professionals have not been the only beneficiaries of their favourable economic climate. Their amateur counterparts have gained from that too, and also because the vast size of the country guarantees that at least some part of it enjoys an ideal golfing climate, weather-wise, throughout the year. The old shrines like Pinehurst in North Carolina and The Greenbrier in West Virginia have been supplemented by a never-ending chain of courses along the coasts of Florida and South Carolina and an intense concentration in the deserts of California, Nevada and Arizona, where an abundance of natural water supplies and/or modern technology have transformed the landscape.

Man will do a lot for a game of golf. This may be the shape of things to come in Japan, which shows that the world has nothing new to offer. This night-golf competition was held at Westchester, New York, in 1924, and Gene Sarazen (putting) was one of the four participants in this floodlit foursomes.

Pleasant condominiums and a lush golf course have sprung up in abundance in the Californian Desert. This is Mission Hills at Rancho Mirage in Palm Springs.

The rocky landscape of St Thomas, in the US Virgin Islands, has been utilized with great skill and imagination to create a spectacular golf course – Mahogany Run – in exotic surroundings.

Outside the immediate confines of the United States, winter golfers can enjoy a languorous and luxurious lifestyle on Caribbean and Atlantic islands like the Bahamas, Puerto Rico, the Dominican Republic, the Virgin Islands, Jamaica, Trinidad, Tobago or Bermuda (where Charles Blair Macdonald built the justly famous Mid-Ocean). In the Pacific is another golfing paradise, a cluster of rocks that make up the heaven known as Hawaii. All these exotic destinations provide quality and quantity of courses, though sometimes, as in Europe, the real-estate developers grab the prime plots. As has been observed more than once before, it is just as well for golf that Jack Neville's brief at Pebble Beach permitted him to devote the spectacular oceanside land to the course. Given that property was his main line of business, it is not only miraculous but ironic that he should have produced the breathtaking masterpiece that he did.

Hale Irwin, the 1974 and 1979 US Open champion, has more reason that most to be grateful for Neville's perspicacity. He hooked his drive on the final hole of the 1984 Bing Crosby Pro-Am so badly that it disappeared over the edge of the fairway towards the beach. Suddenly, it reappeared. It had ricocheted off a rock back on to the fairway. Irwin duly capitalized on this fluke. He birdied the hole to tie Jim Nelford and then went on to take the play-off. Maybe fate owed him a break. The previous summer Irwin had attempted to knock in a two-incher with the back of his putter during the third round of the Open Championship at Royal Birkdale. The club stubbed the ground and Irwin, like Cinderella, missed the ball. It was an air shot, a whiff. The next afternoon Irwin finished a single stroke behind the winner, Tom Watson.

Irwin could understandably have cried with anguish that night. Bobby Cruickshank cried with pain at the 1934 US Open at Merion. His approach to the 11th hole did 'an Irwin', bounding off a stone on to the green. He threw his club skywards with a yell of jubilation; to be shortly followed by another yell when it hit him on the way down. A frustrated Ben Crenshaw emulated that performance after a poor pitch shot to the 18th green at the 1986 USPGA Championship. 'That's the difference between pros and amateurs', he noted. 'The amateurs skull their wedges and the pros wedge their skulls.'

Bobby Jones (well, he had to get in this chapter somewere) benefited from a massive stroke of luck at the 1930 US Open, the third trick of his Grand Slam. His 3-wood to the 9th green in the second round skimmed across the pond protecting the green – though some say it bounced off a lily pad – and left him with an easy birdie four. He won by two shots. Appropriately in the circumstances, the host club was Interlachen.

It falls to few men to have the opportunity to win the US Open but the most humble golfer can dream of the ultimate thrill that a single stroke can bring. A hole-in-one is a statistical freak, though the chances of achieving one are obviously enhanced if the hole is short and the player proficient. It is reckoned the odds range from some 3700–1 for a professional or scratch amateur to 33,000–1 for the average golfer, but fact can be stranger than either fiction or figures. Norman Manley, a fine Californian amateur, had recorded 58 aces by the end of 1986, when he was aged 64; on the other hand, the great Harry Vardon achieved just one before he died. Where does that leave us?

Manley is currently also the only person to have holed-in-one on consecutive par-4s (ie. back-to-back albatrosses) but golf has innumerable other examples of scarcely credible scoring feats and categories of bizarre incidents which are documented in volumes like the *Golfer's Handbook*, the *Guinness Book of Records* and other books specifically devoted to the weird and wonderful. In such publications, Arnold Palmer making a hole-in-one at the same hole on successive days, which he did in September 1986, merits only a footnote. The last word on the subject here has to be reserved for Robert Mitera,

Gene Sarazen celebrates one of the most famous holes-in-one in history, at Troon's 8th hole in the 1973 Open Championship, an unforgettable moment witnessed on television by millions of people around the world.

who holds the record for the longest ace – an incredible 447 yards. The key may lie not so much with the hole playing downhill and downwind as in the name of the Nebraskan course where he did it. Miracle Hills.

Despite the terse remonstration by that dispirited Scottish caddie referred to in the opening chapter, golf is indeed a funny game: both funny laughable and funny peculiar. And caddies have contributed enormously to the game's fund of humour, my favourite being the traditional British response to the visiting American player who's just topped his drive five yards and fancies another go without penalty.

'What do you call a mulligan over here?' he asks politely.

'Three off the tee,' is the caddie's retort.

It is hard to envisage the most gentle of caddies being tolerant with the likes of Walter Danecki, the bogus American 'professional' ('I don't charge if I give a lesson') who amassed a total of 221 strokes in the 36-hole qualifying competition for the 1965 Open Championship. He returned to Milwaukee admitting he had no handicap and had never received tuition, but nevertheless complaining vehemently that it was using the small ball that had really screwed him up. Maurice Flitcroft, a Cumbrian crane driver, pulled the same ruse of pretending to be a professional in 1976, but he withdrew after shooting 121 for the first round. His mother defended him by saying: 'Well, he has to start somewhere, doesn't he?' The R & A simply fumed and have since made

Maurice Flitcroft, the hero of the hacker, scourge of the R & A.

Tommy Bolt in action on the 18th tee at Cherry Hills in the 1960 US Open. After two of his drives had disappeared into the lake, his driver followed. 'I enjoy fishing and I was just trying to spear one with my driver,' Bolt jokingly explained later. At the time he was less good-humoured. A young boy dived in for the discarded wood and retrieved it from the water. Bolt strolled over to him as if in gratitude, a sentiment that changed abruptly to one of anger as the lad made off with the club, hopped over the fence and was gone.

The incomparable Walter Hagen (right) with Archie Compston at Moor Park in 1928. Hagen's agent, Bob Harlow, had arranged a 72-hole challenge match between the two as part of a big promotional tour to be conducted by the Haig in Britain. Compston then ruined their plans by producing some devastating golf to win by 18 & 17. Hagen privately told Harlow, 'I can beat that sonofabitch on the best day he ever had.' Shortly afterwards he went down to Sandwich and won the Open Championship for a third time. Sarazen was second, Compston third.

strenuous efforts to intercept Flitcroft before he reaches the first tee, but his guile and use of pseudonyms have kept them on their toes.

Of course, a couple of jokers like that are a considerable handicap to their hapless playing partners. Danecki and Flitcroft hurt the chances of others. Some of the early post-war players on the US Tour would hurt themselves. Ky Laffoon was

one. He would thump hard objects to punish his hands after he hit a bad shot. His masochism turned to sadism when his putter was to blame. He was once seen trying to strangle it, on another occasion he attempted to drown it in a lake, and he would regularly ride from one tournament to the next with his putter attached by string to the back of his car so that it would be bashed to death on the road.

He wasn't the only man easily fazed. Clayton Heafner was allegedly described by Sam Snead as 'the most even-tempered player on the tour; he's always angry'. Tommy Bolt, the 1958 US Open champion, held most of the circuit's club-throwing records. His motto was: 'If you are going to throw a club, it is important to throw it ahead of you, down the fairway, so you don't waste energy going back to pick it up.' Bolt's caddie once offered him a choice of two clubs for the shot in hand, neither of them being suitable for the purpose, because they were all he had left in his bag.

Ky Laffoon was Walter Hagen's partner in the 1936 Inverness Fourball competition, which is significant only for being the Haig's last

tournament victory. Hagen was not inclined to indulge in Laffoon's buffoonery but he has been responsible for quite a few of the lighter moments in this book. Among his matchless collection of one-liners there has to be room for this unorthodox compliment to a famous female opera singer to whom he was introduced. 'My dear,' he exclaimed, gazing at her ponderous cleavage, 'did you ever stop to think what a lovely bunker you would make?' Few golfers have been blessed with Hagen's verve. None have had more nerve.

It is usually left to the writers to coin the *bons mots*, and nobody ever made that seem more facile than the great Bernard Darwin. One day he covered the first seven holes at Pine Valley in level par. On the 327-yard 8th he took nine shots and was still not in the cup. He picked up. He later remarked: 'It is all very well to punish a bad stroke, but the right of eternal punishment should be reserved for a higher tribunal than a green committee.'

That sentence illustrates both Darwin's flair for language and Pine Valley's infinite capacity to torment, but that Darwin could be even-par standing on the 8th tee demonstrates how he was able to represent his country with distinction in the Walker Cup. Darwin was a very good golfer, which meant he could faithfully reflect the emotions of those he wrote so beautifully about, but he was also a very tortured soul on the course. In his writing there was a genius which has led eminent scholars to acclaim him as one of the best essayists English literature has known. On the golf course there was a devil within him that resembled Ky Laffoon rather than Siegfried Sassoon. There is no better example of the latter than the tale of the day at Woking when Darwin's superb golf from tee to green had been squandered by some miserable putting. When yet another short birdie putt missed its target it all became too much for him. He fell to his knees, bit a chunk of turf from the green, and pleaded: 'Oh God, are you satisfied now?'

Yes, Darwin wrote with delightful serenity but he played golf with deadly seriousness. His humour also had a touch of asperity. He was once horrified to see a Canadian player at the 1955 Commonwealth Tournament at St Andrews wearing a sweater of yellow, pink, black, green and violet stripes. Eventually he could not resist approaching the offender and asking: 'Are those your old school colours or your own unfortunate choice?'

To another author falls the final putt. He is not widely associated with golf but A. A. Milne, the creator of Winnie the Pooh, provided this succinct summary of why golf appeals to the poor player as much as the good. It suggests one of the many reasons that keeps us all coming back for more.

'When he reads of the notable doings of famous golfers, the 18-handicap man has no envy in his heart. For by this time he has discovered the great secret of golf. Before he began to play he wondered wherein lay the fascination of it; now he knows. Golf is so popular simply because it is the best game in world at which to be bad.'

Bibliography

Below is a complete list of the publications which have provided sources of reference in the preparation and research of this book. Some have proved invaluable; others have been of occasional assistance. In addition to these 39 books the author has also been greatly helped by several magazine and newspaper articles, particularly those appearing in the British magazines *Golf World*, *Golf Illustrated*, *Golf Monthly* and *PGA Journal*, the American magazine *Golf Digest*, and the *New York Times* newspaper.

Allis, Peter (with Michael Hobbs) *The Open* Collins, London, 1984

Campbell, Patrick *How To Become a Scratch Golfer* Blond, London, 1963

Cornish, Geoffrey S. and Whitten, Ronald E. *The Golf Course* Windward, Leicester, 1981

Davies, William H. and the Editors of Golf Digest *Great Golf Courses Of The World* Golf Digest, New York, 1974; *100 Greatest Golf Courses And Then Some* Golf Digest, New York, 1982

Davis, William (Editor) *The Punch Book Of Golf* Hutchinson, London, 1973

Darwin, Bernard *The Golf Courses Of The British Isles* Duckworth, London, 1910

Dobereiner, Peter *The Glorious World of Golf* Hamlyn, London, 1973; (with Peter Alliss, Mark McCormack and Arnold Palmer) *The Lord's Taverners Fifty Greatest Golfers* Kingswood/Quixote, London, 1985; (with Arnold Palmer) *Arnold Palmer's Complete Book Of Putting* Stanley Paul, London, 1986; (Editor) *Down The Nineteenth Fairway* André Deutsch, London, 1982; (Editor) *The Golfers* Collins, London, 1982

Henderson, Ian T. and Stirk, David *Golf In The Making* Henderson and Stirk, Winchester, 1979; *Royal Blackheath* Henderson and Stirk, Winchester, 1981

Keeler, O. B. *The Bobby Jones Story* (edited by Grantland Rice) Tupper and Love, Atlanta, 1959

Longhurst, Henry *The Best Of Henry Longhurst* (edited by Mark Wilson and Ken Bowden) Collins, London, 1979

Mackenzie, Alister *Dr Mackenzie's Golf Architecture* Grant Books, Droitwich, 1982 (originally published by Simpkin, Marshall, Hamilton and Kent, London 1920)

McCormack, Mark H. *The World Of Professional Golf* (Annual) Hodder and Stoughton, London 1968, 1969, 1970; International Literary Management, London, 1971; Collins, London, 1972

McDonnell, Michael *The Complete Book Of Golf* Kingswood Press, Tadworth, 1985

Menzies, Gordon (Editor) *The World Of Golf* BBC, London, 1982

Norwood, Bev (Editor) *The Open Championship 1984* Springwood Books, London, 1984

Parsons, Iain (Editor) *The World Atlas Of Golf* Mitchell Beazley, London, 1976

Plimpton, George *The Bogey Man* Harper & Row, New York, 1968

Price, Charles *The World Of Golf* Random House, New York, 1962; *Bobby Jones And The Masters* Stanley Paul, London, 1986

Shelly, Warner *Pine Valley Golf Club, A Chronicle* Pine Valley Golf Club, Pine Valley, 1982

Steel, Donald *The Guinness Book Of Golf Facts And Feats* Guinness Superlatives, Enfield, 1982

Van Hengel, Steven J. H. *Early Golf* Frank P. Van Eck, Vaduz, 1985

Viney, Laurence (Editor) *Golfer's Handbook* Macmillan, London, 1986

Ward-Thomas, Pat *Not Only Golf* Hodder and Stoughton, London, 1981

Warren Wind, Herbert *The Story Of American Golf* Farrar, Straus, New York, 1948; *The Lure Of Golf* Heinemann, London, 1971; *Following Through* Ticknor & Fields, New York, 1985; (Editor) *The Complete Golfer* Heinemann, London, 1954

Wodehouse, P. G. *The Clicking of Cuthbert* Herbert Jenkins, London, 1922

Index

Numbers in italic refer to illustrations; numbers in bold refer to the colour sections between pages 64 and 65 (**1**), 80 and 81 (**2**), 144 and 145 (**3**), and 176 and 177 (**4**).

PICTURE ACKNOWLEDGEMENTS

The author and publishers would like to thank the individuals and organisations mentioned below for their permission to reproduce the illustrations included in this book. At the time of going to press, it proved impossible to determine the copyright owners of a number of the earlier photographs – the publishers would be pleased to hear from those whom they were unable to trace. Where more than one picture appears on a page, the following abbreviations are used: a – above; b – below; c – centre; l – left; r – right.

Front jacket All-Sport/David Cannon ar, b; Lawrence Levy/Yours in Sport al; Mary Evans Picture Library ac. **Back jacket** The Photo Source. **Colour** *Between pages 64 and 65* All-Sport/David Cannon 2b, 3al; Lawrence Levy/Yours in Sport 4al; Brian Morgan/Golf Photography International 1, 2a, 4ar; Phil Sheldon 3ar, 3b, 4b. *Between pages 80 and 81* All-Sport/David Cannon 4al; Phil Sheldon all others. *Between pages 144 and 145* Peter Dazeley Photography 1al; Lawrence Levy/Yours in Sport 1ar, 1b, 3b; Brian Morgan/Golf Photography International 4; Royal and Ancient Golf Club of St Andrews 2a; Phil Sheldon 2bl, 2br, 3a, 3c. *Between pages 176 and 177* All-Sport/David Cannon 1b, 2ar, 3br; Lawrence Levy/Yours in Sport 3a; Brian Morgan/Golf Photography International 2b, 4a; Phil Sheldon 1a, 3bl; Tony Smith 4b; the author 2al. **Black and white** All-Sport/Dave Cannon 32r, 45b, 46, 48b, 49a, 49b, 50l, 51r, 77, 95a, 95b, 110b, 111r, 149, 174, 190a, 200a. Associated Press 24b, 36b, 42b, 43r, 71, 73al, 87a, 94a, 101r, 102a, 117l, 130a, 191,193l, 201a. Promotion Australia, London 187a. BBC Hulton Picture Library 11b, 13, 14, 15br, 17al, 17b, 18a, 19a, 19b, 35b, 38br, 38bl, 40b, 53l, 56b, 58b, 68b, 69a, 96, 113a, 114, 126a, 127a, 127b, 128, 133a, 135b, 136b, 137, 138, 156, 157a, 161a, 199, 202b. Bettmann Archive/BBC Hulton Picture Library 20b, 41. The Trustees of the British Museum 12a. Canadian Government Travel Bureau 184. Frank Christian/Historic Golf Prints 78, 79, 80a, 83, 84r, 158. G. M. Cowie Collection 26, 31a. Culver Pictures 89. Peter Dazeley Photography 17ar, 64a, 82, 100, 102b, 103b, 106l, 107l, 107r, 126b, 140ar, 144, 150, 165b, 167, 169b, 179a, 194. DP Press, Sevenoaks, for special photography. Dunlop Slazenger 29, 173a. The Mary Evans Picture Library 11a, 133b, 195a. Frank Gardner 63bl, 119. Golf Illustrated 24a, 28a, 28b, 32l, 54a, 98, 123, 124a, 134c, 135a, 153, 160a, 162a, 177b and for the loan of various photographs credited elsewhere. Golf World for the loan of various photographs credited elsewhere. Sonia Halliday 8. Peter Haslam/Golf World 190b. Henderson and Stirk Ltd for the loan of photographs 10, 12a and for permission to reproduce 33 from *The Compleat Golfer* (Victor Gollancz, 1982). Gavin Hodge 193r. Illustrated London News Picture Library 34r, 39, 54b, 55a, 55b, 122, 186b. Steward Kendall 51l, 142, 180. E. D. Lacy 63a. Lawrence Levy/Yours in Sport 50r, 76a, 76b, 103a, 109, 110a, 111l, 129a, 129b, 143a, 151a, 151b, 171b, 178, 201b. The Mansell Collection 9b. The Minneapolis Institute of Arts 10. Brian Morgan/Golf Photography International 159a, 164, 171a, 172, 175, 176a, 176b, 177a, 179b, 197b. National Museums of Scotland 18b, 134l. The Bert Neale Collection/Bob Thomas Sports Photography 44b, 45a, 60r, 62a, 104, 117r, 131, 157b. New York Daily News 125a. New York Times 91. North West Counties Press 64b. The Photo Source 30a, 30b, 40a, 42a, 44a, 47b, 56a, 58a, 60l, 62b, 63br, 90l, 93, 99a, 105, 106r, 113b, 115, 130b, 136a, 145, 155b, 185b, 189. Planet News 36al. Popperfoto 97b. Press Association 57, 59l, 118a. Provincial Press Agency 47a. Royal Blackheath Golf Club 15a. St Enedoc Golf Club 161b. Phil Sheldon 36ar, 75b, 80b, 81, 85, 86a, 86b, 87b, 94b, 108a, 108b, 120, 121a, 121b, 141, 147, 152b, 163a, 163b, 166r, 169a, 173b, 182a, 182b, 183, 187b, 188, 198ar. Tony Smith 185a. Sotheby's 16, 31b, 35a. Spadem 195b. Sport & General Press Agency 43l, 48a, 61, 101l, 134r, 139, 152a, 154. Southport & Ainsdale Golf Club 116a, 116b. Times Newspapers/Graham Wood 198al. Topical Press Agency 90r. United Press International 75a, 99b, 118b, 124b, 198b. United States Golf Association 21, 65, 66l, 66r, 67, 67, 69b, 70, 72, 73ar, 73b, 74, 88, 97a, 125b, 140al, 143b, 166l, 202a. Yugoslav National Tourist Office 197a. The author 159b, 160br, 165a, 168, 170, 181a, 181b, 186a, 196, 200b.